③ 6/13
11/15

② 4/12
10/12

INVESTING STRATEGIES

FOR THE

HIGH NET WORTH INVESTOR

Maximize Returns
on Taxable Portfolios

NIALL J. GANNON
The Gannon Group

New York   Chicago   San Francisco   Lisbon   London
Madrid   Mexico City   Milan   New Delhi   San Juan
Seoul   Singapore   Sydney   Toronto

To Gretchen
the love of my life

CONTENTS

Chapter 4

Asset Allocation for the Taxable Investor   53

Chapter 5

Municipal Bonds: The Forgotten Asset Class   **79**

Chapter 9

Chapter 10

Chapter 11

Chapter 12

Chapter 16

ACKNOWLEDGMENTS

I thank

- God for giving me the opportunity to spend my life's work in a profession which gives me such joy
- My parents, Patrick (P. J.) and Helen Gannon for the gift of Life
- My family, friends, and colleagues
- J. Patrick Kearns, for taking a chance on me as a 23-year-old intern at Shearson Lehman Brothers
- Dorothy Garrison, for becoming my first client

Michael J. Blum, who served as senior research associate for many of the models in this book. Mike's diligence in developing, testing, and validating these models has been an irreplaceable contribution to the integrity of this work. Mike currently works as an investment analyst at Madison Capital Management and is a proud alumnus of Washington University in St. Louis.

Kelly Guerrier, who served as co-research associate for this book. In addition to completing his MS in Finance at Washington University and studying for the CFA level III exam, Kelly volunteered to spend hundreds of hours in support of our research effort. Kelly traveled to libraries between New York and St. Louis to dig into old copies of investment charts and records in order to prove our investment theses. Kelly Guerrier is an impressive and hardworking young man with a bright future in this profession.

Lewis Braham served as my personal editor, structural advisor, and coach. Thanks to Jeanne Glasser and Leah Spiro of McGraw-Hill; my agent Ellen Coleman; Thomas Hutchins of SRC Stock Charts; Jack Bogle of Vanguard; Dean Mahendra Gupta, Olin School at Washington University; Dr. Richard Marston, The Wharton School; Charlotte Beyer, Institute for Private Investors; Matt Miller, Forbes; David Swensen, Yale University; Dr. Aswath Damodaran, New York University, Stern School; Matthew Kreps from The Bond Buyer; Jean Brunel, Journal of Wealth Management.

Special thanks to my business partner of 10 years, Matt Rogers; assistant and family office manager Cindy Feaster; and performance analyst Chris Thach who refined our multi-generational model and greatly assisted with charts, analysis, and formatting. I offer gratitude to current and former colleagues Art Stone, Tony Kalinowski, John Kuddes, Philip McCauley, George Friedlander, Bob Seaberg, Bill Miehe, Tim Young, Mark Allenspach, Tony Gallea and his co-founders/board members of the Portfolio Management Institute, Marshall Kaplan, Bob Jerome, Mike Salamida, from the Portfolio Management Group of Smith Barney, James P. O'Connell and R. J. Shook, author of *The Winners Circle*.

To all five living generations of clients served by the Gannon Group, it has and continues to be an honor to work for you.

INTRODUCTION

In May of 2008, I gave a speech at the annual meeting of the Chartered Financial Analyst (CFA) Institute in Vancouver, British Columbia, titled "Rethinking Tax-Efficient Asset Allocation for the High Net Worth Investor." The speech was based on research I had been conducting for years on investment strategies for wealthy investors at my financial advisory firm, the Gannon Group. What we discovered was that in general the advice dispensed by money managers, academics, and the financial media about investing was inaccurate for high net worth investors. And it was that discovery and the speech it inspired that led me to write this book.

One of the basic assumptions of the investment advice business that we found to be inappropriate for our wealthy clients was that over the long run stocks would outperform bonds. What I'd learned through our research was that being in the top tax bracket could drastically alter the stock versus bond equation and that the stock-oriented strategy proffered by many advisory organizations didn't quite work as planned if you were investing outside of a tax-exempt account. This discovery did not rule out stocks entirely but merely leveled the playing field for my clients and forced me to always do the math when comparing asset classes to make informed decisions on the best returns after taxes.

Once we dispelled the stock myth, there were others we felt obligated to investigate to see if the prevailing investment wisdom truly applied to America's wealthiest citizens. Having realized that it didn't, we developed tools wealthy investors and their advisors can use to rethink the investing equation. Our discoveries and the tools constitute the bulk of this book. My hope is that, by reading it, wealthy investors will learn to think differently about their financial strategies and always remember to do the math and calculate what their expected after-tax returns will be before they invest— because, in general, the financial services industry will not do this for them.

Among the many sacred tenets of the investment advice industry we will challenge in subsequent chapters are the long-term outperformance of stocks, the superiority of index funds over active management, and the supposed benefits of hedge funds and alternative investments. I also chronicle a short history of the capital markets to provide some necessary context to the claims made by Wall Street and financial academics. Finally, I explore some of the unique financial issues wealthy investors face. Among them: estate planning for multiple generations, gifting strategies, private equity investing, and tax-savvy asset allocation strategies. Having explained these issues, we will also discuss the unique investment tools and strategies we've developed to help high net worth investors deal with them.

CHAPTER 1

Developing an Understanding of the Wealth Creative Process as a Long-Term Business Owner

How Did the Wealthy Achieve Their Success, and Do Those Same Traits Translate into Investing?

To be a wealth manager is to embrace a paradox: Your most successful clients may know more about making money than you do. One of my favorite stories illustrating this contradiction I heard at a conference for the Institute for Private Investors in San Francisco. Merrill Lynch wealth strategist Ashvin Chhabra described how a prospective client came to him and said, "Before we talk about diversification, I want you to know that if I met you 20 years ago I wouldn't be sitting here today." The point the client was making is that it was his lack of diversification and his ultra-concentration in one family business that grew his family's wealth in the first place. If he had instead invested his money in an index fund, he would have never become rich.

This is not to say that wealthy investors don't need diversified portfolios. The majority of wealthy Americans

1

are "self-made" individuals who've built their own businesses. At the point at which most approach a financial advisor, they're often looking to reduce their exposure to downside risk. They may be about to retire from their business, sell it, or just feel that they've reached a stage in their lives where a diversified portfolio makes sense. But in building that portfolio, it's important to never forget where the wealth originated. And understanding this means realizing that there's a point where a diversified portfolio becomes so diversified and convoluted that it no longer represents a collection of individual businesses but the entire U.S. economy, the global economy, or an arbitrary mix of assets, which may or may not be in as good shape as the wealthy investor's original business. In other words, someone who made his fortune selling the computer company he built from scratch to IBM probably shouldn't be invested with 10 money managers who each owns 100 stocks because it becomes impossible to tell if his money is invested in quality businesses anymore.

All of that said, the true value of diversification is that it can help wealthy people stay rich. Perhaps nothing illustrates this better than the Forbes 400 list. The list published annually by *Forbes* magazine since 1982 ranks the 400 wealthiest Americans by their net worth. As is generally the case with wealthy investors, most of the people on the list are entrepreneurs or the children of entrepreneurs, some 271 of the 400 members in 2008 or 68 percent being "self-made" business owners.[1] And yet the changes to the list reveal how fickle the fate of business can be. Since 1982, only 31 people from the original list have stayed on it until today. Some of the members dropped off because they died, but many others fell off because of a decline in their assets.

Yet the remarkable thing our research has discovered is that a "plain vanilla" portfolio of municipal bonds and stocks would have kept more people on the list.

As you can see from Figure 1.1, a member's net worth of $100 million in 1982 needed to grow to $1.3 billion by 2008 for him or her to stay on the list. That amounts to an annualized return of 9.97 or about 10 percent. Meanwhile, from January 1, 1982, until December 31, 2008, the S&P 500 returned 9.63 percent annualized. A $100 million investment in the market would have turned into $1.2 billion, almost equaling the return of America's wealthiest citizens. Even more significant, in 1982 the average municipal bond yielded a whopping 13.36 percent. If a wealthy investor had bought $100 million

FIGURE 1.1

Minimum Net Worth to Make Forbes 400

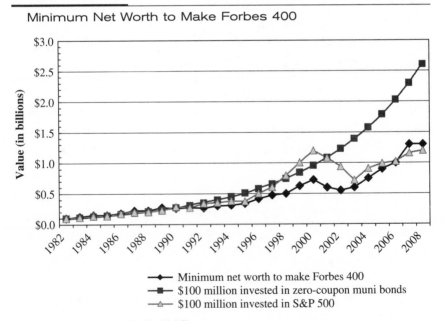

—◆— Minimum net worth to make Forbes 400
—■— $100 million invested in zero-coupon muni bonds
—▲— $100 million invested in S&P 500

Source: Data from Forbes.com and the *New York Times*.

in 30-year zero-coupon municipal bonds in her home state and left the portfolio alone, by the end of 2008 it would have been worth $2.6 billion—an annualized 13.36 percent tax free. The tax-free part of the equation we shall see in subsequent chapters actually led to a significant outperformance of munis for high net worth investors over stocks in recent decades, even when their yields weren't nearly as high.

Of course, such calculations exist only in the purely academic world of indexes. In reality, investors on the list would have spent some of their portfolios' assets over time and in the case of a pure-stock portfolio, management fees and taxes on dividends and capital gains would reduce returns. So the 10 percent growth rate in the net worth of Forbes 400 members was net of all taxes, money management fees, and personal expenses, while the stock or bond portfolio wasn't. And yet a tax-free muni portfolio would still have been enough, even accounting for most expenses and fees. Moreover, $100 million was the minimum net worth to be on the list in 1982. Many of the list's members had significantly more than $100 million that year. If the wealthier members had taken $100 million of their net worth and put it in long-term municipal bonds, or a balanced portfolio containing both stocks and bonds, and left their portfolios alone, more than just 31 of the original Forbes 400 members would probably still be on the list today.

Does this mean that wealthy investors should simply buy a stock or municipal bond index fund? Not at all. One of the key issues we revisit in subsequent chapters is a basic concept of investing that few investors seem to truly understand—"past performance does not equal future results." Ultimately, the future returns of an investment portfolio depend on current economic and securities market conditions—yields and default rates in the case of bonds, and valuations and earnings growth in the case of stocks. So it is important to bear in mind that while in 1982 the average muni yielded 13.36 percent,[2] in 2009 munis yield just under 5 percent. Similarly, the S&P 500 had an average price/earnings (p/e) ratio of 8 at the start of 1982, while at the end of 2008 it had an average trailing one-year p/e ratio of 61, according to Standard & Poor's.[3]

Why after a severe bear market decline in 2008 would stocks in the index still be so expensive? That's because Standard & Poor's rightly incorporates index members with no profits or losses into its calculations of valuations, and many banks and financial companies had losses in 2008. Thus, despite significant stock price declines, there were fewer earnings to be added to the "e" portion of the p/e ratio. Assuming the profitless banks and other failing companies will soon return to profitability and clean up their balance sheets—a big assumption—analysts estimated at year-end 2008 that the index had a forward p/e ratio of 13.8, according to *Baseline*, a much more attractive valuation. But all this begs the question as to why anyone would want to invest in an index in which a significant portion of its members may be in deep financial distress. If wealthy investors made their money building great businesses, why would they want to blindly be diversified into bad ones? Moreover, if stocks have declined so much, aren't there some great businesses with legitimate earnings on sale right now that the index's high p/e ratio masks? I would argue that wealthy investors would be better off investing in those great businesses to diversify instead of in an index fund.

If you talk to America's wealthiest citizens, few seem keen on the indexing concept or broad diversification in general. In an article titled "Secrets of the Self-Made 2008" *Forbes* editor Brett Nelson asked 20 questions to 17 of the 400 list's entrepreneurs who had an average net worth of $4 billion. The last question was, "You have $100,000 to invest. What do you do with it?" Some mentioned buying real estate, biotech startups, or alternative energy stocks, while others would invest more in their own businesses. No one recommended index funds, hedge funds, or diversified investments of any sort.[4]

And yet if we look at this list a few years from now, probably many of its current members will no longer be on it because of bad investments. So clearly some sort of balance needs to be struck between the tendency of financial advisors to build portfolios for their clients that are overly diversified and the tendency of wealthy investors to bet the farm on a single idea and then lose it all.

INSTITUTIONAL MISALLOCATION

Unfortunately, the trends for wealthy investors who have diversified portfolios are equally discouraging. According to a 2008 survey conducted by the Institute of Private Investors,[5] a wealth management, educational, and networking association, the average wealthy investor has 35 percent of his or her portfolio allocated to stocks and 44 percent to alternative assets, 22 percent or half of that alternative allocation in hedge funds. By contrast, "boring" municipal bonds only accounted for 10 percent of portfolios. In fact, as we shall see in subsequent chapters, most wealthy investors' portfolios now resemble the famous Yale University endowment in their asset allocations.

Although such a hedge-fund–oriented strategy has worked brilliantly for Yale, I believe it is inappropriate for wealthy individual investors. It is important to realize that predictable and understandable investment performance is much more significant to a family than it is to an institutional investor. The reason for this is that the high net worth investor, unlike an endowment, charity, or pension plan, can rely only on investment performance for the growth of capital. This is in stark contrast to, for example, a corporate pension plan, which can receive a cash infusion from the company when its investments underperform. And if the pension plan ultimately fails, it can be taken over and bailed out by the U.S. government's Pension Benefit Guarantee Corporation (PBGC).

In particular, with university endowment funds such as Yale's the constant flow of new dollars from fund-raising activities provides their portfolios with the capital to deploy new strategies and not worry so much about short-term losses. Some would argue that the presence of these predictable cash inflows allows the management of these endowments to take on greater risks with hedge funds and other alternative investments such as commodities. But most wealthy investors, when they approach a financial advisor, are of retirement age or approaching retirement age and plan to live off their portfolios. It is therefore imperative that their advisors recognize that the wealth creative event—the success of their business—is in all likelihood a once a lifetime experience and that there will be no entity like the PBGC to bail the family out if the advisor fails to manage the assets properly.

Hedge funds, as we reveal in later chapters, are about the worst possible investment a wealthy investor can make. Their fees are high which incentivizes managers to generate returns by taking on inordinate amounts of risk via leverage. This is true for both institutional and wealthy investors. But for the individual high net worth investor hedge funds have the added drawback of being incredibly tax-inefficient, employing high turnover strategies that produce short-term gains taxed at the highest rates.

So why are financial advisors putting so many wealthy investors in hedge funds, while municipal bonds are often overlooked? Perhaps the reason is that many advisors don't really understand the needs of wealthy investors. Unfortunately, most of the investment advice provided at the major consulting think tanks on Wall Street and across the United States is geared toward nontaxable pools of money. The reality is that the ultra high net worth market is still relatively small compared to the institutional world of pensions, endowments, 401(k) plans, and mutual funds. Less than 1 percent of U.S. taxpayers are subject to the top tax bracket.

Ultimately, a boring portfolio of high-quality stocks and municipal bonds can often satisfy the needs of wealthy investors with better after-tax returns and less downside risk. But not many advisors have been recommending such a strategy, perhaps because it is one that typically for a high net worth investor comes at a relatively low fee. One thing I like to remind my clients is that a $1 billion portfolio compounded at 6 percent (after taxes and fees) over four decades translates into $4 billion. If this can be done in a manner that is completely transparent, generates cash flow along the way, and doesn't require derivatives, margin, or "hoping" for high returns, does it not make sense to consider?

A boring or more appropriately termed traditional portfolio also has a unique advantage in that the income produced by its bond allocation provides a predictable cash flow that can be used to cover a wealthy investor's ongoing expenses. This is especially so if the bonds are bought directly as opposed to through mutual funds. As long as an investor's individual bonds do not default, he knows they will pay him their coupon rate until they mature. That is very useful from a financial planning perspective. It helps the investor to not worry much about stock market fluctuations and focus more on her individual goals, and it helps her budget her expenses according to a predictable income stream. By contrast, no one knows how a hedge fund will perform in any given year, which is why such alternative investments are more suitable for institutional investors that don't pay taxes and can afford to take on the additional risk.

Thus a very basic allocation strategy for a wealthy family might be to live debt-free, to own a portfolio of high-quality tax-free bonds for income, and to own a diversified equity portfolio that will generate dividends and wealth for future generations and fund the philanthropic works of the family. This is straightforward. It is time-tested, completely transparent, and can be understood by even the least sophisticated members of the family. And yet so few wealthy families seem to follow this strategy.

DO THE MATH

It is for all the above reasons that our central message to both wealthy investors and their advisors is to adopt an after-tax view of asset allocation and expected returns. In order to do that, we must clarify the elements of commonly used capital markets assumptions made by Wall Street and academia. Most importantly, we must develop habits for using this information to make informed decisions in the future. When examining the building blocks of capital markets returns and conventional asset allocation studies, we've observed that they often over-state the after-tax returns on equity investments. It is our con-clusion that wealthy investors have been influenced by the studies, causing overstated performance expectations. As a result, they often select asset allocation strategies with a high equity bias, high risk profile, and low tax efficiency.

In order to illustrate the remarkable difference in returns earned by taxable versus nontaxable investors, we should revisit the most popular study of asset class returns. This of course would be the one by Chicago-based financial research firm Ibbotson Associates, which calculated the long-term return of equities, bonds, and T-bills (Treasury bills) since 1926. Though Ibbotson deserves credit for updating founder Roger Ibbotson and Rex Sinquefield's original 1976 study to examine after-tax returns in 2006,[6] its tax analysis unfortu-nately makes certain assumptions, which limit its effective-ness for wealthy investors. First, the study compares equity returns to U.S. Treasury bonds, which generally do not pro-vide as high after-tax returns as do municipal bonds. But more significantly, the after-tax numbers are calculated only for the middle income tax bracket rate of 28 percent rather than the top income tax bracket over time, which at its peak has been as high as 94 percent. Finally, the analysis does not include a liquidation of the portfolio at the end of the study, meaning the study's portfolio contains a large embedded capital gain that remained untaxed. It is essential to under-stand the returns investors would experience if liquidating an asset in the portfolio for either consumption or redeployment into a business or different asset class.

One of the goals of this book is to provide a more accurate analysis of the after-tax returns of these asset classes. Indeed, the primary reason I was speaking in Vancouver was to discuss a study I had published with Michael Blum in 2006 titled "After-Tax Returns on Stocks versus Bonds for the High Tax Bracket Investor" in *The Journal of Wealth Management.*[7] Our study for this book has been updated to include the period from 1957 through year-end 2008. One of our main findings was that the outperformance or "risk premium" of stocks versus bonds for wealthy investors was only 0.77 percentage points rather than the 4 percentage points experienced by nontaxable investors. For our study the untaxed equity portfolio return on stocks is similar to the Ibbotson study, 9.15 percent annualized. However, after subtracting taxes from the portfolio paid at the highest rate in each of the years studied, the return dropped to 6.24 percent. This compared to a compounded return on a high-grade municipal bond of 5.47 percent. We review our study's results in greater detail in Chapter 3.

MULTIGENERATIONAL OBSTACLES

Though investing with taxes in mind is crucial for wealthy investors, developing savvy estate planning strategies is equally significant. Regardless of how well a stock or bond portfolio performs, a wealthy investor's heirs will ultimately be confronted with the estate tax, which in 2009 was 45 percent and is set to rise to 55 percent in 2011. (As an indication of this tax's complete unpredictability, it is set to drop to 0 percent in 2010 because of quirks in the tax policies in The Jobs and Growth Tax Relief Reconciliation Act of 2003.) It is interesting to note then that only 19 percent of 2008's Forbes 400 members were heirs to fortunes.[8] That fact is hardly coincidental.

Although most of the 33 former Forbes 400 members who dropped off the list in 2008 did so primarily because of asset value declines, 6 were removed because they died. If no problems with estate transfers existed, surely heirs to these deceased members would have taken their place on the list. But what the estate tax doesn't take, the multiplication of heirs ultimately will. Consider the case of deceased Idaho potato and French fry king Jack Simplot. In 2007, *Forbes* estimated him to be the eighty-ninth richest person in the United States, with a net worth of $3.6 billion. He was married twice and had 4 children, 18 grandchildren, and 25 great-grandchildren, each of whom will receive a portion of what remains of his estate after his second wife Esther dies—at which point the estate tax will kick in.[9] He also had a charitable foundation, which will receive a significant portion of his wealth. All other things beings equal, the likelihood of his heirs joining the Forbes 400 list solely because of their inheritance is negligible.

Is there a way for heirs to stay on the Forbes 400? If you examine the 2008 list, you will find that one of the few instances where heirs actually advanced in the rankings is the Ziff brothers—Dirk, Robert, and Daniel. The children of publishing magnate William Ziff, Jr., they sold the family business in 1994 for $1.4 billion and used the proceeds to build a hedge fund business, Ziff Brothers Investments. In 2006, the three brothers were equally ranked at number 242 with each having $1.5 billion; by 2008 they ranked ninety-seventh with $3.7 billion each. Given what I've written about hedge funds, some readers may find this ironic. But running a hedge fund and investing in one are two completely different things. For the money management company, running hedge funds can be a great business, especially because the fees collected from investors are so exorbitant—2 percent of assets plus 20 percent of all profits. Whether the brothers remain so high on the list or fall off it after 2008's bear market is unknown. But make no mistake, the best returns available in the hedge fund business is the return, that is, fees on other people's money.

CONCLUSIONS

- Wealthy investors should never forget where their wealth originated.
- No one became rich owning index funds.
- A balance must be struck between portfolio diversification and concentration.
- Always do the math when it comes to taxes and fees in investing.
- After taxes, a balanced portfolio of municipal bonds and stocks can produce better risk-adjusted returns than hedge funds.

CHAPTER 2

Market History

Mark Twain once said that history doesn't repeat itself but it rhymes. And surely investors who don't understand market history will suffer the consequences of their ignorance. Historians would agree that no one can predict what stocks or bonds will do tomorrow, but there are patterns that seem to recur—a cycle of booms and busts, bubbles and inevitable crashes. The booms seem to last longer than the busts, while the busts are sudden and severe. There are reasons for these cycles, and by studying history closely investors and their financial advisors can do their best to, if not avoid the unavoidable declines, at least resist the siren call of the bubble mentality. All around the country we can see evidence of the immeasurable damage done to individual investors who piled in to seemingly hot sectors as they were peaking as well as the hordes who liquidated their portfolios at the market bottom due to incurable fear.

Much has been written about the history of the stock market in books such as Jeremy Siegel's *Stocks for the Long Run*, Burton Malkiel's *A Random Walk Down Wall Street*, and John Kenneth Galbraith's *A Short History of Financial Euphoria*. I do not intend to recount here every single episode they have more than adequately covered, but rather hone in on some of the key elements of booms and busts that will help readers identify the essential patterns in the future.

MISLEADING LONG-TERM RETURNS

Before we proceed, it's important to understand why having a grasp of financial history can help investors avoid making costly mistakes. The reason for this is that if you look at asset class performance data without having an understanding of the historical context to them, the numbers can mislead you into having a false sense of confidence.

The data in Figure 2.1, often referred to as the "History of Capital Markets," is a mainstay of financial advisors, who use it as a marketing/educational tool with clients when trying to illustrate the benefits of investing in stocks or stock mutual funds. But the chart is misleading because it seems to imply that the market always goes up, and if an investor has a long enough time horizon, then is likely to experience a return in the future similar to the mean return of the past. Aside from the fact that few investors plan to buy and hold stocks for more than 80 years, it assumes that they would have had the prescience at the beginning of this tumultuous time period to implement a stock-oriented strategy. Truth be

FIGURE 2.1

Cumulative Returns on an Invested Dollar (1926–2008)

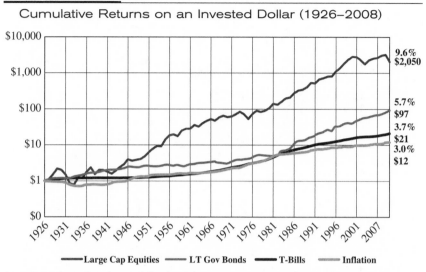

———Large Cap Equities ——— LT Gov Bonds ——— T-Bills ~~~~~ Inflation

Source: Morgan Stanley Smith Barney LLC Consulting Group, 2009. This is for illustrative purposes only and not indicative of any investment. Past performance is no guarantee of future results. Underlying data is from the *Stocks, Bonds, Bills, and Inflation*® *(SBBI) Yearbook,* by Roger G. Ibbotson and Rex A. Sinquefield. Updated annually. March 1, 2001 © 2001. Ibbotson Associates, Inc.

told, few if any human beings on the face of this earth have compounded their money along the lines shown in the chart.

Let's put the chart into perspective. In 1926 one could argue that the United States was a volatile emerging market. Prior to this date the nation was subject to frequent economic booms and busts not unlike the violent swings we've seen in Asian and Latin American markets in recent decades. Consider that 1926 really wasn't that far off historically from a civil war which nearly tore the country apart and ushered in a bubble period and crash comparable to what precipitated the Great Depression. Indeed, a chart of leading blue chip stocks included in Graham and Dodd's famous post-Depression era book *Security Analysis* (Figure 2.2) reveals how the years from 1900 to 1939 were full of violent shocks on the downside that might have discouraged investors from

18

FIGURE 2.2

Dow Jones Industrial Average (1890–1922)

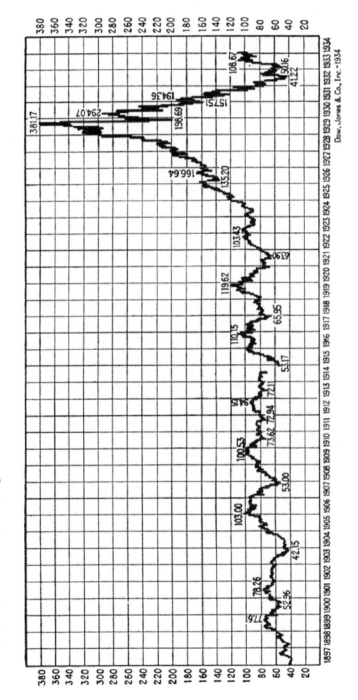

Source: Benjamin Graham and David L. Dodd, *Security Analysis: The Classic 1934 Edition* (New York: McGraw Hill, 2009), p. 2.

buying and holding even if the Great Depression in which stocks lost 88 percent of their value hadn't occurred.[1]

The problem with the more popular capital markets from 1926 through 2008 chart is that it wasn't published until the 1960s and wasn't widely accepted as an instructional tool until the 1980s. Advisors who adopted it were more than 50 years too late. Clients don't want to know how they could have invested their money over the last 50 years. They want to know how to invest it for the next 50. So why didn't we have any of these theories available to our great grandparents in the 1920s?

But even if we acknowledge that stock indexes would have made handsome gains from 1926 until today if left untouched by investors, intermediaries, fees, and taxes, to then extrapolate that the same thing will happen in the next 80 or so years is presumptuous, to say the least. What's more, even if such returns were somehow repeatable, they would be much lower for wealthy investors whose performance after taxes in equities can be drastically reduced depending on the tax rates when they own stocks. Indeed, in subsequent chapters we reveal how, after taxes, wealthy investors have earned more along the order of 6 percent in stocks historically, not the usual 10 percent cited. Moreover, they could have earned that return during several periods in history with a lot less volatility by investing in tax-free municipal bonds.

So it's important to highlight this equity bias in the financial industry because we see these past performance measures being used to market both traditional and alternative investments, and the end result is that investors are lulled, whether intentionally or not, into believing that there is a predictable pattern to the market that will continue into the future. By contrast, truly educated investors know that the performance and volatility of any investment we make in the future will be a function of the economic conditions at the time of purchase combined with the economic realities of the future, most of which are unknown. Investors must learn that rarely if ever will the returns or the volatility that they experience match what's in the sales brochure or prospectus.

HERD MENTALITY

I suspect that the rational side of most investors, even novices, understands that such rosy long-term returns are by no means guaranteed. No one who honestly examines their own lives believes that their past is necessarily a prelude to their future. And yet throughout history investors have used past success in the markets as a justification for future speculation—from the seventeenth century's Dutch tulipomania to the eighteenth century's British South Sea Company bubble, through the repeated booms and busts in America's nineteenth century until today; the attitude, once a bubble is well underway, is that investing in whatever the inflated asset may be is a sure thing.

So why do investors constantly get caught up in these speculative manias? It's easy to identify such behavior as foolishness in retrospect, but in the heart of a bubble the rational side of investors loses out to their tendency to follow the herd, and the end result is a stampede toward overpriced assets. As philosopher and poet Friedrich Schiller once wrote and legendary investor Bernard Baruch was fond of quoting, "Anyone taken as an individual is tolerably sensible and reasonable—as a member of a crowd, he at once becomes a blockhead."

Consider how it must have felt for investors sitting on the sidelines in 1999 to watch commercials for brokers in which truck drivers suddenly owned tropical islands by trading stocks online. Imagine their feelings of being left out knowing the tech-heavy Nasdaq Composite Index rose by 86 percent that year. The temptation to join the party and the peer pressure must have been intense.

Ideally, one would hope that trusted financial advisors would have recognized that markets were overheating and shown more self-restraint. But the harsh reality about Wall Street is that financial advisors often feel more pressure to follow the herd than individual investors do. Advisors and money managers are often paid based on their assets under management or their performance compared to a stock benchmark. If they underperform the stock market, they lose clients and their performance-based bonuses. So when markets are rising sharply, there is an incentive for them to follow the herd even if some voice of reason inside their heads says, "I know this is a mistake."

One piece of anecdotal evidence I had that we were in or dangerously close to a speculative excess occurred in March 2000. When I made the decision that year to cut our tech stock positions in Cisco, Oracle, and EMC in half to increase our weightings in municipal bonds, one of our clients sent me a fax that said, "Why would you be holding onto losers (like Procter & Gamble) and selling winners?" And, "I'm not sure if I can trust you anymore with the remaining shares of these companies, so why don't you have my shares issued in paper stock certificates and sent out to me, so that you won't be tempted to sell them and prevent me from having a future gain?" Today that client and I laugh about that instance. And of course I should have trusted my own valuation work even more and sold all those positions at that point.

Such negative reactions from investors to any dissenting opinions are classic signs of the herd mentality accompanying a bubble. And money managers don't just risk losing clients when they disagree. They risk losing their jobs. Legendary fund managers such as Julian Robertson, Robert Sanborn, George Vanderheiden, Jeff Vinik, and Chuck Clough all quit or were fired from their jobs in the late 1990s and 2000s because they refused to buy or recommend stocks they thought were grossly overvalued. Investors and the press often belittled their underperformance. At the height of the bubble in March 2000, one investor on a stock message board wrote of Robert Sanborn, the erstwhile manager of the Oakmark Funds, "Sanborn should give up stock picking and start sacking groceries. What a joke!" according to *USA Today*.[2] Sanborn's value-oriented strategy went on to vastly outperform the market in subsequent years.

It is experiences like these that make it so hard to be a good financial advisor during a bubble. Advisors who try to be cautious and responsible with their clients' money will generally lose business to more bullish competitors. In the short term telling the truth—that stocks, bonds, or real estate are overvalued—prevents participation in the final wave of speculative returns and that can be too painful for many advisors to handle, or they may experience pressure from their employers to be more optimistic. But in the long term, being disciplined will help soften the blow of the inevitable crash, and the clients who stick around will stay with such an advisor for life.

NEW PARADIGMS

While in reality speculation during a bubble just feeds upon itself as one fool pushes up asset prices for the next, the public justification for such manias has always been that we've entered a new economic era in which asset prices will perpetually rise. This new paradigm often revolves around discovery and innovation, either perceived or genuine. The first tulip bulbs, for instance, arrived in Antwerp from Constantinople in 1562. As Galbraith observes in *A Short History of Financial Euphoria*:

> Speculation, it has been noted, comes when popular imagination settles on something seemingly new in the field of commerce or finance. The tulip, beautiful and varied in its color, was one of the first things so to serve. . . . Attention came to be concentrated on the possession and display of the more esoteric of the blooms. An appreciation of the more exceptional of the flowers rapidly gave way to a yet deeper appreciation of the increase in price that their beauty and rarity were commanding.[3]

By the mid-1630s a single tulip bulb could trade for as much as $50,000 on the Amsterdam Stock Exchange. Houses and land were sold to purchase bulbs at ridiculous prices. People borrowed substantial sums with their property promised as collateral for the debt to buy flowers. A foreign sailor who ate one of the bulbs by mistake, thinking it an onion to garnish his meal at a local tavern, was thrown into debtor's prison when he couldn't afford the outrageous sum to pay for it. And then when the market crashed, average citizens went bankrupt and lost their homes, Holland entered a depression, and the government tried vainly to bolster the prices of falling bulbs. Sound familiar?

The same pattern has repeated itself innumerable times to the present day. In France in the eighteenth century, it was the excitement over the supposed riches to be found in spurious Louisiana gold mines that propelled the Mississippi Company to previously unseen heights. In the same century England's South Sea Company was supposed to control new American trade routes, which never materialized. Its spectacular rise spawned many equally dubious imitators, according to Galbraith: companies to develop a perpetual motion machine, to insure horses, to transmute quicksilver into malleable fine metal, and one completely nebulous enterprise "for carrying on an undertaking of great advantage, but nobody to know what it is."[4]

There were also several notable booms and busts in the nineteenth century to build out the infrastructure of the United States, roads and turnpikes which did benefit the nation at large but few if any investors. Then there was the U.S. railroad boom and bust, a Florida real estate craze, the automobile and telephone stocks that collapsed during the Great Depression, the Nifty Fifty that collapsed in the 1970s, the real estate investment trusts and saving and loans busts in the 1980s, the dot-com bombs of the 1990s, and most recently the real estate, investment banking, and hedge fund collapses.

Each time the promoters of these investments said, "It's different this time"—the oldest sentence in any financial history book. And each time the asset class being sold eventually reached unsustainable heights and collapsed. And each time anyone who dared to suggest that the prosperity created by such irrational exuberance would be ephemeral was publicly raked over the coals. Notes Galbraith about the 1929 crash: "In the winter of 1929, Paul M. Warburg, the most respected banker of his time and one of the founding parents of the Federal Reserve System, spoke critically of the then orgy of 'unrestrained speculation' and said that if it continued, there would ultimately be a disastrous collapse, and the country would face a serious depression. The reaction to his statement was bitter, even vicious. He was held to be obsolete in his views; he was 'sandbagging American prosperity'; quite possibly, he was himself short in the market."[5]

At the same time enough market "experts" and academics always emerge with theories about the new paradigm to justify the madness of crowds. In the fall of 1929, Yale University's Irving Fisher, one of the most famous economists of his day, made the unfortunate remark that "stock prices have reached what looks like a permanently high plateau." Meanwhile, during the dot-com era, I vividly remember market prognosticator Harry Dent's 1999 book *The Roaring 2000s* forecasting a prodigious rise in the Dow Jones Industrial Average. He was very popular at the time making projections of the Dow hitting anywhere between 20,000 and 40,000 depending on when he was interviewed. The hyperbolic rhetoric of the new paradigm was evident throughout the book:

> In fact, we are on the brink of the most exciting boom period since the Roaring Twenties. . . . During the Roaring Twenties, new technologies, industries, products and services seemed to burst forth virtually overnight. Lindbergh's first flight across the Atlantic epitomized the soaring possibilities of the new technology, and the new spirit of optimism that accompanied it. Cars, phones, radios, electrical home appliances, movies, Coca-Cola, and so much more became affordable, mainstream, consumer items. . . . Sounds like a great economy? It was! The Roaring 2000s will be even greater. Now, new technologies, industries and products and services are again about

to burst forth. This will mark the beginning of the information revolution—*but it hasn't really happened yet!"*[6]

Mr. Dent's book was not only a best seller, but he became a regular guest on financial news shows, and then brokerage firms began hiring him to give public seminars, all of which we know now contributed to the bubble. (In 2009 Dent published a new book, *The Great Depression Ahead*. Given his previous track record as a prognosticator, investors might want to interpret it as a contrarian indicator of a market bottom.)

The new paradigm philosophy justifying the bubble of course requires a complete disregard of traditional valuation metrics. I noticed this first in 1998 when the concept of p/e ratios started to change on analyst conference calls with companies. CEOs were no longer talking about price-to-earnings ratios, but price-to-sales or sometimes even price-to-clicks for dot-com companies that had no earnings. When they did speak of earnings, they talked of price-to-next-year's earnings or two or even three years out. They would take last year's earnings and assume an inflated 30 percent annual growth rate going forward so that the stocks did not seem as outrageously valued as they were.

What's interesting about the bubble philosophy Dent so perfectly typified is that from a business or macroeconomic perspective he wasn't exactly wrong. The 1990s and 2000s were revolutionary from a technological standpoint as were the Roaring Twenties. But one of the classic mistakes investors have made throughout history is confusing good ideas, good technology, or good businesses with good investments. Companies like Cisco or EMC may be great businesses, the perfect representatives of the "new economy," and yet be terrible investments at the wrong price as they turned out to be in 2000. Similarly, before the Great Depression companies such as Coca-Cola, Gillette, General Electric, and AT&T were great businesses, but they were a lot better investments after the crash.

But for every great business that emerges during a period of technological innovation, many others in the same innovative industries often fail. While investors may celebrate companies like Amazon.com, eBay, and Google today, scores of other defunct dot-coms such as Webvan, Beenz, and Pets.com have long since been forgotten.

As we will see in subsequent chapters, the key to investing well is buying good businesses at the right price. If either one of these two key ingredients is missing, then you may find yourself becoming more of a speculator than an investor—either overpaying for good businesses or buying into the new paradigm stories of the bad.

REINVENTING THE WHEEL

The 2008 bear market was different from the dot-com crash in that the epicenter of the bubble wasn't in the stock market but in the real estate market and the companies that fueled its advance. Though valuations in equities were not nearly as extended as they were in 2000, the impact of the subprime mortgage implosion sent shockwaves through the entire financial system because home ownership is so central to the U.S. economy and because new types of financial instruments—collateralized mortgage obligations and credit default swaps—and an excess of leverage applied to those instruments by investment banks and hedge funds turned a severe cold in one industry into a global pandemic.

While bubbles often occur when there is genuine technological innovation as in the dot-com era, they also happen
when there is the appearance of some form of financial innovation. The latter is a much more dangerous kind of speculation because there is essentially no real engine of economic
growth underlying it. As economist John Maynard Keynes
once remarked, "Speculators may do no harm as bubbles on
a steady stream of enterprise. But the position is serious
when enterprise becomes the bubble on a whirlpool of speculation. When the capital development of a country becomes
a by-product of the activities of a casino, the job is likely to
be ill-done."[7]

What financial innovation inevitably implies is a repackaging of leverage in some new form or what John Kenneth
Galbraith called reinventing the wheel. Galbraith noted:

> The world of finance hails the invention of the wheel over and
> over again, often in a slightly more unstable version. All finan-
> cial innovation involves, in one form or another, the creation
> of debt secured in greater or lesser adequacy by real assets.
> This was true in one of the earliest seeming marvels: when
> banks discovered that they could print bank notes and issue
> them to borrowers in a volume in excess of the hard money
> deposits in the banks' strong rooms. The depositors could be
> counted upon, it was believed or hoped, not to come all at
> once for their money. There was no seeming limit to the debt
> that could thus be leveraged on a given volume of hard cash.
> A wonderful thing. The limit became apparent, however,
> when some alarming news, perhaps of the extent of the lever-
> age itself, caused too many of the depositors to want their
> money at the same time. All subsequent financial innovation
> has involved similar debt creation leveraged against more
> limited assets with only modifications in the earlier design.

> All crises have involved debt that, in one fashion or another,
> has become dangerously out of scale in relation to the under-
> lying means of payment.[8]

This passage almost perfectly describes what happened
in the 1990s and 2000s with the explosion of "new" debt
instruments and derivatives. The invention of mortgage-
backed securities (MBS) and subsequently collateralized
mortgage obligations (CMOs) enabled mortgage lenders to
bundle all their mortgage loans to individual homeowners
into tradable bonds they would sell to investment banks and
other financial institutions. These securities were sliced up
into different tranches with more or less actual real estate
assets backing them as collateral depending on the tranche
of the debt purchased—hence increasing the disconnect
between the debt and the assets backing it. Investment banks
would sell off the different tranches of CMOs to hedge funds,
mutual funds, and other institutional investors. Because
money managers assumed that housing prices always go up
in classic bubble-mentality fashion, they would leverage their
bets on CMOs, sometimes 10 times or more in the case of
hedge funds. Meanwhile, mortgage companies and banks
started lending to the shoddiest of borrowers to satisfy the
seemingly unquenchable desire for more MBS and CMOs.

Exacerbating the problem was the invention of new
derivatives such as credit default swaps (CDSs), which were
ostensibly designed to reduce the risk to financial institutions. These swaps are essentially insurance contracts on
bonds that cover their buyers' losses in the case of a bond
default. The problem is that such insurance contracts are
highly unregulated and require little or no initial collateral
backing them by their issuers. So they essentially became

another way for their issuers to leverage their bets. Sellers of the contracts receive income for selling the contracts with minimal downpayment to cover the potential losses to the buyers. Meanwhile buyers of these contracts are lulled into a false sense of security. Confusing the matter is that CDSs are heavily traded, so it's often hard to tell who the original issuer is on a contract and who will exactly be on the hook to pay up in the case of a default. Total outstanding CDSs now exceed $38 trillion, according to the International Swaps and Derivatives Association,[9] although this number may be over-stated from double-counting of heavily traded contracts.

As usual, these types of financial innovations, which amplify risk through increased leverage, will always have their boosters among academics and financial industry pundits during boom times. No less a personage than former Fed chairman Alan Greenspan, who accused investors of being irrationally exuberant in 1996, praised the explosive issuance of credit derivatives in the 2000s as being a means for banks to offload their balance sheet risk. In a speech he made to the Federal Reserve Bank of Chicago in May 2005, he famously said: "As is generally acknowledged, the development of credit derivatives has contributed to the stability of the banking system by allowing banks, especially the largest, systemically important banks, to measure and manage their credit risks more effectively."[10] Four years later many of the biggest users of such derivatives, such as insurer AIG (American International Group), were in dire straits.

An excess of debt is always an essential ingredient to a bubble and a stock market crash not only because it allows speculators to borrow increasing amounts of money to inflate asset prices but also because when the debt ultimately has to be repaid, speculators who've run out of money from tapped-out lenders are forced to sell their assets in a rush. As prices fall, margin calls occur and more investors have to sell, and then the psychological dimension of panic ensues. This is why crashes are often so sudden and so severe. There is a terrifying snowball effect to the leverage on the downside that causes an avalanche of selling. Certainly such proved to be the case in 2008 when hedge funds and investment banks had to deleverage their overleveraged balance sheets all at once, causing tremendous downward pressure on stocks and corporate bonds.

And judging by the amount of leverage still outstanding on every level of U.S. society, the U.S. economy may not be out of the woods yet. According to financial research firm Ned Davis Research, total credit market debt outstanding in the United States was $52.9 trillion at the end of 2008, exceeding the country's total gross domestic product (GDP) of $14.1 trillion by 375 percent. In other words, we're still spending a lot more than we produce. And that percentage is the highest in U.S. history, far exceeding the 260 percent debt-to-GDP ratio reached right before the Great Depression began. (See Figure 2.3.)

TUNING OUT THE MARKET

Does a recession or even a depression mean that wealthy investors should avoid the stock market entirely? Not at all. Just as it's important to remember that great businesses can become overpriced in boom times, it's equally important to know that those same businesses can survive, even thrive, during a downturn as weaker companies go out of business. In 2008, Best Buy was strengthened by the demise of competitor

FIGURE 2.3

Total Credit Market Debt as a Percent of GDP (quarterly data 12/31/1922–3/31/2009)

Circuit City. Walgreens and CVS benefited from the weak balance sheet and limited business flexibility of Rite Aid. And the prices of some of the strongest companies can become remarkably cheap during such times, discounting much of the bad news from a valuation perspective so that a severe recession is already priced into their shares. Moreover, because stocks are leading indicators that don't move in lock-step with the economy, share prices can often rise a long time before the economy exits a downturn.

During bear market or recessionary times, should wealthy investors adjust their strategy because financially distressed investors are being forced to sell? The simple answer is that if the investor has not put himself in a position of distress, he should be willing to buy (or continue to hold) undervalued assets regardless of the perceived direction of the market. Failure to do so essentially means that informed investors should abandon their valuation work and take investment cues from the weakest, most damaged investors. This of course makes no sense because we know that distressed and emotionally driven investors are neither informed nor rational in their behavior.

The important thing investors should take away from history is to avoid being uninformed speculators in over-hyped stocks and start being informed investors in undervalued individual businesses. The ultimate goal should be to tune out the daily fluctuations in the market and understand what the private market value of the companies they're invested in would be based on their expected earnings or cash flow. If the private market value of a company far exceeds its current stock price, then it shouldn't matter to the long-term investor if the stock gets cheaper in a bear market. The investor knows that in the long term that private market value should be realized. As we shall see in subsequent chapters, that private market value is determined by examining the future earnings growth of the company and seeing whether its profitability is sustainable.

Despite a 37 percent decline in the fourth quarter, 1987 was a positive year for the U.S. stock market. The investors who exhibited euphoria as the market advanced from January through September fell into despair when most of the gains for the year were wiped out during the October crash. Many inflicted permanent damage to their portfolios as the market troughed. Peter Lynch recalled that week in his book *One Up on Wall Street* describing the pain of having to sell stock in a down market to meet investor redemptions. He summarized the lessons of October 1987 with the following simple advice: "I've always believed that investors should ignore the ups and downs of the market."[11]

Of course, the irrational euphoric psychology of investors in a bubble has its corollary in the irrational panic investors experience in a bear market. Only when fear and pessimism have reached their maximum point has the market truly bottomed. Wealthy investors, unfortunately, are not immune to either manifestation of this irrational psychology, even though from an economic standpoint they are in an enviable position to be truly successful long-term investors. They have the financial wherewithal to tune out the market and ride out the storm with a portfolio of great businesses bought or held at discount prices.

CONCLUSIONS

- History has shown that past performance does not equal future results.
- Avoid herd mentality when investing and think of valuations instead.
- Market experts will often rationalize bubbles by claiming that there's a new paradigm.
- Bubbles go hand in hand with excesses in leverage.
- Tune out the noise during bear markets and stay invested.
- Invest in good businesses at reasonable prices, not story stocks.

CHAPTER 3

After-Tax Returns on Stocks versus Bonds for the High Tax Bracket Investor

Our academic research on after-tax returns was published in the summer of 2006 in *The Journal of Wealth Management*. Our article, "After-Tax Returns on Stocks versus Bonds for the High Tax Bracket Investor," was certainly not the first to study equity risk premiums. I do believe it was the first to approach the topic from the perspective of the highest tax bracket investor, include the effect of state taxes, and study the variations of return under different portfolio turnover rates in comparison to high-grade municipal bonds. Like previous studies, the equity risk premium we examined is the excess return that equity investments provide over historically less risky fixed income investments, but in this case we calculated it on an after-tax basis.

In the fall of 2006, Dr. Jeremy Siegel paid a visit to my office, and I presented him with a copy of the article. I was quite pleased that Dr. Siegel chose to incorporate a chapter on the tax effects of equity returns in his 2008 edition of *Stocks for the Long Run*. Dr. Siegel's research contained a wealth of information and statistics that are helpful in understanding the topic. One notable difference between the approach we chose to take and that of Dr. Siegel's was to include and model for the effect of state taxes and portfolio turnover rates. In doing so, we found that the equity premium over municipal bonds was smaller and even negative in some cases of portfolios domiciled in high-tax states such as New Jersey or New York. Another notable difference was that we tried to communicate that declaring a winner between two asset classes on a historical basis (such as the title of his book *Stocks for the Long Run* suggests) has limited use for the investor who is most concerned with returns in the future rather than those of the past.

Prior to the release of our article, we submitted our findings to John C. Bogle, founder of Vanguard. His comments were invaluable as he has long been a champion of after-tax performance reporting. We've subsequently been in touch with him regarding this book, and he had some interesting insights about the *Stocks for the Long Run* thesis. While Bogle believes in indexing as a means of achieving one's asset allocation and I don't, he also believes in doing the math and not just looking blindly at the indexes' past returns and assuming that those returns are guaranteed to recur indefinitely in the future. In fact, Bogle told me that he doesn't even permit that old Wall Street saying that stocks always outperform bonds over the long term to be uttered in his presence. "What is permitted is to say stocks have done better than bonds in the past," he says. "But in about one out of every six- or ten-year period bonds win, and bonds can win for a lot longer periods than that if you go back in history. So one has to look at the prospective returns on stocks and bonds and try to make some sense as to what to do." (See sidebar for more of Bogle's insights.) If, as we shall soon see, taxes are factored in, the stocks versus bonds equation changes significantly, further emphasizing Bogle's fundamental point.

Bogle Does the Math

It may seem ironic to some readers that the founder of the one of the first stock index funds currently favors bonds. Truth be told, Vanguard 500 creator John Bogle is agnostic when it comes to either asset class, preferring to invest where he thinks the best value is and in assets that are most appropriate for someone his age.

Though "buying the entire stock market" as an ostensible sure thing is how advisors often present index funds to clients, Bogle never really bought into the concept. He believes as I do in comparing the earnings yield of the average stock in the S&P 500 to the yields of bonds to see which is more attractive. "Past returns don't matter," he says. "What matters is the source of returns." In stocks he sees that as dividend yields and earnings growth, and in bonds it's interest rates. "My theory is pretty simple," he says. "Today's coupon in the bond market is a highly accurate indicator of the return over the next 10 years," he says. "So, forget what the history of bond returns has been. If today the [Treasury] bond yield is 4 percent, that's what you can expect to get in the years to come."

Because he is 80 years old, the majority of Bogle's portfolio is currently invested in bonds, but he is selective in the kinds of bonds he owns. With 10-year Treasury notes yielding less than 4 percent in 2009 and high-quality corporate bonds yielding 3 percentage points more than that, he says that the spread is enticing enough to favor corporate debt. "That's a 300 basis point yield premium," he says. "The normal premium is around 50 to 75 basis points. So we really have two different bond markets right now and a diversified portfolio of corporate bonds or a bond index fund which holds both corporates and governments seems to me to be a pretty good choice." Bogle has always done this kind of math for stocks as well.

One equation that doesn't add up for Bogle is the appeal of hedge funds to wealthy investors. He calls their costs "horrendous," citing not only their 2 percent of assets plus 20 percent of profits fee structure but also their high turnover, trading costs, and tax inefficiency, and he says that one could get better after-tax returns with less downside risk by investing in a low-cost balanced mutual fund such as Vanguard's Wellington Fund.

Moreover, Bogle believes that hedge funds and other alternative assets don't do the job they're supposed to do, failing to provide diversification in major downturns when investors need it most. "What we have found time and again is the idea of uncorrelated assets doesn't usually work when times are bad," he says.

Even if some hedge funds are bound to have superlative performance, Bogle thinks that knowing which ones that will be is a daunting task: "Hedge funds cannot be really subsumed by one sentence. They're all over the lot in terms of what they do. The failure rates for them are very high. So the premium on selecting the right one makes the premium on selecting the right mutual fund seem very modest in comparison."

As you review the tables in this chapter, you will understand why I have so forcefully insisted that investors understand the characteristics of shorter time periods, 10 or 20 years, in order to understand the performance of the major asset classes. My reason for cautioning investors from relying too heavily on long-term averages of 50 or 100 years is that the length of these time periods masks the extreme periods of positive or negative performance and the outperformance of certain asset classes during shorter time periods. You will also see where we have proved that the notion of equity outperformance "over the long run" is false for several extended periods in the second half of the twentieth century and that investors should not assume this phenomenon under all circumstances. Because of the equity market declines of 2008, the portfolio returns for the entire period are lower than those we communicated in our 2006 study.

AFTER-TAX RETURNS ON STOCKS 1957–2009

The Standard & Poor's 500 Index was first published in 1957.[1] So our research on the after-tax equity risk premium began with the index's value on January 1, 1957, and ended on January 1, 2009. In Table 3.1, we present the model portfolio illustrating an investor in the highest tax bracket who invested $100 into the model portfolio on January 1, 1957. The portfolio of stocks matched the performance of the S&P 500 including dividends. The portfolio was modeled with a turnover rate of 5 percent for our first illustration. We also modeled for a 20 percent turnover rate, which we believe represents a "core" investment style for active managers. Note that the actual turnover rate of the S&P 500 is assumed to be 5 percent over the same period, while the turnover of the average actively managed mutual fund is assumed to be as high as 90 percent. Later in the chapter we observe the variations in after-tax returns with turnover rates ranging from 0 to 100 percent. In each of the years, the portfolio paid tax on dividends at the prevailing top tax rate, and all gains

TABLE 3.1

S&P 500 Taxed at Top Income Bracket–5 Percent Turnover

Taxes? Y   Turnover: 5.00%   State tax: 6.00%

Year Start	S&P 500	S&P Performance	Dividend Yield	Ordinary Income Tax	Capital Gains Tax	Portfolio Value	Portfolio Performance	Quarterly Portfolio Dollar Change	Dividend Dollar Yield	Net Dividend After Tax	Principal	Gains Tax After Turnover	Retained Capital Gains
1957	44.72	(8.05%)	1.75%	91.00%	25.00%	$100.00	(8.00%)	($2.01)	$1.66	$0.05	$100.00	$0.00	($8.00)
1958	41.12	35.26%	1.75%	91.00%	25.00%	$92.00	35.04%	$8.11	$1.96	$0.06	$99.65	$0.26	$32.24
1959	55.62	4.33%	1.83%	91.00%	25.00%	$124.24	4.03%	$1.35	$2.34	$0.07	$100.69	$0.45	$5.00
1960	58.03	0.14%	1.95%	91.00%	25.00%	$129.25	(0.14%)	$0.04	$2.52	$0.08	$101.75	$0.43	($0.18)
1961	58.11	23.13%	3.41%	91.00%	25.00%	$129.07	22.57%	$7.46	$5.04	$0.15	$102.79	$0.87	$29.13
1962	71.55	(11.81%)	2.85%	91.00%	25.00%	$158.20	(12.07%)	($4.67)	$4.18	$0.13	$104.87	$0.54	($19.10)
1963	63.10	18.89%	3.40%	91.00%	25.00%	$139.11	18.35%	$6.57	$5.29	$0.16	$106.19	$0.92	$25.52
1964	75.02	12.97%	3.13%	91.00%	25.00%	$164.63	12.34%	$5.34	$5.57	$0.17	$108.39	$1.20	$20.32
1965	84.75	9.06%	3.05%	91.00%	25.00%	$184.94	8.40%	$4.19	$5.96	$0.18	$111.24	$1.40	$15.54
1966	92.43	(13.09%)	3.06%	70.00%	25.00%	$200.48	(12.88%)	($6.56)	$5.63	$1.35	$114.54	$0.93	($25.82)
1967	80.33	20.09%	3.59%	70.00%	25.00%	$174.66	20.25%	$8.77	$7.06	$1.69	$117.95	$1.42	$35.36
1968	96.47	7.66%	3.09%	70.00%	25.00%	$210.03	7.68%	$4.02	$6.80	$1.63	$122.81	$1.60	$16.12
1969	103.86	(11.36%)	2.93%	75.00%	26.90%	$226.15	(11.37%)	($6.42)	$6.16	$1.17	$128.01	$1.19	($25.72)
1970	92.06	0.10%	3.52%	77.00%	27.50%	$200.43	0.12%	$0.05	$7.06	$1.20	$131.61	$1.16	$0.24
1971	92.15	10.79%	3.46%	70.00%	32.30%	$200.67	10.84%	$5.41	$7.41	$1.78	$135.10	$1.67	$21.75
1972	102.09	15.63%	3.10%	70.00%	34.30%	$222.42	15.38%	$8.69	$7.57	$1.82	$139.57	$2.37	$34.22
1973	118.05	(17.37%)	2.70%	70.00%	36.50%	$256.64	(17.34%)	($11.14)	$6.18	$1.48	$144.90	$1.43	($44.51)
1974	97.55	(29.72%)	3.70%	70.00%	36.50%	$212.13	(29.00%)	($15.76)	$6.39	$1.53	$148.31	$0.02	($61.52)
1975	68.56	31.55%	5.43%	70.00%	36.50%	$150.61	32.43%	$11.88	$9.79	$2.35	$149.87	$1.03	$48.84

Year														
1976	90.19	19.15%	4.14%	70.00%	36.50%	$199.45	19.37%	$9.55	$9.25	$2.22	$153.61	$1.79	$38.62
1977	107.46	(11.50%)	3.93%	70.00%	39.90%	$238.07	(11.13%)	($6.85)	$8.68	$2.08	$158.24	$1.20	($26.50)
1978	95.10	1.06%	5.11%	70.00%	39.90%	$211.57	1.73%	$0.56	$10.88	$2.61	$161.74	$1.20	$3.66
1979	96.11	12.31%	5.39%	70.00%	39.00%	$215.23	12.91%	$6.62	$12.49	$3.00	$165.76	$1.71	$27.78
1980	107.94	25.77%	5.53%	70.00%	28.00%	$243.01	26.37%	$15.66	$15.60	$3.74	$170.85	$2.29	$64.09
1981	135.76	(9.73%)	4.74%	70.00%	28.00%	$307.10	(9.21%)	($7.47)	$13.67	$3.28	$179.04	$1.67	($28.27)
1982	122.55	14.76%	5.57%	70.00%	23.70%	$278.83	15.51%	$10.29	$16.96	$4.07	$185.57	$2.00	$43.23
1983	140.64	17.27%	4.93%	50.00%	20.00%	$322.06	18.93%	$13.91	$17.59	$7.74	$194.36	$2.38	$60.98
1984	164.93	1.40%	4.32%	50.00%	20.00%	$383.05	2.71%	$1.34	$16.69	$7.34	$208.89	$2.33	$10.38
1985	167.24	26.33%	4.68%	50.00%	20.00%	$393.42	27.83%	$25.90	$21.44	$9.43	$222.87	$3.56	$109.47
1986	211.28	14.62%	3.88%	50.00%	20.00%	$502.89	15.62%	$18.38	$21.30	$9.37	$242.45	$4.34	$78.55
1987	242.17	2.03%	3.38%	50.00%	20.00%	$581.45	2.80%	$2.95	$19.90	$8.76	$264.18	$4.28	$16.27
1988	247.08	12.40%	3.71%	38.50%	28.00%	$597.72	13.52%	$18.53	$23.89	$13.26	$285.11	$6.57	$80.81
1989	277.72	27.25%	3.68%	28.00%	28.00%	$678.52	28.71%	$46.23	$29.22	$19.29	$311.13	$9.39	$194.80
1990	353.40	(6.56%)	3.32%	28.00%	28.00%	$873.32	(5.37%)	($14.32)	$27.81	$18.35	$348.64	$7.95	($46.88)
1991	330.22	26.31%	3.74%	28.00%	28.00%	$826.45	27.82%	$54.35	$35.99	$23.75	$382.42	$11.24	$229.92
1992	417.09	4.46%	3.11%	28.00%	28.00%	$1,056.37	5.49%	$11.79	$33.77	$22.29	$428.00	$11.48	$57.96
1993	435.71	7.06%	2.90%	31.00%	28.00%	$1,114.33	7.86%	$19.65	$33.74	$21.26	$472.58	$12.25	$87.63
1994	466.45	(1.54%)	2.72%	39.60%	28.00%	$1,201.96	(1.02%)	($4.63)	$32.38	$17.61	$517.61	$11.32	($12.21)
1995	459.27	34.11%	2.91%	39.60%	29.20%	$1,189.75	34.50%	$101.46	$42.00	$22.85	$557.20	$18.28	$410.41
1996	615.93	20.26%	2.30%	39.60%	29.20%	$1,600.16	20.23%	$81.06	$41.46	$22.56	$613.69	$23.07	$323.74
1997	740.74	31.01%	2.01%	39.60%	29.20%	$1,923.89	30.63%	$149.14	$46.16	$25.11	$678.71	$32.41	$589.26
1998	970.43	26.67%	1.60%	39.60%	20.00%	$2,513.16	26.43%	$167.56	$46.91	$25.52	$763.50	$31.46	$664.29
1999	1,229.23	19.53%	1.32%	39.60%	20.00%	$3,177.44	19.14%	$155.11	$47.06	$25.60	$878.56	$37.95	$608.08
2000	1,469.25	(10.14%)	1.14%	39.60%	20.00%	$3,785.52	(10.38%)	($95.96)	$40.42	$21.99	$1,012.17	$31.06	($392.90)
2001	1,320.28	(13.04%)	1.23%	39.60%	20.00%	$3,392.63	(13.13%)	($110.62)	$38.33	$20.85	$1,122.57	$23.76	($445.37)
2002	1,148.09	(23.37%)	1.37%	39.60%	20.00%	$2,947.25	(23.19%)	($172.17)	$34.48	$18.76	$1,211.04	$13.62	($683.53)
2003	879.82	26.38%	1.83%	39.60%	20.00%	$2,263.72	26.62%	$149.29	$48.26	$26.25	$1,268.56	$20.70	$602.70
2004	1,111.91	8.99%	1.61%	15.00%	15.00%	$2,866.42	9.69%	$64.45	$48.74	$38.51	$1,353.73	$18.59	$277.74

TABLE 3.1

(Continued)

Year Start	S&P 500	S&P Performance	Dividend Yield	Ordinary Income Tax	Capital Gains Tax	Portfolio Value	Portfolio Performance	Quarterly Portfolio Dollar Change	Dividend Dollar Yield	Net Dividend After Tax	Principal	Gains Tax After Turnover	Retained Capital Gains
2005	1,211.92	3.00%	1.60%	15.00%	15.00%	$3,144.16	3.70%	$23.59	$51.25	$40.49	$1,462.17	$18.65	$116.19
2006	1,248.29	13.62%	1.79%	15.00%	15.00%	$3,260.35	14.47%	$111.01	$63.33	$50.03	$1,572.82	$22.38	$471.69
2007	1,418.30	3.53%	1.77%	15.00%	15.00%	$3,732.04	4.35%	$32.93	$67.51	$53.34	$1,707.05	$22.65	$162.42
2008	1,468.36	(38.49%)	1.89%	15.00%	15.00%	$3,894.46	(37.50%)	($374.70)	$55.90	$44.16	$1,845.58	$5.78	($1,460.43)
2009	903.25			15.00%		$2,434.03					$1,911.47		

Annual return: 6.33%

Return after liquidation: 6.24%

Portfolio Turnover

State tax	0%	10%	20%	30%	40%	50%	60%	70%	80%	90%	100%
0%	7.03%	6.41%	6.19%	6.07%	5.99%	5.93%	5.89%	5.85%	5.81%	5.78%	5.75%
1%	6.98%	6.33%	6.11%	5.99%	5.91%	5.84%	5.80%	5.76%	5.72%	5.69%	5.66%
2%	6.93%	6.26%	6.03%	5.90%	5.82%	5.75%	5.71%	5.67%	5.63%	5.60%	5.57%
3%	6.88%	6.19%	5.95%	5.82%	5.73%	5.66%	5.62%	5.58%	5.54%	5.51%	5.48%
4%	6.83%	6.12%	5.86%	5.73%	5.64%	5.57%	5.53%	5.49%	5.45%	5.42%	5.39%
5%	6.78%	6.05%	5.78%	5.64%	5.55%	5.48%	5.44%	5.40%	5.36%	5.33%	5.30%
6%	6.73%	5.97%	5.70%	5.55%	5.46%	5.39%	5.34%	5.30%	5.27%	5.24%	5.21%
7%	6.67%	5.90%	5.61%	5.47%	5.37%	5.30%	5.25%	5.21%	5.18%	5.15%	5.12%
8%	6.62%	5.83%	5.53%	5.38%	5.28%	5.21%	5.16%	5.12%	5.09%	5.06%	5.03%

resulting from portfolio turnover were taxed at prevailing long-term capital gains rates. We chose to model a 6 percent state tax rate, though we made observations for variance in state tax rates from 0–10 percent.

The annualized, after-tax return for a high net worth investor who began investing in 1957 and liquidated her portfolio on January 1, 2009, was 6.24 percent. To normalize for any long-term investment period since 1957, we have analyzed each rolling 10- and 20-year period[2] and concluded that the average annualized return for a 10-year period is 7.88 percent and 7.43 percent for a 20-year period. The median returns for these two investment horizons are 8.78 percent and 6.96 percent, respectively.[3]

In the model, we simulated an actual portfolio with an initial $100 investment. The dividend yield during the first year was 1.75 percent (which was paid at a quarterly rate of 0.4375 percent). The S&P 500 dropped by 8.05 percent in 1957, so the annual dividend totaled $1.66 resulting from the declining value of the portfolio during the year. The dividend tax in 1957 was 91 percent, and state tax was assumed to be paid at an additional 6 percent. After payment of federal and state taxes on dividends, the $1.66 was reduced to only $0.05. Portfolio turnover was assessed at a rate of 5 percent which resulted in a capital gains tax loss carry-forward for the first year.

OBSERVATIONS OF AFTER-TAX RETURN VARIATIONS BY STATE OF RESIDENCE

The investor or trust's state of residence, or situs, has a remarkable impact on the long-term returns of equity portfolios as a result of the taxation, or lack of taxation, of investment gains and dividends. In the above example, we modeled for a state income tax rate of 6 percent and concluded that the long-term compounded after-tax return of the equity portfolio was 6.24 percent. A portfolio that benefited from zero state tax such as Alaska, Florida, Nevada, New Hampshire, South Dakota, Texas, Washington, or Wyoming would see its annualized after-tax compounded return rise to 6.62 percent. The zero-state-tax portfolio achieved an additional 38 basis point annualized return over the 6 percent state tax portfolio. Measured over many decades on a multi-million dollar portfolio we find a significant capital accumulation advantage for the zero-state-tax portfolios, an effect that is amplified with higher turnover.

Conversely, many portfolios of wealthy families are domiciled in high income tax states such as California with a 10.3 percent state tax, Rhode Island with a 9.9 percent state tax, Vermont with a 9.5 percent state tax, Oregon with a 9 percent state tax, or the District of Columbia with a 9 percent state tax. When we modeled the after-tax equity portfolio with a state tax rate of 10.3 percent, the annualized return dropped to 5.95 percent (while still using a turnover rate of 5 percent). The difference between the zero-state-tax portfolios was a 67 basis point advantage over the California portfolio.

RETURNS FOR DIFFERENT PORTFOLIO TURNOVER RATES

Portfolio turnover results in significant costs to the investor. In building and studying the model, we observed portfolio turnover ranging from 0 to 100 percent. Other studies estimate that the average turnover in an equity mutual fund is as high as 90 percent. The 20 percent turnover rate that we used as the secondary benchmark in our model was an appropriate level in our view based upon observations of large capitalization "core" portfolios. In Table 3.1 it is notable to see how much variance exists in the after-tax returns of portfolios that had identical gross returns but varied turnover rates. Equally notable is the benefit or detriment that state taxes caused on the net returns under varying portfolio turnover rates:

- The most favorable return (7.03 percent) was experienced by the portfolio domiciled in a 0 percent income tax state and a 0 percent portfolio turnover rate.
- The least favorable return (4.59 percent) was experienced by the portfolio domiciled in a 10 percent income tax state and a 100 percent portfolio turnover rate (366-day holding period in order to qualify for long-term capital gains tax rates).
- The difference between the first and second portfolios above is 2.44 percent. This difference would also have significant accumulation implications on a multi-million dollar portfolio over several decades for a wealthy family. In dollar terms if the two portfolios were to begin with $100 million, the portfolio with no state tax and no portfolio turnover costs would earn an additional $2.3 billion over the 52 years of the study.

The more we studied the model and made adjustments for state income taxes and portfolio turnover rates, the more we were compelled to study shorter time horizons in order to spot patterns, trends, and characteristics that would have been visible to the investor before implementing the portfolio. In performing this analysis, we found convincing evidence that the most reliable time horizon for equity portfolios is 20 years because of the high correlation rate between earnings yield and rolling 20-year compounded performance. We have concluded that an effective tool for estimating the long-term after-tax rate of return of equities is to use the earnings yield (which is the inverse of the price/earnings ratio). In observing the earnings yield of the portfolio in each year and the corresponding annualized returns that the portfolio would achieve for each rolling 20-year period, we found a 74.5 percent correlation with the after-tax return which the portfolio would ultimately achieve at the end of the same 20-year rolling period. In essence, the earnings yield at the beginning of the investment is a fairly reliable predictive indicator of the annualized, after-tax, returns over the next 20 years (see Table 3.2).

The 10-year returns were more volatile than the 20-year periods, with a correlation rate of 36.6 percent between the earnings yield at the beginning of each 10-year rolling period and the after-tax return which the portfolio would ultimately achieve at the end of the same 10-year rolling period. This data proves that the effect of p/e ratio expansion and contraction has such a strong impact on actual returns of shorter time periods (such as 10 years) that simple valuation observations become less reliable as predictive tools.

The lowest after-tax return of any 20-year period for equities began on January 1, 1959, and ended on December 31, 1979. The annualized return for this period was 2.49 percent. The highest after-tax return of any 20-year period began on January 1, 1980, and ended on December 31, 2000. The

TABLE 3.2

Twenty-Year Equity Rolling Returns (1957–1989)–5 Percent
Turnover, 6 Percent State Tax

Correlation	74.5%

Start Year	Annual Return	After Liquidation	Beginning of Period P/E Ratio	Beginning of Period Earnings Yield
1957	4.43%	3.56%	13.69x	7.30%
1958	4.19%	3.56%	11.87x	8.42%
1959	2.94%	2.49%	19.10x	5.23%
1960	3.38%	2.92%	18.7x	5.34%
1961	4.59%	3.86%	21.2x	4.71%
1962	3.19%	2.77%	17.2x	5.81%
1963	4.48%	3.97%	18.1x	5.51%
1964	4.63%	4.06%	17.8x	5.62%
1965	4.25%	3.73%	17.5x	5.73%
1966	5.16%	4.50%	14.8x	6.74%
1967	6.50%	5.75%	17.7x	5.66%
1968	5.81%	4.89%	18.1x	5.51%
1969	6.12%	5.16%	15.1x	6.63%
1970	7.98%	6.82%	16.7x	5.98%
1971	7.65%	6.64%	18.3x	5.46%
1972	8.47%	7.32%	19.1x	5.23%
1973	8.05%	6.96%	12.3x	8.16%
1974	9.32%	8.20%	7.3x	13.64%
1975	10.89%	9.75%	11.7x	8.55%
1976	11.14%	9.82%	11.0x	9.07%
1977	11.27%	9.88%	8.7x	11.43%
1978	13.32%	12.21%	8.3x	12.11%
1979	14.53%	13.36%	7.4x	13.48%
1980	14.86%	13.67%	9.1x	11.04%
1981	12.99%	11.94%	8.1x	12.39%
1982	12.66%	11.75%	10.2x	9.83%
1983	10.41%	9.78%	12.4x	8.06%
1984	10.80%	10.18%	9.9x	10.07%
1985	11.14%	10.50%	13.5x	7.42%
1986	10.05%	9.46%	16.8x	5.96%
1987	10.03%	9.41%	15.4x	6.49%
1988	10.08%	9.48%	12.2x	8.20%
1989	6.86%	6.68%	14.7x	6.80%
Average	8.25%	7.43%	14.0x	7.81%
Median	8.05%	6.96%	14.8x	6.80%

Source: Data from Standard & Poor's and Bloomberg.com.

annualized return for this period was 13.67 percent. The average after-tax return for all 20-year rolling periods was 7.43 percent, and the median was 6.96 percent. We thought the period from 1989 to 2009 was particularly interesting. Despite the fact that this period contained three recessions (1991, 2000, and 2008) and two bear markets of a nearly 50 percent loss each (2000–2002 and 2007–2008), the annualized return for a portfolio that began investing on January 1, 1989, and was liquidated on January 1, 2009, was 6.68 percent.

The question is, what statistics were available to investors at the beginning of these periods that would have given clues to the ultimate return that would be earned over the 20-year periods? Our objective in studying these periods of history is to extract statistics that would have been available to investors to enable them to make informed decisions as to the future returns of their portfolios and the outperformance of either stocks or bonds over various periods. Future rates of inflation, GDP growth, earnings growth, and multiple expansion/contraction are not easily predictable for investors who are beginning a 20-year investment portfolio. The earnings yield (earnings/price) is the one statistic that seems to have given a predictive clue as to the actual after-tax returns of portfolios at the time of investment. We noted that the earnings yield, with a few exceptions, was one of the best predictive measures of future returns on an after-tax basis.

LIQUIDATION

As important as the year in which an investor begins investing in equities is the year in which he liquidates his investments. Using the 10-year investment periods, an investor who started on January 1, 1991, and liquidated on January 1, 2001, achieved a 13.71 percent return, while an investor who began on January 1, 1993, achieved a 7.05 percent return. The two periods shared eight years of the same returns, but during 2001 and 2002 the S&P declined by 13.04 percent and 23.37 percent, respectively. The intuition to liquidate a portfolio after subpar returns can eliminate a large portion of the gains experienced in the previous years. Furthermore, if the same investor who had begun in 1993 had waited two additional years, his annualized return after taxes would have increased to 9.03 percent. It must be noted that ordinary income taxes and capital gains taxes were reduced during year 12, affecting the final liquidation return.

BONDS VERSUS EQUITIES

The after-tax equity risk premium over municipal bonds from 1957 through 2009 was 0.77 percent. Comparing the 20-year return data with the Bond Buyer Index yield over a similar time period, the average equity premium is 1.43 percent with a median of 1.04 percent. Of the 32 rolling 20-year periods we studied, there were 6 periods in which bonds outperformed equities (see Figure 3.1). The first observation of bond outperformance was the 20-year period beginning in 1959 and ending in 1979. The bond portfolio returned 3.05 percent, while the equity portfolio returned 2.49 percent. The period of the greatest bond outperformance was from 1969 through 1989. During this period, the bond portfolio returned 6.61 percent, and the equity portfolio returned 5.16 percent for a total outperformance of 1.45 percent. The period of greatest equity outperformance was from 1979 through 1999. In that

FIGURE 3.1

Bond Buyer versus 20-Year Equity Rolling Returns— 5 Percent Turnover, 6 Percent State Tax

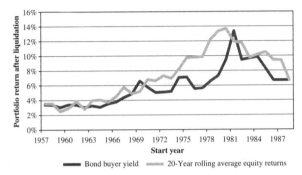

Return Comparison (Bond Buyer Yield versus 20-Year. Equity Rolling)
–5 Percent Turnover, 6 Percent State Tax -

Year	Bond buyer yield	20-year rolling	Outperformance	Equity premium
1957	3.41%	3.56%	Equities	0.15%
1958	3.37%	3.56%	Equities	0.19%
1959	3.05%	2.49%	Bonds	–0.56%
1960	3.41%	2.92%	Bonds	–0.49%
1961	3.37%	3.86%	Equities	0.49%
1962	3.05%	2.77%	Bonds	–0.28%
1963	3.26%	3.97%	Equities	0.71%
1964	3.07%	4.06%	Equities	0.99%
1965	3.53%	3.73%	Equities	0.20%
1966	3.76%	4.50%	Equities	0.74%
1967	4.38%	5.75%	Equities	1.37%
1968	4.85%	4.89%	Equities	0.04%
1969	6.61%	5.16%	Bonds	–1.45%
1970	5.74%	6.82%	Equities	1.08%
1971	5.03%	6.64%	Equities	1.61%
1972	5.08%	7.32%	Equities	2.24%
1973	5.18%	6.96%	Equities	1.78%
1974	7.08%	8.20%	Equities	1.12%
1975	7.13%	9.75%	Equities	2.62%
1976	5.54%	9.82%	Equities	4.28%
1977	5.64%	9.88%	Equities	4.24%
1978	6.58%	12.21%	Equities	5.63%
1979	7.32%	13.36%	Equities	6.04%
1980	9.49%	13.67%	Equities	4.18%
1981	13.36%	11.94%	Bonds	–1.42%
1982	9.48%	11.75%	Equities	2.27%
1983	9.66%	9.78%	Equities	0.12%
1984	9.87%	10.18%	Equities	0.31%
1985	8.33%	10.50%	Equities	2.17%
1986	6.70%	9.46%	Equities	2.76%
1987	6.70%	9.41%	Equities	2.71%
1989	6.70%	6.68%	Bonds	–0.02%

Average	5.93%	7.36%		1.43%
Median	5.59%	6.89%		1.04%

period the bond portfolio returned 7.32 percent, and the equity portfolio returned 13.36 percent for a total equity out-performance of 6.04 percent. As further evidence of the link between earnings yield and future returns, the earnings yield of the equity portfolio in 1979 was 13.48 percent. The earnings yield predicted the forward 20-year after-tax performance with a difference of only 12 basis points (13.48 percent earnings yield versus 13.36 percent actual performance).

In order to compare the compounded after-tax returns of the equity portfolio, we illustrated a best- and worst-case municipal bond portfolio. While the straight-line average of the Bond Buyer Index from 1957 through 2009 was 5.72 percent, we wanted to illustrate the benefit or detriment that the timing of bond purchases would have had on a real-life portfolio. (See Figure 3.2.) Thus we created 20 different municipal bond

FIGURE   3.2

Growth of $100 (1957–2009)–5 Percent Turnover, 6 Percent State Tax

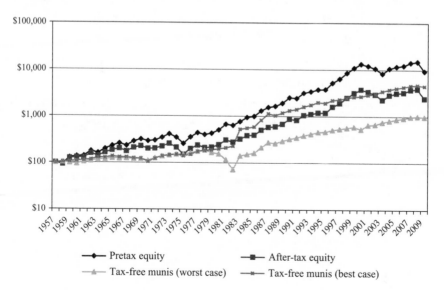

portfolios, each with different starting years until maturity to minimize the impact of the yields at which time a new bond was purchased. The best-case portfolio had a compounded after-tax return of 7.6 percent (meaning that the bonds outperformed equities by 1.36 percent) and the worst-case portfolio had a 4.5 percent compounded return (meaning that equities outperformed bonds by 1.74 percent).

CONCLUSIONS

- After taxes, the average risk premium for stocks over municipal bonds was 0.77 percent.
- 20-year rolling returns are the most reliable period for comparing stock and bonds.
- Earnings yields provide a 75 percent correlation to the after-tax return earned by stocks over 20-year periods.
- Municipal bonds beat stocks after taxes in 17 percent of the 20-year rolling periods—6 out of 36.
- A general correlation was observed between tax-exempt bond yields and the after-tax returns of equity portfolios over 20-year rolling periods.
- High-turnover portfolios matching the return of the S&P 500 index have underperformed municipal bonds after taxes and fees.

CHAPTER 4

Asset Allocation for the Taxable Investor

Often when I turn on the television or pick up a financial magazine, I'll see an interview with a famous money manager telling me his top five stocks to buy right now. So-called "hot stock tips" are what sells, but anyone who investigates the subject knows that individual security selection determines only a fraction of portfolio performance. According to a well-known study by Gary P. Brinson, L. Randolph Hood, and Gilbert L. Beebower titled "Determinants of Portfolio Performance," 90 percent of the average portfolio's returns are attributable to asset allocation.[1] So although the individual companies or bonds in which you're invested are of course important, the proportions of your portfolio invested in stocks as compared to bonds and cash overall is far more significant.

There are three primary mistakes most people make with their asset allocation plans. They think that the past performance of stocks or bonds is indicative of their future. They don't match the cash flow being produced by their portfolio with their financial needs. And they don't consider the tax and fee consequences.

The biggest mistake is generally the first one. Despite that disclaimer in every hot stock fund's prospectus that "past performance is no guarantee of future results," people often buy at the top and sell at the bottom because they mistakenly take history as a prologue to the future. And so they observe a 10 percent historical rate of return on an asset class, and then they deem that return to be akin to a law of nature like gravity—that stocks will always revert to a mean return of 10 percent. Such an assumption is very dangerous and, unfortunately, commonplace. Japanese investors had every reason to believe in mean reversion and that there was a positive long-term trend line for their Nikkei stock index until it peaked in 1989. In 2009, two decades have passed, and the Nikkei is still trading around 77 percent below its 1989 level. This horrific investment experience for investors in the world's second largest economy should give U.S. investors pause when betting the ranch on a repeat of the past.

Like Japan's Nikkei, the U.S. stock market has performed very poorly since 1999. Yet that hasn't stopped investors and their financial advisors from allocating 60 percent, 70 percent, sometimes even 100 percent of their assets to stocks simply because they believe the historical record somehow guarantees them a 10 percent return if they just hold on long enough to achieve that desired return.

EARNINGS DRIVE STOCKS; COUPONS DRIVE BONDS

So if you can't trust past performance, what can you trust? Though I admit that investing over short periods of time produces essentially arbitrary results, earnings—and the price you pay for those earnings—have been a better indicator of future long-term performance than are past returns. When we evaluate how much to invest in stocks in our portfolios, we compare the earnings yield of stocks, which is the inverse of their price-to-earnings ratios, to the yields of bonds after taxes.

Before we even think about purchasing shares in a single company, it is important for us to understand the macro valuations of the broad market and its respective subsectors. This valuation work is inclusive of the relative level of U.S. large-cap equities compared to small capitalization stocks, mid-capitalization stocks, and developed foreign markets. Within each of these categories we must assess the character of the markets and their respective valuation at any given time. For example, by year-end 2000, the Standard & Poor's 500 index traded at a p/e level of over 30 times. However, technology stocks, which accounted for over 35 percent of the market capitalization of the index, were trading at a p/e multiple of over 130 times. Therefore, it was important for investors to understand that the nontechnology stocks were trading at a significant discount when compared to technology issues. These observations are critical when determining the expected rate of return available to investors at a given time.

I must continually remind myself that I cannot declare an asset to be attractive or overvalued until I do the math by determining what I must pay (in terms of a stock price) relative to the earnings I am expecting to receive as a shareholder. So a stock trading at $20 a share that produces $1 a share of earnings would have a p/e ratio of 20 and an earnings yield of 5 percent before taxes. We must make realistic assumptions as to the rate of earnings growth that could come from an expansion in the business. In order to verify whether the $1 of earnings is truly available to investors, we perform a process to "purify" the earnings. This process exists to determine whether the earnings reported by the company have been achieved through the organic growth of the business or by use of accounting gimmicks. The bottom line on asset allocation is to determine the relative values and expected returns of the major asset classes before investing.

In a 2008 study we conducted of the pension plans of the 10 largest stocks in the S&P 500—or the "Big 10" as we like to call them—we also found evidence of how closely these companies' stock prices tracked their earnings. (In our study we substituted IBM and Berkshire Hathaway for Microsoft and Intel, which do not maintain large defined benefit pension plans.). If you examine Table 4.1, you can see the Big 10's results for the past 35 years from 1974 through the first quarter of 2009. Keep in mind that this time span included all or part of three bear market declines of over 50 percent each (1973–1974, 2000–2002, and 2008) and several more moderate bear markets including 1976, 1981, 1987, 1990, and 1998. Matt Rogers, my partner at The Gannon Group, has developed a system of tracking the earnings produced by the businesses we own in our portfolio. In short, the model shows us what we would have received in dividends at the end of each year if 100 percent of earnings were distributed to shareholders.

TABLE 4.1

Do Stocks Follow Earnings? (1973–2008)

Company	Stock Return	Earnings Growth	Total Return (Including Dividends)
Exxon Mobil	10.30%	10.30%	10.90%
General Electric	9.70%	10.60%	10.60%
Procter & Gamble	9.20%	10.20%	9.80%
Johnson & Johnson	9.90%	13.80%	10.50%
JP Morgan	5.70%	4.90%	7.10%
Bank of America	6.30%	7.60%	7.60%
AT&T	6.50%	6.00%	8.00%
Chevron	8.60%	8.90%	9.50%
IBM	5.30%	7.70%	5.90%
Berkshire Hathaway	23.40%	19.70%	23.40%
Averages	**9.49%**	**9.97%**	**10.33%**

Source: 2008 SRC Green Book of 35-Year Charts, Securities Research Company, 2008.

Though the actual performance of portfolios is rarely in sync in any individual year, we believe that long-term performance will be highly correlated to earnings as we have proven in the Big 10 example.

Yet because of the constant barrage of Wall Street hype, most of the time I find myself convincing people not to take as much equity risk as they think they want to take. When I meet clients for the first time, I make sure that they understand what drives returns in each component of the portfolio. Communicating the effects of different portfolio mixes as well as the effects of fees and taxes leads to a more informed view of the portion of the portfolio that will be available to them for income or long-term compounded growth. We also discuss the interest-rate and valuation environment and show them how portfolio returns over time are less a function of the return they desire and more a result of the assets they own and the ability of those assets to produce a competitive rate of return.

MELTDOWN MATH

The example I often give clients to educate them is from my own practice in the year 2000. The market was trading at 35 times earnings, and many people had it baked into their heads that they could compound equity returns at 10 percent, or more. They just didn't understand how mathematically difficult it was going to be to compound at 10 percent while beginning the process with an earnings yield of just 3 percent. And at the same time you could get 6 percent tax-free on a long-term high-grade municipal bond. And, so, regardless of their desire to compound money at 10 percent, I convinced my clients to acknowledge that the bond was showing them two times the cash yield of stocks, and thus warranted a higher than normal allocation in their portfolios.

Yet I understand the difficulty of convincing clients because I once needed to be convinced myself. When I started in the financial advice business in 1991, my typical allocation of stocks for clients was 80 to 85 percent, and it stayed that way through much of the 1990s. I went along with the conventional wisdom that stocks outperform bonds over the long run and that growth-oriented investors should have a heavy stock allocation. But gradually as my portfolios grew in size and my clients aged, I became more concerned about preserving their capital and generating cash flow.

A turning point for me occurred in December 1996 when Alan Greenspan made his "irrational exuberance" speech to the American Enterprise Institute. At that point the market was hanging on to his every word, and after two straight years of 20 percent plus returns, he was suggesting that stocks were starting to reach bubble capacity. It was an alarm that was only temporarily heeded by the rest of the market. But it kicked me into a much deeper study of valuation multiples.

Security Analysis was written by Benjamin Graham and David Dodd in 1934 (two years after the market bottomed during the Great Depression), and it very vividly shows the speculative buildup to the Great Depression from 1925 to 1929, and then the 88 percent decline from 1929 to 1932. Having seen the damage that kind of collapse could do, I grew increasingly alarmed in the 1990s at how many economic commentators and television strategists would write off the possibility of major market corrections. They would make all kinds of excuses that in retrospect seem ridiculous today: The banking system was so much safer now; modern securities laws supposedly prevented most corruption; and technology and never-ending increases to productivity would keep the economy rolling indefinitely. Other "silly" evidence of market excesses would be dismissed by the existence of trading curbs on the New York Stock Exchange (NYSE).

It seemed almost as if the investing public felt like we had legislated ourselves away from the ability to ever have an overvalued market. And so the more I saw those books by Harry Dent about the *Great Boom Ahead* and others that advocated high allocations to equities, the more skeptical I became.

By August 1999, my valuation work started to keep me up at night. So gradually from that point through February 2001, we brought our stock allocation down from 85 percent to between 45 and 50 percent of our clients' accounts. We also paid off every client mortgage and wiped leverage of any kind from our clients' balance sheets. By the fourth quarter of 2007 we switched our money market accounts to those containing only U.S. Treasury securities as we anticipated the upcoming problems that would affect funds holding Collateralized Debt Obligations (CDOs) and Structured Investment Vehicles (SIVs).

AFTER-TAX CALCULATOR

But our allocation to municipal bonds is by no means a static one. We made this decision to invest in them because we did the math. It was during this post-1999 period that we developed our after-tax calculator. It was our attempt to build a valuation model specific to the clients who have to pay taxes at the highest tax bracket. And the model prevents us from developing a bias toward or against any asset class, the same kind of bias that induced investors to put too much faith in stocks. Since munis have been such a valuable asset over the last eight years, there is a risk that we fall in love with them. Falling in love with any asset class is dangerous, whether the attraction be driven by safety or total return potential. But the model removes emotion and allows us to compare the economic realities of each asset class. And if municipal bonds are no longer a good value because the math says so, then we will modify our strategy or evaluate another way to accomplish the goal of capital preservation and the generation of cash flow.

After taxes, wealthy investors experience drastically different investment results from their institutional peers in tax-sheltered retirement plans and endowments. Certainly they are going to get different returns from taxable bonds. If a junk bond pays 10 percent to a pension plan, that will be about 6 percent to a wealthy client, after you factor in both federal and state income taxes, which are typically 35 percent and 6 percent, respectively. The calculator reveals how every asset class has its own unique tax traits. Private equity happens to be treated very well by our current tax system as are municipal bonds. Hedge funds, junk bonds, taxable bonds, and high-turnover equity funds are not treated favorably by the current tax system.

With equities there's an additional wrinkle because the risk is higher. One of the most desirable traits of bonds is the requirement that their issuers pay a predetermined coupon rate for a finite number of years until maturity (or call) and that the full face value of the bond is due to the investor at that time. No such promises exist for stock investors. Equity earnings are variable, which, on the plus side, means that a stock's earnings yield and subsequent earnings growth can far exceed that of the fixed interest rates on a bond, but on the negative side this can mean that earnings decline or disappear completely.

Because of this additional risk, in order for stocks to be attractive relative to bonds, they must pay a premium to investors—which is known as the *equity risk premium*. And to pay that premium from a Graham and Dodd valuation perspective, the earnings yield on stocks must be greater than the yield on less risky bonds. Moreover, to be attractive to our wealthy clientele, the actual after-tax liquidation value of the stock—or privatization yield, as we call it—must be greater than the equivalent yield on high-grade municipal bonds.

In our after-tax calculator we replace the 30-year U.S. Treasury with a 30-year high-grade general obligation (GO) municipal bond. As of April 2009, that GO muni would be yielding 4.5 percent in my home state of Missouri. Just like comparing stocks with Treasury bonds, in the calculator any other asset class needs to be able to provide a risk premium. The calculator is designed to extract the equity risk premium, the junk bond risk premium, or the hedge fund risk premium, if there is one, and measure it as a spread over what is available in that low-risk GO bond—4.5 percent after taxes. Because tax rates may rise or fall, we may modify the inputs for the various top tax rates on ordinary income and stock dividends. We are also able to change the expected rate of portfolio turnover which our research has proven to highly influence the effective tax bite of trading. We are able to model for an expected default rate within the individual fixed income issues. Finally, because clients live in different states, we model for the effects of the state income tax rate in our clients' state of residence, which may range from 0 to up to 10 percent.

MANAGING EXPENSES

Once we've established the yields and premiums of the different asset classes, we match the expected cash flow generated by a portfolio of the asset classes with the clients' income needs. Managing the clients' expectations and making sure their expenses do not exceed the cash flow from their investments is an essential part of our asset allocation plans. And here is where the second most common mistake occurs: Investors either miscalculate their expected cash flow or their financial needs. Finance professor Richard Marston of The Wharton School has cautioned investors not to expect stock dividends and bond yields to remain stable. His advice to investors is to formulate a spending rule that incorporates real (post-inflation) returns into consumption planning. In recent years we have adapted our client spending rules by using a portfolio-based cash flow generation model that allows clients to consume a blended mix of bond coupon income and stock dividends.

When people use a financial calculator to compound their money at a rate of 10 percent, it looks like a very large number, especially if the modeling occurs over several decades. Even a blended return of stocks and bonds at 6 percent can be quite compelling. That adds up to a tenfold increase in your investment over four decades. But then if you're working with high net worth investors who live off their assets, you also have to deduct their spending. And you have to deduct taxes and fees as well. So the investor's long-term expected return of 10 percent gets knocked down to 6 percent after taxes. And if you take out 3 percent for spending, you're down to 3 percent. If you factor in inflation, you're not really left with much gain at all. And so with the asset allocation mix for such clients, it is important for us to look out a decade, two decades, or three decades, and be aware of what the portfolio size might be if we are correct in our modeling.

Since most wealthy investors are familiar with the concept of compound interest and longer-term trends in the capital markets, we like to begin the financial planning process with them by sharing our view on the forward-looking expectations for the broad asset classes. We ask them to verbalize their preference for cash flow and how they envision the assets with respect to their extended family or charities. We have witnessed client preferences for portfolio spending rates at 2.5 percent on the low end and 8 percent on the high end. The spending rate is an important discussion at the outset of a client relationship because the lower it is, the higher the likelihood of a growing portfolio. Similarly a high spending rate, such as 8 percent, leads to a frank discussion of the limited shelf life of the portfolio as a younger retiree may possibly risk spending the portfolio down to zero.

It is imperative for us to communicate the importance of spending predictable cash flow from the portfolio rather than relying on capital gains or total return, as is often the case in the pension and endowment world. Ideally, most of the income for expenses comes from the bond side of our clients' portfolios, allowing the remaining assets in their portfolios to grow. The end result of this first part of our interaction with new clients is that we aim to view portfolio returns net of taxes, fees, and spending. This exercise certainly creates a more muted portfolio return than they may have seen from other advisors, but we feel that it is imperative that they understand that their portfolio will not compound based upon gross returns.

Regardless of the mix of stocks and bonds, we ask the client for the discretion concerning where we will harvest the cash flow to pay their expenses. In the past decade, because muni rates have been between 4 and 6 percent, we were able to rely 100 percent on the interest income from the municipal bonds and leave the stock portfolios untouched. This was very beneficial in 2008 as our clients didn't miss a penny of expected portfolio cash flow. Investors whose portfolios were relying on "total return" for income were forced to liquidate highly depreciated assets in 2008. When you are forced to sell stocks in a down market to meet cash flow requirements, it is mathematically impossible for the portfolio to ever recover from losses on assets that were sold. But we have acknowledged the fact that interest rates can and do go down, and there could be a point where municipal bond yields are below 3 percent. In this case, we would want the discretion to be able to harvest some of the stock dividends or accumulated portfolio cash and not disrupt the optimal long-term portfolio mix.

One thing clients pay us for is to tell them the truth. They're expecting us not to withhold the bad news, and this means telling them if we think their portfolio can't produce enough cash flow to cover their expenses. There are some clients who fully expect to eat into their principal, and there is nothing wrong with that. They figure that if they have $100 million and they die with $70 million, so what? But there are other clients who say, "This is all I've got, and I'm not going back to work," so we have to be very up front and open, and we must communicate the first sign of overspending. We even have clients who insist on overspending. On their performance reports we give them an estimated time when their assets will run out. This is a difficult task for many financial advisors, but it must be done for the sake of full disclosure.

PORTFOLIO MANAGEMENT

Because financial planning for wealthy clients is so complex, we manage their assets ourselves rather than outsourcing the stock and bond picking to external fund managers or divvying up the assets among different advisors. Such a strategy has many unique advantages. First, we have shortened the distance between the clients and the assets they own in the portfolio. We have reduced the number of intermediaries who expect to be paid a fee. And the clients always have direct access to their portfolio manager instead of a relationship manager or salesperson.

Among other benefits, a direct client relationship brings tax efficiencies and a greater level of understanding between clients and their advisor. If we need to harvest any capital losses in a portfolio, we know where to find depreciated stock to sell because we're investing in stocks directly. Such losses can be used to counteract any realized capital gains in the portfolio and thus reduce a client's tax bill. Also, when a client has a large exposure to appreciated company stock in their family business, if we have control of all of the assets, the client can direct us to transfer those shares (or appreciated shares of the diversified portfolio) to the family's charitable foundation, which can then sell those shares with little or even no tax consequences.

Often my clients who own businesses engage us right before "liquidity events." The sale of a business is probably going to be the biggest taxable event in the history of the family. So it's important for us to make sure that things like philanthropic intent and gifting to other family members are discussed well ahead of time. If it's a private business, gifting can be done to other family members in advance of an acquisition or sale so that the appreciation that will occur when the deal closes can occur outside the estate. Therefore, if a founder's stock is worth $2 per share on a stand-alone basis and the business might be sold for $3 or $4 per share, you'd want to consider gifting those shares to the younger family members well in advance of having a deal on the table.

Perhaps a greater benefit of our management of client assets could be likened to the benefit of having an airbag in a car. When conditions deteriorate, the direct asset management relationship can protect the clients from bad decisions by providing them with up-to-the-minute information from principal decision makers. For instance, I telephoned the principals of every family on each of the tumultuous 10 days following 9/11/01 to update them on our strategy and our plan. We made similar contact for each of the other market-shaking events of subsequent years including the London subway bombing, the failure of Bear Stearns, and the demise of Lehman Brothers. Consultants and financial planners who have to wait weeks for newsletters, e-mails, and updates from different funds and money managers simply didn't have that luxury. Many mutual funds and institutional money managers were not answering their phones. When they did, clients did not have access to the principal decision makers.

PICKING STOCKS

Buying individual stocks and bonds gives us a chance to improve a client's portfolio performance. Over the short run, I am less concerned about relative performance compared to an index than I am in maintaining a portfolio mix that will allow it to produce a suitable long-term tax-adjusted return. Although I believe that asset allocation is the ultimate driver of performance, as I've explained previously, I do not subscribe to the idea that index funds are the way to achieve one's target asset allocation. The index fund's objective is to perform in line with an index whether that be positive or negative. The objective in our equity portfolios is to make money over time.

Since my clients have achieved above-average profits from their businesses, I seek above-average profits from the businesses I invest in for them. But I also try to purchase that earnings growth at a reasonable price—a strategy financial advisors call GARP (growth-at-a-reasonable-price) investing. Just as with the asset classes as a whole, I look at the earnings yields of individual companies and try to make a reasonable assessment of the earnings they could accumulate over the next 3, 5, or 10 years. Then I calculate the privatization yield or what the earnings of the company would net my clients after taxes. This is where the heavy lifting comes in: where we model a company's 10-year normalized earnings growth and attack it from different angles to come up with a reasonable and accurate assumption.

The "privatization yield" is an earnings model we developed. We analyze every stock as though we plan to purchase the whole company with cash to determine its ability to generate a return on investment based on its ability to generate profits for shareholders (often referred to as owners). We cannot own a business with historical annualized earnings growth rates of 8 to 9 percent and simply assume that this growth rate will continue indefinitely. We want to know what the economic benefit of owning the company will be in the future based upon the price we pay today for the earnings.

In our analysis we look at the number of stores, divisions, units sold, net profit margin, debt-to-capital ratios, and other fundamental characteristics. Next, we try to determine what we are going to earn net of all expenses and taxes as a shareholder of that business for one year, and then we apply reasonable growth rates into the next decade. This helps us avoid making irrationally exuberant earnings projections. For instance, it is relatively easy for a company with five stores and $1 million in sales to grow to ten stores and $2 million in sales. But if a company like Wal-Mart has 3,500 stores, it is difficult to assume that Wal-Mart's store growth is going to be similar over the next decade to the way it was over the past decade. So we apply reasonable assumptions for same store sales and for new store growth and other possibilities, and we build an earnings model that will show us what we would accumulate in after-tax profits at the end of a decade.

When we purchase shares in a company, we are looking for a high mathematical probability that the earnings (manifested in dividends and price appreciation) provide a competitive return to shareholders based upon the current market price. Though we would hope that stock prices compound in lockstep with earnings in each and every year, this rarely happens over the short term. On the upside, a company's price/earnings multiple can expand rapidly as a result of earnings growth, and an investor might view this as being paid early for future shareholder earnings. Because we aim to ensure that all client portfolios contain our freshest ideas, we refuse to hold a company in an existing client portfolio if we deem the shares to be too expensive to purchase for a new client.

This process has served us very well over time. On the downside, we must be crystal clear on this point: the concept of buy and hold is risky and ineffective. Investors should remember that in the early 1970s one of the top-selling beer brands was Schlitz, retail was dominated by Sears and Roebuck, and Wal-Mart wasn't even on the radar. As a rule of thumb, if an investor believes in long-term ownership of successful companies, I would replace the practice of "buy and hold" with "buy and verify." Buying and holding Bethlehem Steel, Woolworths, or Kresge for 20 years makes no sense if those businesses are losing customers, market share, and earnings. In the short-term, stock prices can be pretty random, but over a decade or two, our research proves that shareholders will be rewarded by the profits of the business they own provided they acquired them at a reasonable price.

CASE STUDY

Generally we let the earnings growth of a company and the quality of its business determine our buy and sell decisions. Yet sometimes the market and stock valuations force our hand. So, for example, in April 2000 we initiated an investment in Anheuser-Busch, Inc. (NYSE: BUD) at a split-adjusted price of $34.05. The company was trading at a trough valuation to the rest of the market as investors were fleeing "stable" companies like beverages and other consumer staples for the excitement of the tech bubble. BUD posted earnings per share in 2000 of $1.69, giving it an earnings yield of 5 percent compared to the overall stock market's 3 percent, and yet many analysts on the Street had neutral to negative ratings on the stock. Analysts had abandoned the possibility of BUD being able to institute a price increase or any margin improvement as the company's domestic market share had surpassed 50 percent. The Street was wrong. By the midpoint of 2002 net profit margins had widened from 12.7 percent to 14.3 percent. Earnings per share jumped to $2.21. The stock rallied from nearly a 40 percent p/e discount in the market to a premium of nearly 25 percent.

We were pleased with the performance of the stock, especially in light of the fact that the broad stock market had dropped by nearly 50 percent since our initial purchase.

Despite this, there was a thematic problem that existed for owners of BUD: Young people were migrating their consumption patterns away from beer toward wine and spirits. Distributor and industry research confirmed this trend which made it very difficult for Anheuser-Busch to improve from its current market position. To our surprise, we found that Constellation Brands, a leading manufacturer and marketer of wine and spirits, was trading at a 50 percent p/e discount to BUD. Between June 2002 and September 2002 we exited the bulk of our position in BUD at approximately $51 per share. We acquired Constellation Brands (NYSE: STZ) between September 2002 and January 2003 at an average cost of $13.27.

By June 2005, Constellation Brands rallied by over 100 percent from our initial cost. Similar to Anheuser-Busch, Constellation had seen its p/e swell from 12 to 21. The company had recently closed on the acquisition of Robert Mondavi Corporation, a deal for which it paid a hefty price. When we viewed Constellation in light of record earnings, sales, and margins, this company, too, was beginning to look expensive. We trimmed 50 percent of our position at $30.37 and sold the balance at $24.82. Constellation's p/e would eventually drop to 7 as its price fell by over 60 percent.

Only two weeks from our sale of Constellation, Anheuser-Busch was trading at an even lower valuation than when we had sold the position in 2002. On October 17, 2005, we initiated a position in BUD at $42.55. By the second half of 2007, Bud was looking expensive again, and we exited our position at between $50.82 and $53.46.

In hindsight, our sale of Anheuser-Busch was early because the company received a bid from Inbev, NV for $70 per share. What if we had simply "bought and held" BUD for what would have been ultimately a 105 percent share price return excluding dividends? In this case our practice of owning companies when they can be bought at a value was superior to buy and hold. Our investments in the alcoholic beverage industry produced nearly four times the shareholder return than if we had simply held our original BUD position and received the $70 buyout price.

Two important points come to mind after reviewing the above example. First, we have had our share of disappointments and losses in portfolio decisions. It is nearly impossible to accomplish a successful economic result such as we have described above without knowledge of what can go wrong when assumptions fail to materialize. I also wish to remind investors and money managers that some of their best "trades" will turn out to be those instances in which hours of work went into the analysis of a possible sale of a company they owned, but the fundamentals justified holding the position. In a simple mathematical sense, a portfolio that demonstrates 20 percent annual turnover is affected more by making the right "hold" decisions than it is by making the right buy or sell decisions. This fact will be familiar to CEOs with respect to their history of acquisitions and divestitures, since many successful companies are aware that making the wrong deal or divesting the wrong division could be disastrous to the corporation's survival.

A GLOBAL APPROACH TO PORTFOLIO MANAGEMENT

Author Thomas Friedman's 2005 edition of *The World is Flat*,[2] encouraged investors and businesses to view their existence in terms of a global economy filled with numerous opportunities that were simply unavailable in the twentieth century. Wharton's Dr. Richard Marston has strongly advocated that investors refrain from becoming trapped in an overly localized approach to investing. I couldn't agree more. As we have stressed in other parts of the book, I'll add that investors should be aware of the price they are paying for a global portfolio, in that foreign markets are as subject to booms and busts as the market in the United States is.

There are two schools of thought with respect to gaining foreign exposure in equity portfolios. The first is based upon the location of the company headquarters and legal domicile. The second focuses more on the company's footprint with respect to its customers and revenue stream. Let's take a look at an example of each. Halliburton's headquarters is located in Dubai, United Arab Emirates, but 46 percent of its revenues come from North America. Nike is based in Beaverton, Oregon, yet only 34 percent of its revenues come from the United States (30 percent Europe, 16 percent Asia, 20 percent South America, and "other"). McDonald's is clearly an iconic U.S. company, yet only 34 percent of its 2008 sales came from the United States. Which of the above is truly an international company?

The important point to remember about international investing is that if earnings are what the investor is truly interested in, then he or she must trace the source of those earnings in order to determine a company's global footprint. The location of the corporation's headquarters and home currency is simply not enough.

Valuation also matters in international investing. Many investors allocated heavy amounts of their portfolio to non-U.S. assets toward the end of 2007 as the global approach to investing made more sense to them. The goal of this portfolio move was to gain diversification, reduce the weighting of the portfolio exposed to the U.S. dollar, and gain access to the growing economies of India, China, and other high-growth economies. If they had done their valuation work, they might have hesitated to make such a move because international and emerging markets were generally trading at extended valuations compared to stocks in the United States and thus experienced a greater decline in 2008.

MUNI STRATEGY

When we invest in municipal bonds, we also buy them directly (as opposed to using an outside manager or fund), but we approach this asset in a completely different fashion from the way we approach equities. With equities there are a large number of variables that affect the ultimate return to shareholders. When purchasing a bond, on the other hand, there are essentially two primary outcomes. The bond will either pay interest and then mature or be called, or the bond will default. True, the price of the bond may fluctuate above or below par value over time in response to changes in the overall interest-rate environment, but a bondholder knows at the day of purchase exactly what return he or she will receive until maturity. For this reason, the construction of a bond portfolio is less focused on predicting future returns than it is in capturing yield and controlling risk: risks of interest rates, reinvestment risk, diversification risk, and issuer risk.

As is the case with equities, buy and hold is an ineffective portfolio strategy. There is no such thing as a static bond portfolio in today's bond market. Opportunities continually change with respect to the sweet spot in the yield curve. Bonds are rarely noncallable in today's bond market meaning that a diversified portfolio will see bonds called before maturity, or they could be pre-refunded by the issuer. Failure to acknowledge these factors leads to missed opportunities in the best case or a loss of optimal portfolio cash flow or default in the worst case.

Though it is a rare event for us to sell an individual bond because of credit concerns, it does indeed happen. I can recall selling only five bonds for credit concerns over my career. Two of the issues were municipal bonds, and the other three were corporate bonds which we held in our family foundation accounts. The sell decision on the bonds is similar to that of equities. If we would not be willing to purchase the issue at current prices based upon the knowledge of the situation that we now possess, the bond is sold. It makes no sense to hold an issue for existing clients if our attitude is that we wouldn't touch it with a 10-foot pole for a new client. As basic as this seems, many portfolio managers do the opposite by having one set of rules for new accounts and a different set of rules for existing ones.

That said, for investors who hire bond managers hoping to "add value," outperform the index, or time interest rates my advice is this: Be careful. Your bond portfolio probably exists for preservation of capital and the generation of cash flow. Trading bonds can be quite expensive as spreads can be wide, meaning there needs to be a significant move in a bond price before the investor makes money on the trade. More importantly, getting cute in a bond portfolio can rob the investor of the very reason she allocated to bonds in the first place: to have predictable, risk-controlled issues with finite maturity dates. We depend on a steady stream of income from our bonds, so we're not looking for capital appreciation through trading within this asset class. Equity risk should be taken in the equity portfolio, not in the bond portfolio.

With respect to the decision to build a home-state bond portfolio (thus possibly being exempt from both federal and state taxes) rather than a diversified national portfolio, several factors must be studied. First, investors must ask how much concentration risk in their home state are they willing to accept, and does the additional yield they receive on such issues after taxes compensate them enough for that risk? A state like Missouri encompasses a large geographic area with a mix of large and mid-sized metropolitan areas as well as rural communities. Though part of the state sits on the New Madrid seismic zone and has two major rivers running through it, geographic risk control is readily accomplished with a range of issuers to build a Missouri portfolio. We use an interactive map that divides the state into six separate geographic areas. Then we overlay the flood plain areas and earthquake prone areas in order to understand where we have concentrated bond issues.

The hurricane Katrina case is a good illustration of why geographic diversification is important, not because there were a large number of defaults but because if the damage had been worse, investors who maintained exposure to a concentration of coastal communities would have experienced severe losses. Missouri has a relatively high income tax rate of 6 percent which makes Missouri paper more attractive than out-of-state issues which would produce income subject to Missouri taxes. The Missouri case does not mean that every state or investor should build a home-state portfolio. Some states are too small to accomplish geographic or economic risk diversification. We also stick to bonds that are highly rated and prefer to heavily weight general obligation bonds, school districts, and essential revenue issues which have a lower likelihood of default than lower credit issues. We focus on municipal bond defaults and how to evaluate this risk in the next chapter.

An important point should be made with respect to bonds and inflation. Conventional wisdom says that bonds do not provide an adequate hedge against inflation. This statement is sometimes true, but we must understand the economic situation at the time to know if a bondholder is compensated for inflation risk. Consider the year 1980. The average inflation rate as measured by the consumer price index (CPI) in 1980 was 13.5 percent.[3] In 1981, the Bond Buyer 20 Index of general obligation bonds had a yield of 13.36 percent.[4] Though the bond investor in 1981 did not maintain a hedge against inflation rising above 13.5 percent, we can say that he was compensated for the presence of inflation in the coupon rate of a new bond. In the 1980/1981 case, inflation peaked and dropped steadily for the next two decades. The buyer of the bond, however, maintained his yield of 13 percent as long as he held the bond.

The challenge with respect to inflation is best illustrated by using the example of a buyer of bonds in 1978 or 1979 where bond yields had not yet risen to double-digit levels. If a bond investor was able to purchase an issue in 1979 and bought a bond with a yield of 7 percent and inflation subsequently rose to and stayed above 13 percent, this investor would have received a negative yield net of inflation. A strategy a bond manager would use in this case would be not to deploy all of the investable capital at the long end of the curve. Instead, she would employ diversification along the yield curve in a laddered portfolio of bonds with short-, intermediate-, and long-term maturities. This of course is no magic bullet in that some portion of the portfolio will indeed be exposed to the inflationary risk. However, because the bond portfolio would never exist on its own without other assets in a diversified portfolio, the inflation risk could be significantly dampened. If we expect inflation to be high, we may invest more in short-maturity bonds in order to be ready for an interest-rate increase. If we can't find anything attractive, we will hold cash.

CONCLUSIONS

- Asset allocation is more important than individual security selection.
- Look at earnings yields for stocks and interest rates for bonds instead of past returns.
- Invest according to the after-tax premium of an asset class compared to the forward yield of high-quality municipal bonds.
- Make sure to match the cash flow produced by your portfolio with your cash flow needs.
- The fewer intermediaries between investors and their money, the better.
- Buy and hold is an ineffective strategy. Instead, buy and verify.
- The location or a company's customers and earnings source is more important than the location of its headquarters.

CHAPTER 5

Municipal Bonds

The Forgotten Asset Class

Recent surveys by the Institute for Private Investors,[1] the Wharton Global Family Alliance,[2] and Northern Trust[3] confirm that most U.S. wealthy families maintain little to no exposure to municipal bonds. Throughout much of our research, we have found that the "sticker shock" of municipal bonds has led investors to believe that they are a low-return asset class and thus should be minimally weighted in portfolios. As we have proved, when factoring in taxes, fees, and risk, the value of municipal bonds increases as a tool for providing income or a predictable long-term return. Yet we often hear from prospective clients that they have heard of but do not fully understand municipal bonds as an investment. The truth is that because of the low nominal coupon rate of high-quality municipal bonds, they are often overlooked.

WHAT ARE MUNICIPAL BONDS?

The Securities Industry and Financial Markets Association defines municipal bonds as debt obligations issued by states, cities, counties, and other governmental entities to raise money to build schools, highways, hospitals, sewer systems, and many other projects for the public good.[4] When investors purchase municipal bonds, they are essentially lending money to the issuer who promises to pay a specified amount of interest (usually semiannually) and return the principal to the investor on a specific maturity date.

Municipal bonds may be issued in nontaxable tranches (which constitute the bulk of issuance) or in tranches subject to federal tax (suitable for purchase by nontaxable entities such as foundations, endowments, or pension plans). The vast majority of wealthy investors favor investment in high-quality tax-free issues. Although the attractiveness of this asset class varies widely, it is relatively simple to understand in that it carries a predictable coupon rate and a predictable value at maturity. Issues purchased in some states enjoy the benefit of double tax-exempt status in that the interest earned on such issues are exempt from federal and state income taxes.

In April 2009, the U.S. Government introduced federal assistance to municipalities (through a federal subsidy payment), which allowed them to finance any capital expenditures for which they otherwise could issue tax-exempt governmental bonds as a part of The American Recovery and Reinvestment Act of 2009. Build America Bonds, however, are not exempt from federal taxes as are traditional municipal bonds. The program, according to the IRS website, describes the purpose of the bonds as, "intended to assist state and local governments in financing capital projects at lower borrowing costs and to stimulate the economy and create jobs." Though the bonds seemed to be well received in the retail and institutional marketplace, some traditional tax-exempt investors and money managers fear that the presence of these new bonds could shrink the available supply of traditional tax-exempt bonds.

HISTORY OF MUNICIPAL BOND YIELDS

To understand the significance of the taxable equivalent yield, it's important to know how municipal bonds have traded historically relative to taxable issues. Established in 1891, *The Bond Buyer* is the only daily newspaper committed to serving the municipal bond market. It maintains an index of 20 general obligation municipal bonds with 20-year maturities, known as the Bond Buyer 20 Bond Muni Index.[5] Figure 5.1 depicts the yields of the municipal bond market over the period from 1946 through 2004.

In general, the yields on high-grade municipal bonds have historically traded at a discount to U.S. Treasury bonds as taxable investors are willing to accept a lower tax-exempt yield than they would be on a similar maturity taxable issue. Beginning in 2007, however, as interest rates began to drop in U.S. Treasuries, the yields on municipal bonds did not follow as the coming recession sparked fears of municipal bankruptcies and resulted in a higher perceived risk profile for the asset class as a whole. When viewing the yields in the Bond Buyer chart, it is important to remember that the yield or return to investors did not necessarily change with the yearly

FIGURE 5.1

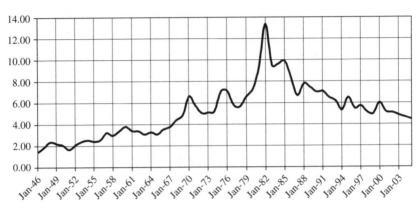

Bond Buyer 20 Historical Yields (1946–2004)

Source: The Bond Buyer.

change in the Bond Buyer yield. Rather, the yield or return to investors was a function of the yields available at the time of their purchase as well as whether the bonds were held to maturity or were traded.

Many investors and advisors make the mistake of studying the historical default rate or the historical average yields without understanding that such statistics are useless to them unless they are able to purchase exactly the same bonds under exactly the same conditions. Since this is impossible, I will share the results of our research in the municipal bond market and render my opinion as to which components of historical statistics are useful and which are not.

On September 9, 2008, the Municipal Bond Fairness Act[6] was submitted to the U.S. House of Representatives in order to clarify and codify regulations surrounding the credit rating agencies and the methods they use to gauge creditworthiness of municipal issuers. A table included in the report described what was characterized as the "low" default history of municipal bonds rated by Standard & Poor's and Moody's. The period included in the default study was from 1970 through 2006. The relative brevity of this time period highlights the mistake investors often make when attempting to justify risk or return. Because the economic history of the United States includes periods of deeper financial crisis than the period from 1970 through 2006, I believe it is prudent to study a longer period of time as well as the nuances of each period of economic distress and prosperity.

The most comprehensive study on municipal bond defaults and credit quality was published in 1971 by George Hempel of Washington University in St. Louis.[7] His report, "The Postwar Quality of State and Local Debt," was brought to my attention by my colleague and municipal bond legend in his own right, George Friedlander. The Hempel paper provided a deep insight into the character of municipal bond defaults from 1820 through 1968. It is available in many libraries for further study. Below I share my observations of some important points in history based upon study of the Hempel paper and our own research.

HISTORY OF MUNICIPAL BOND DEFAULTS

Following the credit crisis of 2008, the area that garners the highest amount of interest from individual investors with respect to municipal bonds is the period of the Great Depression. Though it's important to understand and study defaults of the Great Depression, it should be understood that an even deeper and more severe depression began 56 years earlier in 1873. The highest period of default observed from

1837 through 2008 was during the post-Civil War depression from 1873 to 1879. During this period estimates range from a total default rate of 15 percent (Hempel) and 24 percent (1988 Enhance Reinsurance Company study[8]). A recent commentary in *The Bond Buyer* by James Spiotto, a municipal bankruptcy expert at Chapman and Cutler, LLP, in Chicago claims that 11 U.S. states repudiated their debts in the 1800s, the majority of them Southern states that didn't think they should pay back debts incurred by Northern "carpetbaggers" after reconstruction.[9]

DEFAULTS DURING THE GREAT DEPRESSION

One notable item with regard to the default rates of the period 1929 to 1937 is the varied incidence of default by issuer type. In reviewing Table 5.1, you will notice that the lowest rate of default by category was that of towns and townships (2.9 percent default rate in proportion to total outstanding debt), state general obligation bonds (6.8 percent default rate), and school districts (7.8 percent default rate). The highest rate of default was revenue bonds (25 percent default rate) which included reclamation, levee, irrigation, and drainage districts. In total, the default rate (defined as the percentage of issues in default in proportion to total outstanding debt) for the period from 1929 to 1937 was 16.2 percent.

It is critical for investors and advisors to study the character and timing of the default rate in order to understand the ultimate impact it has on the bondholder. We believe that the investor must be aware of the total default rate (total dollar amount of defaulted issues as a percentage

TABLE 5.1

Muni Bond Defaults (1929–1937) (Dollars are in Millions)

Type of Government Unit	Total Number[1]	Number in Default[2]	Percent of Total Number in Default	NEBT Debt of All Units, 1932[3]	Indebtedness of Defaulting Unit[4]	Proportion of Debt in Default
States	48	1	2.1	$2,361	$160	6.8%
Counties	3,053	417	13.7	2,391	360	15.1
Incorporated municipalities	16,366	1,434	8.8	8,842	1,760	19.9
Towns and organized townships	20,262	88	0.4	344	10	2.9
School districts	127,108	1,241	0.9	2,040	160	7.8
Reclamation, levee, irrigation, and drainage districts	3,351	944	28.2	1,599[5]	400[5]	25.0[5]
Other special districts	5,229	646	12.4			
Total	**175,417**	**4,771**	**2.7**	**17,577**	**2,850**	**16.2**

[1] Based on number in William Anderson, *The Units of Government in the United States*, Public Administration Service, Chicago, 1934, pp. 1 and 24.
[2] Based on all defaults reported to *The Daily Bond Buyer* from 1929 through 1937.
[3] U.S. Bureau of the Census, *Financial Statistics of State and Local Governments*, 1932, Washington, D.C., 1933. NEBT–Net Earnings Before Taxes.
[4] Indebtedness at time of default as reported to *The Daily Bond Buyer.*
[5] Combination of reclamation, levee, irrigation, and drainage districts and other special districts.

Source: The Postwar Quality of State and Local Debt, George H. Hempel, Washington University in St. Louis, National Bureau of Economic Research, New York, 1971. Distributed by Columbia University Press, New York and London.

of total municipal debt outstanding) during periods in which defaults were high. Equally important is the recovery rate for defaulted issues and overdue interest that was eventually repaid by the issuer, restructured maturities, or federal government intervention.

CHARACTERISTICS OF THE 1929–1937 DEFAULT PERIOD

The recovery rate experienced by investors who held the bonds to maturity, settlement, or complete default is more important than the default rate because it reflects a more complete picture of total loss. The total loss of principal and interest resulting from the default of municipal issuers is estimated to be 0.5 percent of the average amount of all outstanding state and local debt. In other words, 99.5 percent of all outstanding municipal debt obligations were eventually repaid to the bondholders including the interest owed to them under the terms of issue. The surprisingly low total loss rate (lost principal and interest) was minimized by the Federal Municipal Bankruptcy Act of 1937. Early in the Great Depression, many distressed counties, municipalities, and townships received assistance from their home state governments. The states' assumption of various local debts naturally caused an increase in the financial instability of their own balance sheets.

By 1934, 14 states (Arizona, Florida, Louisiana, Michigan, New Jersey, North Carolina, Ohio, Texas, Alabama, Kentucky, Mississippi, Oklahoma, South Carolina, and Tennessee) had defaulted securities. Cities with large populations were observed to emerge from default at a faster rate than did smaller cities with fewer than 25,000 people. All 48 cities with populations of over 25,000, which were in default during the Great Depression, were reported to be out of default by 1938. Smaller cities had a less impressive performance during the same period. The records of the cases filed under the Federal Municipal Bankruptcy Act of 1937 showed 353 municipal units that filed petitions for assistance. Nearly all the municipalities and issuing entities had populations of less than 10,000. Over 50 percent of the petitioners represented special districts that had issued revenue bonds. (See Table 5.2.)

POSTWAR PERIOD, 1945–1965

The postwar period from 1945 through 1965 is interesting for study because the defaulted issues were heavily weighted by several large bond issues rather than by the broad defaults of the period from 1929 to 1937. The postwar period represented a total of $325 million of principal and interest in default. This number translates to about 0.3 percent of all municipal debt outstanding by the end of the 1965 fiscal year. Thus, 99.7 percent of all municipal debt and interest payments from municipal debt were paid to bondholders over the period. Of the $325 million in default, $294 million was the responsibility of 27 municipal units. Of the 27 issues, 21 were revenue bonds. Two particular issues, the $133 million West Virginia Turnpike and the $101 million Calumet Skyway represented 72 percent of the entire amount of defaulted municipal debt for the two decades of the postwar period.

DEFAULTS DURING 1965–2008

By studying data on defaults throughout history, we conclude that the ratings system has been generally effective in

TABLE 5.2

Defaults by State and Local Units (1837–1937) (Dollar Figures in Thousands)

Period	Average State and Local Debt Outstanding	Total Indebtedness of Defaulting State and Local Units	Percent of Debt Outstanding	Past Due Interest and Principal[1]	Percent of Debt Outstanding	Loss of Principal and Interest[2]	Percent of Debt Outstanding
1837–1843	$245,000	$125,000	51.0	n.a.	–	$15,000	6.1%
1873–1879	1,000,000	245,000	24.5	n.a.	–	150,000	15.0
1893–1899	1,300,000	130,000	10.0	n.a.	–	25,000	1.9
1929–1937	18,500,000	2,850,000[3]	15.4	320,000[3]	1.7	100,000	0.5

[1] Does not include interest on unpaid interest.
[2] Does not include interest on unpaid interest, interest due after debt was repudiated, or interest lost due to refunding at a lower interest cost.
[3] Overdue interest plus debt upon which interest is in default was $1,355,000 or 7.3 percent of debt outstanding in 1929–1937. This figure is not available for the earlier default periods.

Source: The Postwar Quality of State and Local Debt, George H. Hempel, Washington University in St. Louis National Bureau of Economic Research, New York, 1971, Distributed by Columbia University Press, New York and London.

identifying the quality of municipal issuers relative to their likelihood of default. The investment grade category shows a .07 percent cumulative default rate (Moody's) and .20 percent (Standard & Poor's). The noninvestment grade category shows a cumulative default rate of 4.29 percent (Moody's) and 7.37 percent (Standard & Poor's). The only exception was the Moody's AA rated bonds had a slightly higher default rate (.06 percent) than the A rated bonds default rate (.03 percent).[10]

The decade of the 1990s was the subject of a default study conducted by Standard & Poor's. The overall cumulative default rate for the period from 1987 to 1997 was 1.28 percent. Similar to the findings in the Hempel paper, the S&P study found the highest incidence of defaults within the broad category of revenue bonds, which represented approximately 50 percent of all defaults.[11]

PRICE SENSITIVITY OF MUNICIPAL BONDS OVER TIME

Municipal bond investors should be aware of the reality of fluctuating bond prices between the time of purchase and maturity. Understanding this concept requires patience. It is equally important for the investor to be aware of the reason for a bond's purchase. Investors who purchase bonds with the intent to hold them to maturity or call may mentally disassociate themselves from fluctuating bond prices since they have no intention of selling the bonds prior to maturity. Investors who purchase bonds to trade them or time the bond market must be aware of the dynamics of the effect of interest rates on bond prices. Once a bond is issued, its market price and yield will fluctuate according to changes in market conditions, current interest rates, or credit quality. This is characteristic of bonds in general not just municipal bonds. When prevailing *interest rates rise, prices of outstanding bonds fall* to bring the yield of older bonds into line with those of new issues at a given point. Similarly, when prevailing *interest rates fall, prices of outstanding bonds rise*, until the yield of older bonds is low enough to match the level of new issues.

Municipal bond investors must be aware of the fact that a temporary dip in a bond price does not change the maturity value. Temporary price increases, resulting from falling interest rates, cause the bond investor to see a gain in the price of his or her bond. This gain also does not change the value of the bond held to maturity because it will dissipate toward par value the nearer in time it gets to maturity or call. Failure to understand the dynamics of fluctuating interest rates (including the possibility of an inverted municipal yield curve or an instance of municipal bonds trading at a yield premium to U.S. Treasury bonds) contributed to the catastrophic losses incurred by municipal bond arbitrage hedge fund investors during the period from 2007 to 2008.

CLASSES OF MUNICIPAL BONDS

Municipal bonds fall into three general categories: general obligation bonds, revenue bonds, and special assessment bonds. The safest category of bonds (relative to observed historical defaults) is general obligation or GO bonds. GOs promise to repay based upon the full faith and credit of the issuer. GOs can be issued by states, cities, municipalities, and school districts. Revenue bonds are generally subcategorized into two groups: essential revenue and nonessential revenue. An example of an essential revenue bond is a metropolitan water and sewer project in which the monthly user fees are used to pay interest on the bonds. Nonessential revenue bonds are offered by a wide range of issuers including hospitals, nursing homes, convention centers, and retail centers. Earlier in this chapter, we discuss the higher incidence of default in the revenue bond category compared to other types of issues. Special assessment bonds include specific projects of a school district or municipality in which the revenues from the specific project are used for payment of interest. Special assessment bonds should not be confused with general obligation bonds because they do not carry the full faith and credit of the issuer.

With respect to credit quality, investors should be aware that some municipal bonds carry insurance; these are known as insured municipal bonds. In these cases, the credit quality of the insurer—not the issuer—determines the primary credit rating. In 2008 many municipal bond insurance companies were downgraded from their AAA credit rating when losses from subprime mortgage pools, which they had also insured, hurt their balance sheets. The reduced credit ratings of the monoline insurance companies created a conundrum for many municipal bond investors. Those who had purchased a "diversified" portfolio of insured revenue bonds found that the underlying issuers' credit ratings were, in some cases, junk rated (noninvestment grade). It is important for investors and advisors to understand that careful selection of municipal issues at the time of purchase is inadequate as the sole due diligence on the creditworthiness of issuers. Municipal issuers, like corporations and individuals, make decisions about their operations that either strengthen or weaken their credit quality over time. As we advised with respect to equity investing, the concept of "buy and hold" is dead and should be replaced with "buy and verify."

The three main rating agencies for municipal bonds in the United States are Standard & Poor's, Moody's, and Fitch. These agencies can be hired by the issuer to assign a bond rating, which is valuable information for potential bondholders as well as secondary market purchasers. One of the key concerns of the sponsors of the Municipal Bond Fairness Act was that corporate bonds had a higher incidence of default among the same rating classification as municipal bonds. It should be noted that the rating agencies essentially got the credit assessment of the monoline insurers wrong prior to 2008. Investors should be aware that a seemingly well-diversified portfolio of insured revenue bonds may hinge on the credit-worthiness of a handful of bond insurers. In these cases, investors who ignore underlying credit ratings of issuers for the perceived safety of the AAA insured bonds make a gross miscalculation.

STRATEGIES FOR INVESTING IN THE MUNICIPAL BOND MARKET

As is the case with other asset classes, there are multiple approaches to investing in the municipal bond market. The strategies vary according to fees, risk, taxes, and the purity of the asset class. By "purity," we mean that a municipal bond strategy should contain as high a level of the pure asset as is possible. Purity does not just pertain to the presence of an asset within a strategy. It means that a strategy should aim to capture the best attributes of the asset and remain free of derivatives and leverage which could add risk under certain circumstances.

Earlier in this chapter, we talk about the benefits and risks of municipal bonds. With respect to the benefits, many of the indirect or "impure" strategies dilute those benefits to the investor. For example, one of the greatest attributes of the holder of a general obligation bond of a city is that the investor has a direct creditor relationship with the city with no intermediaries. The only way for this direct creditor relationship to exist in the truest sense is for the investor to own the bond outright. A fractional ownership or participatory ownership of municipal bonds through mutual funds, exchange-traded funds, hedge funds, or unit trusts dilutes this creditor relationship. With respect to income and fixed maturity, the same rule applies. The owner of a bond is aware of the exact dollar amount of interest due in a given year as well as the exact date in the future the principal of the bond is to be redeemed by the issuer. In fund or pooled structures, this benefit is diluted since bonds must be constantly purchased and redeemed to meet the cash inflows and net investor redemptions. There are cases, however, in which smaller investors may be better served through a fund even after considering the above.

TRADITIONAL MUNICIPAL BOND PORTFOLIO

A traditional municipal bond portfolio is a long-only strategy, i.e., one that involves no leverage or derivatives. It involves acquiring municipal bonds for interest, the payment of a future liability, or absolute return over a long period. The traditional portfolio would most often be constructed and maintained by a manager skilled in this area or by an in-house portfolio manager within a larger family office. The portfolio would not engage in leverage, derivatives, swaps, or other high-risk strategies.

One of the simplest strategies to consider is the controlled ladder. In its most basic form, a laddered portfolio aims to assemble maturities of different issues in a semisymmetrical pattern with regard to maturity. For example, the portfolio manager may believe that the 10-year part of the municipal curve is the "sweet spot" (meaning the point on the yield curve at which the investor can maximize return while controlling maturity risk). In such a case, the ladder would be built by staggering maturities between 5 to 15 years, thus creating an average maturity of 10 years. The proponents of the laddering concept believe that the ladder creates flexibility if rates rise (at which point shorter maturity bonds could be swapped for longer-term higher-yielding bonds). Should rates fall during the life of the portfolio, the owner of a laddered portfolio has at least captured higher yields on the portion of the portfolio at the long end. As we have stated throughout this book "buy and hold" is an ineffective strategy for even a simple municipal bond ladder. Periodic bond maturities, calls, changes in the "sweet spot" in the yield curve, fluctuating credit quality, and prerefundings require laddered portfolio owners to perform periodic due diligence and portfolio maintenance.

Other portfolio strategies include the barbell approach, in which maturities are accumulated in similar quantities at opposite ends of the yield curve. The barbell approach requires an opportunistic portfolio manager with conviction because this structure requires him to have an opinion on where he believes interest rates are headed. In a perfect world there would be an ample supply of home state GO bonds at every point in the yield curve which could be acquired at attractive valuations. Because this is seldom the case, investors are best served when the portfolio managers have the flexibility to build a portfolio where value is present in the marketplace. Building a perfect bond ladder with exactly the same dollar amount in each 10 to 15 years of maturities would be less beneficial than the portfolio that had a few holes (missing a few years of maturity) because the values were so compelling at or near the same maturity.

Credit quality is obviously an important factor in determining the risk of default. While we continually run our after-tax portfolio modeling to compare equities with municipals, we model for the high-quality/investment grade sector of the market. I am firmly of the opinion that the bond portfolio's role of providing income and principal protection should not be compromised by treating core investments as risk capital. When we cover the fund/hedge fund approach to this asset class, you will understand why I feel so strongly on this topic.

Once the investor or manager has established the targeted credit quality of the portfolio, a determination must be made as to where she sees value on the yield curve. A flat yield curve, where yields are similar on the short as well as the long end of the curve, might convince the manager that longer maturity bonds do not adequately compensate the investor for interest rate risk, so she may opt to target the maturity at the short to intermediate part of the curve. A normal or upward sloping yield curve pays the investor with higher yields for the longer maturity issues. Based upon the role the bond portfolio will play for the family, the manager will determine a targeted maturity and portfolio structure and then shape the portfolio around this bias. It is common for older investors to question the sense of a long-term average maturity when they believe that the portfolio will outlive them. In most cases, if the investor believes that the role of the municipal bond portfolio is as valuable to his heirs as it would be to him personally, this concern is alleviated.

HOME STATE VERSUS NATIONAL PORTFOLIO

Some municipal bond investors favor building a portfolio exclusively within the borders of their home state, especially if their home state bonds are exempt from income tax in that state. As of 2009, 35 U.S. states exempt their home state municipal bonds from state tax. In some cases, this exemption applies only to general obligation bonds. For the investor who resides in a state in which home state municipal bond income is exempt, he or she must determine the out-of-state yield that must be achieved (after the payment of state tax) in order to match the double tax-exempt status of a home state portfolio. For example, Hawaii has a maximum state income tax rate of 8.25 percent.[12] If a Hawaiian investor (in the top income tax bracket) were to purchase a new issue Hawaii municipal bond with a 5 percent yield to maturity, no tax would be assessed on this cash flow. If he were to purchase a new issue California municipal bond at 5.25 percent yield to maturity, he must subtract the effect of Hawaii's income tax on the California bond in order to determine his after-tax yield. In this case, the true after-tax yield on the California bond would be 4.97 percent.[13] The conclusion is that as the portfolio manager begins building the portfolio for the Hawaiian investor, she must be able to find an out-of-state yield of nearly 30 basis points higher in the same maturity and credit quality for it to be considered over the 5 percent Hawaii bond.

The traditional municipal bond portfolio should be reviewed periodically by the portfolio manager to determine if the targeted maturity is still in line with the goals of the portfolio and that credit ratings, pre-refundings, and pending call issues are considered for reinvestment. One obvious issue with respect to portfolio construction is the price the manager is willing to pay for a bond he wishes to place into the portfolio. Since municipal bond trades are now publicly available, it is evident that price discipline is not regularly practiced by municipal bond buyers. Unlike stocks where prices are quoted in spreads, which may be only pennies, municipal bond spreads are much wider and varied because of factors such as retail markups (broker commission added to the price of a bond) or motivated sellers and buyers. In 2008 and 2009, it was not at all uncommon to see a bond trade at prices 3 to 4 percent apart in the same day. The municipal bond buyer must be choosy about the type of bonds he wishes to own and be disciplined about the price he is willing to pay. If the investor is to own the bond for 10 years, a 2 percent difference in acquisition price has a significant effect over the life of the bond.

For all these reasons, a bond portfolio should receive the same effort, due diligence, and discipline as the equity portfolio.

ZERO COUPON MUNICIPAL BONDS

Zero coupon municipal bonds were introduced to the fixed income market in 1982. Traditional municipal bonds typically provide semiannual interest payments and are redeemed at their "par" or face value. Zero coupon municipal bonds are issued at a discount to their face value and make no income payments prior to maturity. Longer-term zero coupon municipal bonds are purchased at a substantial discount from their full face value. For example, a bond maturing in 20 years might trade for 37 cents per dollar of face value. The purchase of a bond at $0.37 that matures in 20 years at a price of $1.00 equates to a yield to maturity of approximately 5 percent.

There are several benefits that are unique to zero coupon municipal bonds. First, because the bonds do not provide current cash flow, zero coupon bonds have tended to command a "yield premium" over coupon bonds of the same maturity. For example, if 20-year coupon bonds are trading at a yield of 4.85 percent, a zero-coupon buyer may be able to capture a 5 percent yield in a similar credit rating 20-year issue. Another reason for the yield premium in zeroes is that the buyer demands it because the zero will be generally more volatile in response to changes in interest rates. A second unique trait about zero coupon bonds is that they offer what I refer to as "true compounding." In our example above the migration of the zero coupon bond at $0.37 to maturity at $1.00 in 20 years offers a compounded return of 5 percent. This cannot be said of coupon bonds for two reasons. In order for a coupon bond to offer a true compounded return of 5 percent, each and every coupon payment over the 20-year period (40 in all) must be invested by the bondholder in another instrument that offers at least a 5 percent rate of return. Since it is unlikely that over a 20-year period the investor will be able to consistently reinvest coupon income into a similar credit quality issue at 5 percent, it becomes difficult to claim that the coupon bond offers a true compounded rate of return.

Drawbacks or risks to consider with zero coupon bonds include the fact that their price volatility tends to be higher than that for a coupon bond. Zero coupon bonds tend to be less liquid than coupon bonds since I believe the demand for them is smaller. The bid-ask spread in the market is therefore wider.

There are several strategies where a wealthy family can use zero coupon bonds to fund specific liabilities due at a specific date. One of my favorites is for college funding. Using our example of the 20-year issue which would be purchased at $0.37 per $1.00 of face value, the family would be able to fund a $75,000 future tuition payment for a current cost of $27,750. If the buyer were to purchase these bonds using general obligation bonds in their home state (assuming home state tax deductibility of municipal interest), the $75,000 would be received in the year it was needed for the college tuition without a penny due of federal, state, or capital gains taxes. Assuming supply of such issues was available, I would structure the maturities of the zero coupon bonds to match the years in which the children were to be enrolled in college.

BLACK SWANS, THE UNFORESEEN, AND STRESS TESTING

In 2009, most would now admit that black swans[14] always appear on the horizon and will usually be undetected and "shock" the market. For this reason, municipal bond investors should consider the range of events that have taken place in every 20-year period of the last century and then determine if they should risk the very existence of their bond portfolio hoping to squeak out a few extra basis points of yield. The most grievous example of an investment train wreck occurred in the realm of the municipal bond arbitrage hedge funds. Many investors claim that these funds were sold to them as safe and that volatility "back-tested" studies proved them to perform like a AAA investment portfolio. The strategy of the "muni arb" funds, as they were called, was to purchase a portfolio of investment grade bonds with a majority of the portfolio and fill the remainder with derivatives and short trades against U.S. Treasury bonds. When the municipal bond curve inverted in late 2007 and early 2008, the derivative trades went against them and in some cases destroyed 90 percent of the portfolio value. In the aftermath, investors would learn that the portfolio of AAA bonds was leveraged 8 to 10 times and that on a few select days the amount of the fund's margin balance exceeded the underlying value of the entire portfolio. Some consultants and wealth managers sold or recommended these strategies to investors as enhanced municipal bond alternatives in place of a traditional portfolio. The only thing alternative about these strategies is that those who used them would find that their "low-risk" assets turned out to produce losses worse than the major equity indexes of 2008. Investors should do the math, study history, and fortify their portfolios with discipline and common sense.

CONCLUSIONS

- Municipal bonds are often underweighted in wealthy investors' portfolios.
- Although municipal bond yields have historically traded at discounts to other bonds, investors shouldn't assume that they always will.

- Investors must consider the entire history of muni defaults when considering new investments.
- Recovery rates on munis are as important as default rates.
- Buy individual municipal bonds as a pure asset class rather than intermediary pooled funds.
- Consider factors of economic and geographic diversification when deciding on a single state or national portfolio.
- Demand strict ongoing portfolio due diligence: "buy and verify."

Are Alternative Investments a Necessary Component of a Diversified Portfolio?

I am a relentless skeptic of alternative investments as a so-called asset class. I like to invest with a transparent method that can be understood by my clients. I like to limit the effects of fees and taxes on portfolio assets. Since these criteria are generally not met by venturing into the alternative investment world, that may be enough of an explanation for most of you. And yet because such investments are marketed so heavily to wealthy investors, I feel they need to be addressed. In the wake of such books as Yale endowment manager David Swensen's *Unconventional Success: A Fundamental Approach to Personal Investment* and Allianz Funds and former Harvard endowment manager Mohamed El-Erian's *When Markets Collide: Investment Strategies for the Age of Global Economic Change*, investing like the bigwigs at endowments and pension plans has become all the rage.

And if in a post-Bernard Madoff world, the shine on hedge funds has tarnished some, they still possess enough of wealthy Americans' assets to warrant further analysis.

I first warned of wealthy investors' dangerous infatuation with alternatives at a 2005 Institute for Private Investors forum in New York titled "What's Wrong with This Picture: Are Wall Street 'Alternatives' Truly a Prudent Alternative to Quality Long Only Investing?" In my talk, I tried to communicate that the advice of "the great ones" has been discarded by investors and replaced with a "new paradigm" of distressed debt, leverage, mortgages, indexing, and alternative investments. Though I now feel vindicated by this unpopular stance, it's notable how offensive my remarks seemed to some investors and advisors at the time. Post-bear market and post-Madoff, I suppose, many feel differently.

It is true that those who study what has become known as the alternative asset classes (hedge funds, private equity, futures, and real estate) have observed periods of low correlation to their traditional counterparts. In 2008, however, this was not the case as these assets which were placed in many investor portfolios in order to reduce risk actually had the opposite effect. I believe the experience of 2008 coupled with the insidious fee and tax consequences have shed new light on one of the wealth management industry's sacred cows. If an investor chooses to invest in alternatives, I suggest a rigorous process of due diligence and a laser focus on individual managers. Broadly diversified fund of fund strategies and other packaged approaches will yield results which will result in outcomes ranging from the mediocre to disastrous.

Still, I don't want to dismiss every alternative asset. Each has its pluses and minuses that should be understood in relation to the particular needs and unique tax sensitivity of wealthy investors. As Chapter 8 will reveal, every asset class can be analyzed with our after-tax calculator to determine what sort of risk premium, if any, it provides over low-risk assets. We encourage all investors and money managers to equip themselves to view these assets in light of their own assumptions for long-term returns and the tax burden unique to their own portfolios. The term "alternative" suggests that the investment attraction lies in what it is *not* as opposed to what it *is*. So let us consider each category of alternative in turn.

COMMODITIES

Commodities differ from stocks and bonds since bonds actually pay a coupon rate, while stocks provide ownership in businesses that aim to produce a profit for investors. A piece of metal, a bushel of corn, a barrel of oil produces nothing other than the fact that the investor owns that asset. So with commodity investing, unlike stocks and bonds, the only way you can make money is to make a bet on the direction of the price. And that becomes quite difficult to do over the long run, first of all, because commodity prices are so volatile; and, second of all, you've got to be right twice. You've got to be right on the buy, and you've got to be right on the sell. Finally your degree of correctness in your trading must produce a competitive return for investors net of taxes, fees, and the cost of leverage. Commodity-managed futures funds generally exist with the same fee and taxation structure as hedge funds. That is 2 percent of assets and 20 percent of profits for funds and 3 percent of assets and 30 percent of profits for fund of funds. Because the funds rely on short-term trading strategies, positive returns are generally taxed at ordinary income rates.

People supposedly buy commodities as an inflation hedge. When I entered the business in November 1991, the Commodity Research Bureau Index, the oldest commodity futures index, was trading at a level of 213. In February 2009 the index closed at a level of 211. Though I'll admit this to be a somewhat random time period, it is safe to say that in my investment career the general commodity index did not provide a hedge against inflation or anything else.

Admittedly, commodity futures do rise in anticipation of inflation. But people forget that when inflation was peaking in 1981, long-term Treasury bond yields got as high as 11 or 12 percent. So inflation's back was broken on high interest rates, and the bonds were actually compensating the investor for the fact that inflation could have remained at 11 or 12 percent. Of course, if inflation advanced past 12 percent and stayed there until the maturity of the bond, the investor would have experienced a negative return on the bond net of inflation (even worse after taxes and inflation). And when inflation died down again after 1981, commodity prices fell.

Since 1981, commodity prices have risen and fallen and risen again ultimately producing little total gain for the long-term investor because they produce no cash flow. Meanwhile, the holder of long-term Treasury bonds has made 11 percent annualized, vastly exceeding subsequent inflation levels. All of which is not to say buy 30-year Treasury bonds to combat inflation. Rather, if you're worried about inflation cropping up, there are alternative means of combating it. You can shorten the average maturity of your bond portfolio. An investor in a laddered bond strategy might proactively lengthen maturities to capture higher yields. Who knows if you might even be able to lock in a guaranteed 11 percent return again one day?

As an investor, I'm looking to make a profit from viable business entities. Thus, when I view oil, natural gas, corn, or even gold, I would prefer to look for business opportunities by owning a company which produces, mines, or processes these commodities. Though I am in no way suggesting that prices of commodity producers are correlated to the underlying commodities, I choose to approach these assets as a business owner rather than as a short-term price speculator. If you own shares of Chevron or Exxon, you not only have exposure to the underlying commodity, but you own a business that takes that underlying commodity, performs a process on it, and then marks it up to a profit to be sold on the open market. As long as the stock valuations make sense, I would prefer to process and mark up that commodity rather than to own it directly because the markup provides a quantifiable return to me. Whereas if I am simply buying the barrel of oil, it can either go up, stay the same, or go down; but there is nothing that says that I am going to make money unless I trade it, unless I buy it right, unless I sell it right, and unless my margin costs and my trading costs from buying and selling oil futures are offset by good decisions.

Futures contracts are by nature short-term investments because they have expiration dates typically only a few months out, and those with longer dates do not track the spot prices of their commodities effectively. That increases your transaction costs of owning them since expiring contracts must be rolled over into new ones. On top of that futures must be purchased on margin, so there are additional interest costs as well as additional volatility to your portfolio from that leverage.

There are some exchange-traded funds (ETFs) and exchange-traded notes (ETNs) that invest in commodities for lower fees than managed futures funds. But in the case of the ETFs they have the same tax problems as investing in futures directly and in the case of ETNs they are really debt instruments that track commodity prices. Issued by banks, which have suffered mightily in the recent bear market, ETNs have credit risk in them that may wipe out their investors in the event of a default.

Finally, investors must be aware that just like stocks, bonds, or hedge funds which can trade to bubble proportions, so too can the spot prices of commodities. In another similarity, the mania for the purchase of these assets tends to occur once most of the upside move has been made. When oil was trading at $146 a barrel in 2008, all I heard about was the "new paradigm" for energy. Today oil trades for $70, and the new paradigm seems an awful lot like the old one.

CURRENCIES

Like commodities, currencies produce no cash flow. So buying a foreign currency is simply a speculative bet that your home currency will fall against that currency. There is a lot of such speculation currently about the U.S. dollar because of America's large fiscal and current account deficits.

I acknowledge the risks and implications of a weak dollar on the U.S. and global economy. That said, I know that by investing in the stocks of large multinational companies, I have an implicit hedge against a dollar decline. In the businesses we own right now in our portfolios, 40 percent of the earnings are derived from non-dollar sources because products are being sold to customers in Asia, Europe, and

South America. And of course owning currency futures to gain exposure is as costly and tax-inefficient as owning commodity or gold futures.

Moreover, the executives running multinational companies (in our equity portfolio) already practice currency and commodity hedging in the normal course of their business. I would not want to enact a trade that would amplify or counter the effects of these programs.

HEDGE FUNDS

Are hedge funds an asset class? The hedge fund industry might like you to think so. But the truth is there are many different hedge fund strategies—long/short, market neutral, merger arbitrage (arb), convertible arbitrage, distressed debt, systematic macro and muni arbitrage, to name just a few. Each of these strategies has its own peculiar nuances, but two things common to almost every hedge fund makes the whole investment category unattractive—high fees and leverage. Throw in the fact that many of the most effective hedge fund strategies—merger arb and convertible arb—are highly tax inefficient, and you have a challenge for high net worth investors.

Unfortunately, the high fees and leverage go hand in hand. Because fees are so high at 2 percent of assets and 20 percent of profits for hedge funds and sometimes 3 percent of assets and 30 percent of profits for funds of hedge funds, the hurdle rate for managers to produce a profit for their investors becomes obscenely high. Because the margin on the safest hedge fund strategies such as merger arb tends to be narrow—and gets narrower and narrower the more hedge funds there are pursuing the same strategy—hedge funds need to use leverage to amplify the returns on those strategies. Otherwise, after deducting their fees and taxes, many funds' returns would be minuscule or nonexistent.

Leverage dramatically amplifies the risk of ostensibly low-risk strategies. A mistake that might cause an unleveraged manager only 1 or 2 percentage points may cause a leveraged hedge fund manager 10 or 20 percentage points. It also increases the total fees—or investment costs—investors pay to the funds. And those leverage costs grow as assets shrink in a falling fund because the cost of servicing the debt remains the same on an asset base that is shrinking. Ask any veteran of the investment business and he'll remind you of a disastrous trade that resulted from a "sure thing" that was leveraged to the hilt. The veterans know what happens when the leverage goes bad and that successful arbitrage strategy that they had identified as being set in stone for 70 years stopped working one day.

Even if fees were more reasonable and the leverage exposure less extreme, most hedge funds would be inappropriate for high net worth investors because they tend to be very tax-inefficient. Many of the strategies managers employ to produce "absolute" returns in any kind of market are based on short-term anomalies in valuation that disappear relatively quickly. The discrepancy in value, for instance, between the announced acquisition price of a merger target and its current price disappears as soon as the merger closes. And when the merger does close, the hedge fund manager moves on to the next merger, thus creating a short-term capital gain.

And yet since U.S. securities law requires a minimum net worth of $1 million or an annual income of at least $200,000 to invest in hedge funds, they are almost exclusively marketed to high net worth investors and institutions.

Institutional investors in hedge funds such as endowments and pension plans will fare better because they are not subject to taxes and because they have the insight and institutional clout to find and hire the best managers. For this reason even successful endowment managers like Yale's Swensen who've employed hedge funds extensively say not to try this at home. According to Swensen's book, for the average hedge fund investors: "The hefty fee arrangements typical of hedge funds erode the already low cash-like return to an unacceptable level, especially after adjusting for risk." He also says, "In the hedge fund world, as in the whole world of money management industry, consistent superior active management constitutes a rare commodity."[1]

Swensen has also called funds of hedge funds, which have even higher fees, "A cancer on the institutional investor."[2] And if such funds are cancerous to tax-sheltered endowments and pension funds, they are absolutely lethal to wealthy investors whose returns are even less after taxes.

I'll freely admit that there are talented managers who have produced impressive results even with high fee structures and leverage. I have learned of other hedge fund managers who employ a long-only strategy with no leverage. I agree with Swensen and Mohamed El-Erian and believe that investors should refrain from viewing hedge funds as an asset class. In doing so, those who find managers or funds that can produce positive tax, fee, and risk-adjusted returns can perform more accurate due diligence. Yet whenever I hear investors say, "There is a lot of money to be made in hedge funds," I agree with them and then remind them that the finest homes in the Hamptons, New York are owned by the managers of hedge funds rather than the investors in the funds themselves.

PRIVATE EQUITY

Is there any alternative investment that may be worthy of consideration for wealthy investors? Although we don't own any positions now, we are evaluating the private equity arena. This may seem contradictory on our part since the fees for private equity funds are often as high as those for hedge funds, if not higher. But the unique advantage private equity funds have for wealthy investors is that the value of private businesses accumulates on a tax-deferred basis for the investor until a liquidity event occurs such as an initial public offering (IPO) or acquisition of the business. That can mean years of accumulation without any realized gains and then, when gains are realized, they are taxed at the lower rate of long-term capital gains, not as ordinary income.

The private equity world breaks down into three categories with numerous subcategories within each. In the first category are venture capital funds with managers bringing tiny brand-new companies to the next stage of financing and are thus funding them at an infancy level. In the second group are private equity funds buying successful small to midsized manufacturing or services companies from their present management teams. Managers of such businesses may not want to take the company public. Such companies are often family-run, and the children of the founders may have no interest in the business, and so private equity funds can purchase these companies often at significant discounts to companies available in the public markets. The third category of funds is the leveraged buyout groups who borrow money and buy public or private companies in order to recapitalize them and make a profit by either selling the company or doing an IPO.

It is the second group that interests us the most—what we would call the true private equity space. I believe that un-leveraged private equity funds may represent today what small-cap funds were in the late 1970s. Many people are aware of the fact that small capitalization companies had a very good run coming out of the 1973 to 1974 recession and that their out-performance is notable even over a 30-year period because of what happened during that period.

One of the reasons I believe that private businesses may possess some of the same traits as the small capitalization stocks of the late-1970s is that new securities laws such as the Sarbanes-Oxley Act of 2002 have made it increasingly difficult costly for small companies to go public. As a result, many remain undervalued and will defer their IPO until they reach a much larger size. Others will forego the IPO process completely and instead seek to be acquired by other companies.

Because of the difficulty of taking a small family-run business public, there is an opportunity for talented private equity managers to identify those companies that have management teams who are tired and do not want to pass on the family business. If the private equity managers believe they can make a profit for these owners and for fund shareholders by buying these companies, it's a win-win for everyone.

Since I and most of my clients believe in long-term business ownership as opposed to short-term stock speculation, we feel that in many ways private equity is more of a pure ownership strategy. Certainly such funds will be delivering more long-term capital gains than will public equity mutual and hedge funds. And the mentality of their managers and investors is more long term. You don't see private equity valuations on your Yahoo! Log-in screen every time you check your e-mail. The funds very often have a five- to ten-year lockup to them and they are not valued that often, so the lack of visibility has probably been a benefit to some of their owners who are concerned about taxes and who prefer long-term gains.

And yet we do see drawbacks to private equity funds that give us pause. Aside from the high fees, which are inherently problematic, the returns on private equity funds can vary dramatically depending on the quality of their managers. According to a study by Josh Lerner, a professor at Harvard Business School, whom Allianz's El-Erian cites in his *When Markets Collide*, the dispersion of returns between private equity funds in the top quartile of performance and those at the bottom was immense, especially when compared to other asset classes. As El-Erian states: "For the period [Lerner] studied the average difference amounted to almost 15 percentage points—that is, the representative top-quartile fund returned an extra 15 percentage points of return per year as compared to the representative fund in the bottom quartile. This is a large absolute number; and it compares to around 3 percentage points for equity mutual funds and 1 percentage point for bond funds."[3] Moreover, El-Erian reveals that the average private equity fund has underperformed the S&P 500 after fees while taking on more risk.

Obviously, if we invest in a private equity fund, we will need to do extensive due diligence to make sure it does not employ leverage that amplifies the risk of blowups and cost of operations. What's more, we will insist that the equity risk premium on high-risk illiquid private investments be significantly higher than what we find in public stock markets. So, for instance, if a private equity fund was seeking to purchase a manufacturing business and it was valued at a 50 percent discount to what we'd pay for shares of big industrial manufacturing companies in the public marketplace, then the discount would be big enough for us to pay the high fund fees and take on the risk.

And yet there may be a better alternative for our high net worth clients. As we shall see in Chapter 13 on multigenerational planning, one of the best ways for wealthy families to stay wealthy is to preserve the entrepreneurial spirit that helped make the family rich in the first place. That would involve investing in private businesses directly instead of through a fund and encouraging family members to become entrepreneurs instead of just the beneficiaries of trust funds. We have, for instance, a client who is investing about 5 percent of his net worth in a custom home-building business in which his son has experience and skill. Such a setup could be ideal for certain wealthy investors.

CONCLUSIONS

- After adjusting for taxes, fees, borrowing costs, and risk, alternative investments may diminish in their attractiveness to taxable investors.
- Commodities produce no cash flow, unlike stocks or bonds.
- Multinational companies already have exposure to foreign currencies including foreign currency hedging strategies.
- Leverage dramatically increases the risk of "safe" hedge fund strategies.

- Most hedge funds exhibit high turnover, and thus are not tax-efficient.
- Private equity funds can be tax-efficient because they generally benefit from gains taxed at long-term capital gains rates.

A History of Taxation at the Top Bracket and the Effect of Taxation on the Long-Term Compounding of Assets

Taxes are as old as civilization. The earliest records date back to at least 3000 BC in ancient Egypt. Citizens would pay biannual levies on their cattle and grain during an event called the "Following of Horus," a royal tour in which the pharaoh appeared before his people for the express purpose of collecting taxes. This gave birth to one of the first tax shelters during the fourth dynasty (2625–2500 BC)—royal charters of immunity often granted–the priesthood staff and property of Egyptian temples.[1]

Perhaps today Americans who can e-file their tax returns have it easier than their ancient counterparts who sent caravans of cattle and grain. But often taxes today seem no less capricious and arbitrary than they did back then. This is especially so for wealthy investors who throughout history have been subject to on-again/off-again estate taxes at widely varying rates and top-income tax rates that are constantly in flux.

INCOME TAX

The first income tax in recorded history was levied in the year AD 10. Emperor Wang Mang of China instituted a tax on the profits of merchants and artisans to finance loans to the needy.[2] Amid widespread famine and outbreaks of pestilence, Wang died in a peasant rebellion in October AD23. Little was heard or seen of the income tax after that until November 24, 1797, when British Prime Minister William Pitt made his famous budget speech pleading for a "general tax on persons possessed of property commensurate as far as practical with their means" to help finance the war against Napoleon.[3]

After much debate and protest and an ever-increasing deficit from the war, what was initially called a triple-assessment tax, metamorphosed into a more conventional graduated income tax in Pitt's Act of 1798, which became effective on January 9, 1799. The tax rates at the time ranged from 1 to 10 percent of income. The tax was repealed in 1801, then brought back in 1803, and vanished again from 1816 through 1842 until it became a permanent part of British society. As Edwin R. A. Seligman notes in his book *The Income Tax: A Study of the History, Theory and Practice of Income Taxation at Home and Abroad*: "In the main, however, all discussion of the tax was silenced in the face of the gigantic struggle against Napoleon. . . . As the war drew to a close, however, a movement was set on foot to compel the government to redeem its pledge and to drop the tax."[4] That agitation led to the temporary repeal, but in the wake of mounting budget deficits and the failure of customs taxes to foot the bill, the Act of 1842 brought the tax back.

The income tax in the United States followed a similar pattern. What initially started out as customs and property taxes in the colonies became an income tax in the wake of the bloody and immensely costly Civil War. While prior to the war, some individual states had imposed a crude kind of income tax called the *faculty tax* to tax those who didn't own property, mounting war costs prompted Congress to pass the Revenue Act of August 5, 1861, which authorized the country's first federal income tax of 3 percent on all citizens earning more than $800 a year. The following year the Revenue Act of 1862 was passed, creating the country's first graduated income tax of 3 percent on annual incomes above $600 and 5 percent on those above $10,000. That same year Congress created the Bureau of Internal Revenue, a precursor to the Internal Revenue Service, and Abraham Lincoln appointed its first commissioner, George S. Boutwell, a former governor of Massachusetts.

When Boutwell was sworn in on July 16, 1862, he was given an office on the first floor of the Treasury building and assigned three clerks. By January 1, 1863, his office had grown to employ nearly 4,000 people, including 365 tax collectors and property assessors.[5] The subsequent Revenue Act of 1864 raised rates to 5 percent for people with incomes over $600, 7.5 percent for incomes between $5,000 and $10,000, and 10 percent for incomes greater than $10,000.[6] And yet despite this predictable explosion in federal bureaucracy, what may seem remarkable to modern readers is that the income tax act actually had a sunset clause built into it so that Congress allowed it to expire in 1872 as the populace mainly viewed it as an emergency measure for wartime situations. From that point until the ratification of the Constitution's Sixteenth

Amendment in 1913 the federal government was supported primarily by excise taxes and tariffs.

The Sixteenth Amendment ushered in the modern income tax era, and I suppose from the high net worth investor's perspective it may seem all downhill from there. But first it's important to remember that high excise taxes and tariffs on trade were ultimately very bad for a burgeoning economy, so the income tax provided some necessary relief. Second, paying income taxes at 35 percent rates in 2010 and 39.6 percent in 2011 may seem like a lot, but that's nothing compared to their peak rate of 94 percent in 1944. So it's absolutely crucial for wealthy investors to keep abreast of tax trends and study tax history, and to factor after-tax returns into their portfolio strategies.

Consider Figure 7.1 showing the top marginal income tax brackets from 1916 through 2011 and you will see how variable they can be.

FIGURE 7.1

Top Marginal Tax Bracket

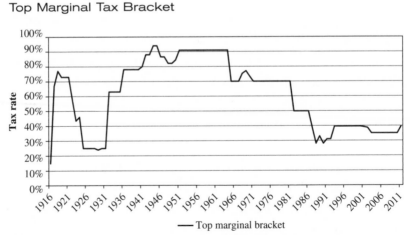

— Top marginal bracket

Source: Citizens for Tax Justice, May 2004; 1930 & 1940's Estate Tax data provided by *The Estate Tax History: Ninety Years and Counting* by Darien B. Jacobson, Brian G. Raub, and Barry W. Johnson.

As you can see, the lowest U.S. top marginal brackets in the modern tax era were 24 percent in 1929 and 25 percent throughout the latter half of the Roaring Twenties, a time of major economic growth in the United States. Unfortunately, that growth and the excesses it inspired created a major stock market bubble that ushered in the Great Depression. Similarly, rates were also relatively low in the 1990s, another bubble period and a time of accelerating economic growth and technological innovation, which also ultimately led to two major stock market crashes from 2000 through 2002 and in 2008. Some might argue whether the low tax rates helped create the economic boom or were a reaction to it as the government needs less tax revenues per capita when the economy is soaring and the federal coffers are already full. This debate cannot be resolved easily, but for wealthy investors all that matters is that they position their portfolios accordingly.

The highest top marginal tax brackets as we've seen throughout history seem to reach their peaks as a result of wars or severe economic stress. The first twentieth-century peak of 77 percent occurred in 1918 as a reaction to the United States entering World War I in 1917. After the war ended, the top rates fell back down to 25 percent.

According to Sheldon David Pollack, author of *The Failure of U.S. Tax Policy: Revenue and Politics*: "America's entry into World War I resulted in an increase in the federal government's demand for revenue that far exceeded all initial estimates. Revenue projections from [the] Treasury were constantly revised upward as estimates by the military of the costs of war invariably proved to be understated. In fact, the cost of the first full year of American participation in the war was $26 billion—more than the total cost of the entire federal government from 1791 through 1917. Such an explosion in federal expenditures could hardly have failed to occasion a fiscal revolution. As had been the case during the 1860s, the revenue crisis of war led to fundamental changes in the structure of the federal income tax."[7]

The second major twentieth-century increase in income taxes occurred in 1932 as the country was neck deep in the Great Depression, and President Franklin Roosevelt's New Deal caused federal expenditures to expand. Top federal tax rates rose from 25 percent in 1931 to 63 percent in 1932 and then to 78 percent by 1936. The Social Security Act of 1935 created not only retirement benefits, but also unemployment benefits and welfare benefits for the poor and disabled. That of course caused expenditures to grow significantly. Then during World War II income taxes peaked at 94 percent in 1944. Top rates subsequently hovered around 90 percent until 1965 when they dropped to 70 percent because of President Lyndon Johnson's Revenue Act of 1964 and then to 50 percent in 1982 as a result of President Ronald Reagan's Economic Recovery Tax Act of 1981 (rates subsequently dropped to 28 percent during his presidency). Unfortunately, as a consequence of these tax cuts and a large increase in military spending, the federal deficit grew significantly during Reagan's tenure. So it seemed inevitable that taxes would bounce back up, and they did to 33 percent during George H. W. Bush's presidency and then 39.6 percent under Bill Clinton. And of course, 2010's 35 percent top bracket will revert to 39.6 percent in 2011 when former President George W. Bush's tax cuts expire.

ADJUSTING YOUR PORTFOLIO TO SUIT THE TIMES

Although little can be done about the taxation of employment income for wealthy business owners and executives, there's no reason they should have to suffer high taxation on their portfolio assets as investors. As the above history reveals, income tax rates can be incredibly volatile and unpredictable. But whatever the prevailing rates are at the time, investors should do the math and calculate what the returns on their investments will be after taxes and invest accordingly. As we shall see in Chapter 8 on portfolio optimization, there are some investment strategies and asset classes that are more affected by income taxes than others.

Stock dividends are an interesting case, as sometimes they have been taxed as income and sometimes they haven't. From 1913 through 1935 dividends were completely tax exempt, and then from 1936 through 1939 they were fully taxable as income, only to be exempt again through 1953. From 1953 through 2002, dividends were again taxed as income, only the IRS allowed minor dividend exemptions of up to $100. Then with the Jobs and Growth Tax Reconciliation Act of 2003 dividends became taxed at the 15 percent rate which will expire at the end of 2010, and will go back to being taxed at income rates again.[8] If this kind of taxation has the dizzying affect of a merry-go-round, get used to it because tax policies are likely to change. And wealthy investors must change their strategies along with the policies or build portfolios that are less subject to taxation at the top bracket. Right now for instance in 2009 it makes little sense for investors to be piling into dividend stocks (solely because of current preferred taxation rates) if they know that by 2011 the 15 percent tax rate will become 39.6 percent.

Although the tax-free status of municipal bonds seems relatively secure, even they haven't been completely immune from controversy. According to a 1988 ruling by the U.S. Supreme Court on a case titled *South Carolina v. Baker*, there is no Constitutional guarantee of municipal bonds being exempt from federal taxes, and Congress could pass legislation to tax the bonds if it wanted to.[9]

Given all the historical instability of tax rates we've just discussed, ultimately the question will crop up when designing a portfolio as to where they are heading in future years. Obviously, there is a degree of unpredictability to the answer. But if history is any guide, during times of war, economic stress, and large budget deficits, income tax rates on the wealthy tend to go up. All three of these conditions are being met right now (2009). So it should come as no surprise to wealthy investors if income taxes rise significantly.

An increase in taxes will force investors to adjust their net portfolio return expectations. That leads us to a fork in the road where we must decide whether we are going to allocate our portfolio assets based upon the returns that we desire or whether we are going to allocate them based upon the returns that are possible. I believe that this is a point where there will be a divergence between two groups. Some will acknowledge those lower rates of return in traditional asset classes but will still try ever so hard to capture 10 to 11 percent compounding and the only mathematical way to do that (since it will be difficult in equities or in bonds) will be to speculate on hedge funds, private equity, and commodities. Those who choose this route should consider this startling fact: should taxes rise to the level of those of the Carter administration (1977–1980), a commodity or hedge fund would need to produce a gross return of 33.75 percent in order to produce a 6 percent return to investors net of all taxes and fees. This is because during that period, the fund returns would have been taxed at the top marginal bracket of 70 percent and would have been combined with the 2 percent/20 percent fee structure of the hedge fund.

The other group is going to say that I'm unwilling to gamble everything that I have accumulated and amassed in my business by betting on the price of agricultural goods or metals, and I'm going to adjust either my spending rates or my multigenerational view of how these assets will affect my family. This group I think will have a more realistic understanding of what's possible in this environment.

CAPITAL GAINS TAX

Generally speaking, through much of U.S. history long-term capital gains tax rates have been lower than have income tax rates. The reason for this is the belief that capital investment spurs economic growth and shouldn't be penalized with onerous taxes. And yet rates have crept up significantly from time to time. If you review Figure 7.2, you can see how they've changed since 1916.

FIGURE 7.2

Top Capital Gains Tax Bracket

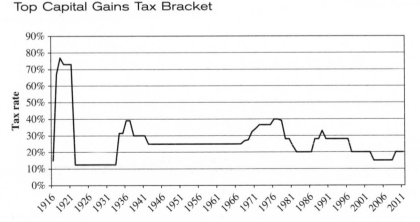

Source: Citizens for Tax Justice, May 2004; 1930 & 1940's Estate Tax data provided by *The Estate Tax History: Ninety Years and Counting* by Darien B. Jacobson, Brian G. Raub, and Barry W. Johnson.

As you can tell, initially capital gains tax rates mirrored those of income taxes because such gains were originally treated the same as income under the Sixteenth Amendment. So in 1918 the top capital gains tax rate was a shocking 77 percent. But investors soon complained that such high rates were an impediment to the flow of capital. According to *Stocks for the Long Run*'s Jeremy Siegel: "Until 1921 there was no tax preference given to capital gains income. When tax rates were increased sharply during World War I, investors refrained from realizing gains and complained to Congress about the tax consequences of selling their assets. Congress was persuaded that such 'frozen portfolios' were detrimental to the efficient allocation of capital, and so in 1922 a maximum tax rate of 12.5 percent was established on capital gains income."[10]

Subsequent to 1922, maximum capital gains tax rates were always lower than maximum income tax rates, except in 1989 when both were capped at 33 percent in an attempt to simplify the tax code. The lower rates are meant to encourage people to invest in the capital markets and have been generally structured to encourage long-term investment. Sometimes the rates have been complicated by various "exclusions." This policy meant capital gains were still considered income, but a portion of the gain was completely excluded from taxation. According to Leonard Burman and Deborah Kobes of The Tax Policy Center: "Since 1934, capital gains tax preferences have generally been affected by means of an exclusion—that is, a portion of long-term capital gains were excluded from tax. For example, from 1982 to 1986, 60 percent of long-term capital gains were excluded from tax. Since the top tax rate on ordinary income was 50 percent, this implies a top effective tax rate on capital gains of 20 percent."[11]

That 20 percent effective rate is derived by taking half of the remaining 40 percent of capital gains taxed as income after factoring in the exclusion.

The use of the exclusion has led to some interesting benefits for the long-term investor. For instance, in 1934 and 1935, 20, 40, 60, and 70 percent of gains were excluded on assets held 1, 2, 5, and 10 years, respectively, while investors who held stocks less than one year received no exclusion. Since the maximum income tax rate at the time was 63 percent, the effective maximum capital gains tax rate for the truly long-term investor who held stocks 10 years and sold in 1934 would have been just 18.9 percent—that is 63 percent of the 30 percent remaining of the capital gain that was taxable as income. Meanwhile, the investor who held his stocks less than one year would be taxed at a maximum rate of 63 percent. If such a taxation system were instituted today, the differences in after-tax returns between low-turnover and high-turnover strategies would be extreme.

Although long-term capital gains rates have generally been lower than income tax rates, it is always important to pay attention to the difference between the two because it can affect your portfolio strategy. For instance, in 1922 and 1989 when income and capital gains tax rates were the same, there was no apparent tax benefit (assuming equal return potential) to owning stocks over taxable bonds such as Treasuries because they were taxed identically. There was also no tax benefit to being a long-term investor. But the wider the gap is between income tax rates and capital gains tax rates, the greater the tax-wise advantage long-term stock investors have. In a year like 1944 when income tax rates were as high as 94 percent while capital gains taxes were only 25 percent, stocks would have a distinct advantage over taxable bonds.

Of course, one unique advantage nondividend paying stocks always have over taxable bonds, regardless of the tax rate, is the control they give investors. If you invest in nondividend stocks (assuming the realization of long-term earnings accumulation in the stock price), the investor is able to capture earnings which were only taxed once at the corporate level. The double taxation of dividends (once at the corporate level and once at the individual level) is seldom understood by investors. If you invest in taxable bonds, you have no choice but to pay the taxes on the bonds as the income is paid. The timing of such a stock sale can have a huge significance to wealthy investors whose net worth is tied up in shares of public or private businesses they founded or run. For them, it is absolutely essential to pay attention to what the current capital gains tax rates are when they're thinking of selling and to calculate what the comparable after-tax returns will be for other investments they are thinking of purchasing with the proceeds of their sale. This is especially true for a family that is considering a sale of its business.

The prevailing capital gains tax rate will have a large impact on how a stock investment compares to a tax-free municipal bond investment. The higher the capital gains rate is, the less attractive stocks look compared to bonds after taxes if you are considering a full liquidation of your stock portfolio. That said, in my own experience as an investor, portfolio strategy should not be trumped by tax strategy unless the fundamentals dictate as such. Consider the example of a CEO of a Nasdaq-listed technology company who received an offer to sell the company in 2000. She may have been convinced that long-term capital gains rates were headed lower and that delaying the sale until that time would save money on taxes. Though she would have been correct in this fact, waiting would have saved her 5 percent in taxes but likely exposed her to 50 percent or more in losses (as valuation levels in the market dropped from 2000–2003). Clearly, this investor would have experienced better economics by paying the higher capital gains tax than the lower one (assessed on a lower valuation).

ESTATE TAX

The modern estate tax in the United States can trace its roots back to 1906 and President Theodore Roosevelt who felt that robber barons such as Andrew Carnegie and John D. Rockefeller wielded too much power and that allowing them to pass their massive estates down from one generation to the next in perpetuity posed a threat to the U.S. democracy. Although some form of "death tax" existed in ancient times and in the United States prior to 1916, mostly such taxes were considered temporary measures to raise revenue during wartime. But it was Roosevelt who in his famous 1906 State of the Union and "The Man with the Muck-rake" speeches pushed for the progressive reforms that led to the Sixteenth Amendment in 1913 and the Revenue Act of 1916.

Politics aside, the ostensible impetus for the estate tax part of the Revenue Act of 1916 was to pay for America's involvement in World War I. The initial tax was just 1 percent on estates over $50,000 to 10 percent for amounts over $5 million. As you can see from Figure 7.3, the maximum rate has changed dramatically over time.

Throughout history there were always various exemptions and exclusions that would allow families to protect a certain portion of their estates from taxes. According to a history of the estate tax compiled by John R. Luckey of the Congressional Research Service, "The 1916 estate tax allowed

FIGURE 7.3

Estate Tax Rates

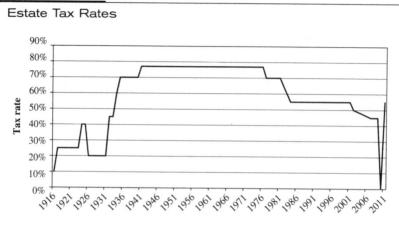

Source: Citizens for Tax Justice, May 2004; 1930 & 1940's Estate Tax data provided by *The Estate Tax History: Ninety Years and Counting* by Darien B. Jacobson, Brian G. Raub, and Barry W. Johnson.

the executor to reduce a decedent's estate for tax purposes by a $50,000 exemption and the amount of any funeral expenses, administration expenses, debts, losses, and claims against the estate."[12] But while such exemptions and exclusions grew over time, so did the top tax rate on the wealthiest estates.

In many respects, the rates followed a pattern similar to that for income taxes. So while estate tax rates rose during World War I from 10 percent to 25 percent in the early 1920s, the anger over high taxes after the war ended, and the unbridled enthusiasm of the Roaring Twenties inspired Congress to cut the rate to 20 percent in 1926 and to double the estate exemption to $100,000. But as with income taxes, estate tax rates soared during the Great Depression from 20 to 45 percent in 1932 and then to 70 percent from 1935 to 1940, peaking finally at 77 percent from 1941 through 1976. And then, like income taxes, they declined again.

One of the unique quirks of the estate tax code though is as a result of former President George W. Bush's tax policies.

There will be no estate tax in 2010, and then it will bounce back to 55 percent in 2011 to the estate tax rate previous to the passage of the Economic Growth and Tax Relief Reconciliation Act of 2001. Some advisors joke that wealthy parents shouldn't leave their drinks unattended around their children at their 2010 Christmas party.

What is also interesting is how dramatically the dollar amount to be taxed at the maximum estate tax rate has changed over time. If you review Figure 7.4, you will see that the dollar amounts by no means follow in lockstep with the rates themselves.

So, for instance, while estate tax rates went up in 1917 from 10 to 25 percent, the dollar amount to be taxed at that rate also rose from $5 million to $10 million, a curious fact in a country with a government hungry for revenue during wartime. The dollar amount stayed at $10 million through the 1920s, but the desire to tax only the super-rich at the highest

FIGURE 7.4

Historical Estate Tax Rates versus Dollar Amounts

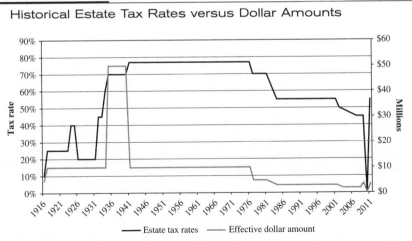

Source: Citizens for Tax Justice, May 2004; 1930 & 1940's Estate Tax data provided by *The Estate Tax History: Ninety Years and Counting* by Darien B. Jacobson, Brian G. Raub, and Barry W. Johnson.

rate grew even stronger during the Depression-era 1930s. According to Luckey of the Congressional Research Service: "Between 1934 and 1942, social policies and wartime demands led to a series of estate and gift tax rate increases, though the gift tax rates continued to be maintained at three-quarters of the estate tax rates. The Revenue Act of 1934 raised the maximum estate tax rate to 60 percent, on a net estate over $10,000,000, and the Revenue Act of 1935 further raised it to 70 percent, on net estates over $50,000,000."[13]

But after 1940, the government started applying the maximum estate tax rate on increasingly smaller dollar amounts—an alarming trend given that in inflation-adjusted terms a million dollars was actually worth a lot less in the decades after 1940. So 1940's 70 percent tax on estates over $50 million became a 77 percent tax on estates worth $10 million in 1941. Rates and dollar amounts remained there through 1976. Then in 1977 the rate became 70 percent for estates over $5 million, and the dollar amount for the maximum tax rate continued to shrink. Meanwhile the exclusions and exemptions started to rise so that the estate tax began to apply only to a narrower range of wealthy people. So, for instance, in 1976, anyone with an estate worth more than $60,000 was subject to a minimum estate tax of 3 percent, while those with over $10 million were subject to the maximum 77 percent rate. But by 2007, only people with a minimum estate value of $2 million were subject to the minimum estate tax of 18 percent, while anyone with an estate worth more than $3 million was subject to the maximum estate tax rate of 45 percent.

Inflation and the decreasing dollar amount required to be subject to estate taxes can have a serious impact on small businesses and family farms. Although in Depression-era America a family farm or small business having a net worth of more than $3 million was relatively uncommon, by the year 2000 when estate taxes were 55 percent for estates that size, there were a number of occurrences in which, in order to pay the estate tax, the family business or farm needed to be sold, sometimes at distressed prices to vulture investors, because the family didn't have the liquid cash to pay the tax.

For this reason alone wealthy families should have ironclad estate plans long before the founding generation of a business passes away. As we have seen, liquidating a business in retirement to build a diversified portfolio not only protects the family's assets but should also provide the necessary cash to pay the estate taxes when the business's founder dies. Illiquid assets pose a unique threat to heirs because they lose the ability to time the sale of assets for payment of estate taxes. A decedent who had a high allocation to an illiquid private business, real estate, or hedge fund and died in March 2008 may have lost his entire estate because of that year's recession. If the decedent's portfolio had a market value of $100 million on the date of death, March 31, 2008, the 45 percent effective estate tax would result in a tax of $45 million. If he were a resident of the state of New Jersey, he might be subject to up to an additional 16 percent of the gross estate[14] or $16 million. If the value of the estate fell in line with the broad stock market averages (−48.9 percent)[15] the value of the combined federal and state estate tax bill would exceed the value of the entire portfolio. Though the above example is a rare "perfect storm," wealthy investors should consider the mathematical effects of such events.

One family I work with had 99 percent of its portfolio invested in its company stock from 1981 through 1996. It experienced six 50 percent corrections in its portfolio resulting from declines in the value of its company stock in the 1980s and 1990s. Near the end of the 1990s it sold the company and invested the entire proceeds of the sale into our balanced portfolio. This was fortunate, because in the subsequent bear markets of 2001 to 2002 the company stock (via the merger) declined by 75 percent. Meanwhile, the two bear markets of 2001 to 2002 and 2008 to 2009 had muted effects on the family's total portfolio because of the presence of bonds, a reduced equity exposure, and the absence of alternative investments. In the case of this family, had the first generation chosen to continue to hold the bulk of its portfolio in the concentrated holding and died any time between July 2001 and April 2004, the estate tax bill would have completely wiped out any residual value for the heirs. Because the stock was publicly traded, the family would have had a difficult time arguing for a discount on the actual value of the estate on the date of death.

We have already discussed that gifting strategies during the founder's life are generally a more efficient means of transferring assets to one's heirs. Unfortunately, given that the 55 percent estate tax rate will resume in 2011 for estates greater than $3 million, we will in all likelihood hear of many more "fire" estate sales of small businesses in coming years.

As we shall see in Chapter 13 on multigenerational planning, the sheer size of the estate tax often means that even with astute planning, estates generally run out of money within three to four generations. But investing wisely with taxes in mind and gifting assets while family members are still alive will produce a more extended existence of the family portfolio.

GIFT TAXES

The origin of the gift tax really goes hand in hand with the estate tax. Luckey of the Congressional Research Service puts it best in his tax history: "The gift tax has developed as a necessary concomitant to the death tax because the easiest way to escape a tax on the gratuitous transfer of property at death is to divest oneself of the property during life. The impact of either tax alone would be diminished by the escape offered by the alternate transfer."[16] The tax was first introduced in the Revenue Act of 1924 to close the loopholes in the original 1916 estate tax law, then repealed by the Revenue Act of 1926—during that by now familiar Roaring Twenties period of antitax activism—and then reintroduced permanently by the Revenue Act of 1932 during the Great Depression.

As you can see from Figure 7.5, gift tax rates have been as capricious and all over the map as the estate tax.

FIGURE 7.5

Gift Tax Rates

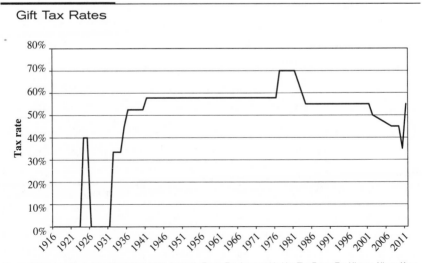

Source: Citizens for Tax Justice, May 2004; 1930 & 1940's Estate Tax data provided by The Estate Tax History: Ninety Years and Counting by Darien B. Jacobson, Brian G. Raub, and Barry W. Johnson.

And yet one of the key advantages of the gift tax historically has been that it has often been lower than the estate tax.
Up until 1977 the gift tax rate was generally about three-
fourths of the prevailing estate tax rate. With such a discount
it always made sense to give your heirs their inheritance
during your lifetime. But as we shall see in subsequent chapters, even when gift tax rates have matched estate tax rates as
they have in recent years, it still generally makes more sense
for wealthy investors to gift because of the potential for
greater capital appreciation and the way gift taxes are calculated. This is due to the fact that the gift tax is assessed on the
net amount received by the heirs whereas the estate tax is
assessed on the gross amount of the estate. For example, an
individual with a $100 million dollar estate would be able to
pass $66 million to his daughter after paying a gift tax of $33
million (gift tax is 50 percent of the $66 million received by
the daughter). If he waited to pass the assets in his estate, the
daughter would only receive $50 million because the estate
tax would be 50 percent of the $100 million dollar estate.

As you can tell from Figure 7.6, the dollar amounts subject to the maximum gift tax rate have generally mirrored that
of the estate tax. But it's important to note that the lifetime
unified tax credit on the gift tax differs from the annual gift
tax exclusion. Currently, for instance, wealthy investors can
gift $13,000 per year to each one of their heirs, and this activ-
ity in no way reduces the $1 million lifetime gift tax exclusion
in 2010.

Perhaps the most significant reform to both estate and
gift taxes occurred in the Tax Reform Act of 1976. According
to an estate tax history compiled by the IRS's Statistics of
Income Division (SOI): "This act created a unified estate and
gift tax framework that consisted of a 'single, graduated rate

FIGURE 7.6

Historical Gift Tax Rates versus Dollar Amounts

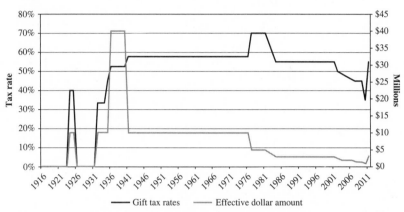

Source: Citizens for Tax Justice, May 2004; 1930 & 1940's Estate Tax data provided by *The Estate Tax History: Ninety Years and Counting* by Darien B. Jacobson, Brian G. Raub, and Barry W. Johnson.

of tax imposed on both lifetime gifts and testamentary dispositions.' Prior to the act, 'it cost substantially more to leave property at death than to give it away during life,' due to the lower tax rate applied to gifts. The Tax Reform Act of 1976 also merged the estate tax exclusion and the lifetime gift tax exclusion into a 'single, unified estate and gift tax credit, which may be used to offset gift tax liability during the donor's lifetime but which, if unused at death, is available to offset the deceased donor's estate tax liability.'"[17]

The 1976 act also introduced a tax on generation skipping trusts, thus closing a loophole whereby the children of the estate's founding family benefitted from the income produced by the estate without paying estate taxes because the parents put the assets in a trust for the grandchildren, thereby "skipping" the generation to be subject to the estate tax. As the existence of the estate tax proves in more ways than one, there are two things you can't escape in life—death and taxes.

CONCLUSIONS

- Taxes are an inescapable part of history.
- Income tax rates tend to go up during times of war and economic crisis.
- The wider the gap between income and capital gains tax rates, the more attractive stocks become versus taxable bonds after deducting taxes.
- Stock investors shouldn't let taxes alone dictate their sell decisions.
- Family businesses are at risk if the estate lacks the liquidity to pay estate taxes.
- Gifting during life generally carries less of a tax burden than estate taxes at death.

CHAPTER 8

Strategies for Optimizing Portfolios

Taxation, Performance, and Fees

The efficient frontier wasn't designed with taxable investors in mind. Nor was the concept of risk premium. When Harry Markowitz and Bill Sharpe were developing the building blocks of modern portfolio theory, their analysis did not include how the frontier curve might look if they factored in capital gains and income taxes or money management fees and how those factors might affect portfolio optimization. Their research was targeted toward nontaxable institutional investors. Moreover, their basic assumption was that investors were rational and that markets were efficient or "perfect," having no taxes, transaction costs, illicit manipulation, or management fees to invest in them. In other words, the frontier truly was a theory, not reality for taxable investors. I am not refuting the historical studies and observations of returns and standard deviation conducted by

Markowitz and Sharpe. I'm simply questioning the way investors and advisers have applied them to taxable portfolios where the risk/return equation is drastically different.

Building an optimized portfolio in the real world is difficult enough for any investor. For high net worth investors, exposed to taxes on dividends and income that have been as high historically as 94 percent, it can be extremely so. It was for this reason that we created our after-tax calculator. Obviously, it can't solve every wealthy investor's asset allocation problems, especially investors on the verge of selling their businesses. As we discuss later in this chapter, there are various solutions to optimizing a portfolio around such a liquidity event, but each situation is different and requires careful planning on the advisor's part. Nor can a calculator truly measure all the fees investors experience when they hire an advisor since some—such as transaction costs, soft dollars, and placement fees—are hidden.

That said, the after-tax calculator is a good place to start the asset allocation process and can be a springboard for discussing a more customized strategy to suit each client's individual needs. As we describe in Chapter 4, we developed the crudest version of the calculator in 1999, when stock prices were high, and we had become intrigued with Graham and Dodd's valuation models. Their model for determining equity undervaluation or overvaluation compared the yield on the 30-year U.S. Treasury bond to the price-to-earnings ratio or earnings yield of equities. Implicit in our after-tax calculator's assumptions is an idea popularized by Harry Markowitz of an equity risk premium—that investors should be compensated for taking on the additional risk of owning volatile stocks by receiving a return in excess of less risky bonds and cash. So if, for instance, the 30-year Treasury bond is yielding 5 percent, this means that pension fund managers know they have a safe 5 percent return readily available to them. If they are going to purchase any other asset class, there must be an expected return that is above 5 percent because of the unpredictability of the return. The volatility normally experienced in those asset classes suggests that investors should demand compensation for the volatility.

What we did with our after-tax calculator is the same kind of analysis, only substituting the highest rated 30-year municipal bonds for Treasuries. The reason people use 30-year bonds as a basis of comparison is that riskier asset classes are generally considered long-term investments, the true value of which can be realized only over lengthy periods of time. This, as we show in Chapter 3, is especially true of stocks, which can move in unpredictable directions over the short term but tend to follow their underlying earnings growth over periods of at least 20 years. So if we plug the long-term earnings yield of a stock portfolio into the calculator and then calculate and compare its after-tax yield to the yield on 30-year municipal bonds, we should get a pretty good idea of what sort of risk premium the stock portfolio has.

CALCULATOR CASE STUDIES

If we examine Table 8.1, we can get a good idea of how the calculator works and how it can be used to optimize a portfolio:

This example of the calculator is designed to estimate the premium of different asset classes over a 30-year municipal bond with its current 5 percent yield. That 5 percent number is in the upper right-hand corner of the calculator. There are some important assumptions to this example that

TABLE 8.1

Example 1: After-Tax Returns Calculator

		Municipal Bond Yield to Maturity:	5.00%		
			After Fees		
Asset Type	Fees	Assumed Return	Assumed Return After-taxes	Premium Over Muni	Required Return to Equal Muni
Core stocks	0.48%	8.50%	6.63%	1.63%	6.77%
High-turnover stocks	1.01%	10.50%	4.25%	-0.75%	12.00%
Cash	0.40%	3.00%	1.10%	-3.90%	10.78%
Hedge fund*	2.00%/20.00%	12.00%	3.81%	-1.19%	14.98%

* Hedge fund fees are taken before taxes.

Full Liquidation (Y or N)	Ordinary Income Tax Rate	Dividend Taxation Rate	Capital Gains Tax Rate	Turnover Rate	Investor's State	State Income Tax Rate	Dividend Rate
N	39.60%	39.60%	20.00%	20.00%	California	10.30%	2.00%

we should review. On the left side of the calculator we have the asset types compared to the municipal bond. The "core stocks" asset class is a portfolio of equities run in a low-turnover fashion, having a turnover ratio of just 20 percent or an average holding period for each stock in the portfolio of five years. "High-turnover stocks" is an aggressive growth type of portfolio with a turnover of 100 percent, meaning that no long-term capital gains are realized because every stock is sold in less than one year. These different turnover ratios will have an obvious impact on how the portfolios are taxed. The cash and hedge fund categories are self-explanatory although it's important to note that we assume that the hedge fund is a high-turnover strategy as most are. Modifications can be made to the calculator to model for the effects of other asset classes including taxable bonds, real estate, and private equity.

Directly to the right of the asset class column is the "fees" column, which is a measure of the fees as a percentage of assets under management. The core stocks category has a 0.48 percent fee which might be charged for a $100 million portfolio by a balanced core manager. The high-turnover stocks category has a 1.01 percent fee because that is the average fee for 182 institutional mutual funds that invest in U.S. stocks and have turnover ratios in excess of 100 percent, according to fund tracker Morningstar's Principia database. We assumed that wealthy investors would have access to institutional-style money management for this category. For cash, 0.40 percent is a typical fee for money markets, and for hedge funds the standard rate is 2 percent of assets plus 20 percent of profits.

In the "assumed return" column we have 8.50 percent for the core stocks strategy. This assessment is based on the privatization earnings yield (14 times earnings) of the stocks in our portfolios plus 10 years of normalized earnings growth. For high-turnover stocks we have a higher 10.50 percent assumed return partially because we want to illustrate how a high-turnover strategy will perform for high net worth investors after taxes even if pretax returns are significantly higher. But we also put in 10.50 percent because that is close to the 10 percent return famed Yale endowment chief David Swensen estimates for stocks in his own portfolios after factoring in inflation. An endowment investor like Swensen can afford to have a high-turnover strategy without worrying about taxes. In the hedge fund column we assumed a high 12 percent rate of return for illustrative purposes.

Below the asset class rows you will see a separate set of data points. The leftmost is the "full liquidation" column. Answering "Y," or yes, to this question on the calculator would mean that the entire portfolio is liquidated and any embedded capital gains in the portfolio would be realized and taxed. In this case, we've answered "N," or no, although we shall see later what the results of a liquidation will be. It's important to measure the embedded capital gain because families are not interested ultimately in what the portfolio looks like on paper. They are interested in what the portfolio can do to produce either a dollar for consumption or a dollar to invest in another business after all taxes are paid.

To the right of "full liquidation," are the ordinary income tax, dividend tax, and capital gains tax rates, which we have at 39.60 percent, 39.60 percent and 20 percent, respectively. Although rates were lower in 2009, they will revert to these rates when the Bush tax cuts expire at the end of 2010. If we are building a portfolio right now and we're looking out a decade from now, it's safe to say that for eight of those years the top tax rates are going to be a minimum of 39.60 percent on ordinary income, 39.60 percent on dividends, and 20 percent on capital gains, and that's easy to predict because the higher rates are already written into the law. They become effective on December 31, 2010. (Should the tax rates change either up or down, we would obviously change these variables to observe the changes in terms of our macro asset allocation.) To the right of that, we have the investor's state of residence. This can have a dramatic impact on an asset class's performance, depending on whether it's a high income tax state or a zero income tax state. Currently, we have California, which has the highest state tax rate of 10.30 percent. As a result, any income from taxable bonds or dividends after the Bush tax cuts expire will be taxed at an additional 10.30 percent in that state. Later, we will see the results in a 0 percent tax state. To the right of the state income tax rate we have the dividend rate, shown at 2 percent is what stocks currently pay on average.

After factoring in the taxes and fees, we can see how different risk premiums or lack thereof. Of the four asset types only core stocks produced a 1.63 percentage point premium over municipal bonds. We can also see in the "required return to equal muni" column how high the gross pretax/prefee returns would need to be in the lagging asset classes for them to begin to have an after-tax risk premium. For hedge funds, that return would be an extraordinarily high 14.98 percent.

But how would returns look if we liquidated the portfolio? In Table 8.2 you can see the results. Here we changed the answer to the "full liquidation" column to "Y" for yes, and just to make the competition between asset types more interesting, we also lowered the high-turnover stocks fee to 0.48 percent to make it equal to the core stocks portfolio fee. As you can see, the after-tax returns of the core stocks category are still higher than every other asset type, and yet the liquidation forces that portfolio's embedded capital gains to be realized and taxed at the long-term capital gains rate, thus reducing the after-tax return from 6.63 percent preliquidation to 5.05 percent postliquidation. This is still enough to edge out the high-turnover stocks category after-tax return of 4.78 percent, even though the high-turnover stocks category had a significantly higher pretax return of 10.50 percent. That's because all high turnover's gains are taxed at the much higher short-term capital gains rate.

And yet core stocks' 5.05 percent full liquidation return should give investors pause, forcing them to recognize that the 0.05 percent risk premium that core stocks has over a high-quality municipal bond's 5.00 percent yield is slender indeed. As a consequence, in this case of a California resident these assumptions may not justify a meaningful overweight to equities compared to a benchmark 50 percent stock/50 percent bond mix.

LIQUIDITY EVENT OPTIMIZATION

Though the calculator is a good springboard for discussion, many wealthy investors are in a unique situation tax-wise when they hire an advisor because they are often entrepreneurs who wish to liquidate or reduce their exposure to their businesses in order to build a more diversified portfolio. As most of their net worth may be tied up in their business, making

TABLE 8.2

Example 2: After-Tax Returns Calculator

		Municipal Bond Yield to Maturity:	5.00%

				After Fees	
Asset Type	**Fees**	**Assumed Return**	**Assumed Return After-taxes**	**Premium Over Muni**	**Required Return to Equal Muni**
Core stocks	0.48%	8.50%	5.05%	0.05%	8.42%
High-turnover stocks	0.48%	10.50%	4.78%	-0.22%	10.94%
Cash	0.40%	3.00%	1.10%	-3.90%	10.78%
Hedge fund*	2.00%/20.00%	12.00%	3.81%	-1.19%	14.98%

* Hedge fund fees are taken before taxes.

Full Liquidation (Y or N)	**Ordinary Income Tax Rate**	**Dividend Taxation Rate**	**Capital Gains Tax Rate**	**Turnover Rate**	**Investor's State**	**State Income Tax Rate**	**Dividend Rate**
Y	39.60%	39.60%	20.00%	100.00%	California	10.30%	2.00%

147

this change will in all likelihood be the biggest taxable event in their lifetimes.

There are a lot of liquidity strategies for founders of public companies. The most simple and the most widely known is open market sales using Rule 144. The Securities and Exchange Commission's (SEC) Rule 144 allows corporate insiders to sell stock on the open market as long as the insider is not in possession of material nonpublic information, SEC reporting is current, and the insider observes certain other restrictions regarding how shares are sold so that there is no price manipulation. This is one area in which I happen to believe that it is in the investor's best interest to pay the tax that is due, especially if the long-term capital gains rates are favorable as they are right now. For instance, in 2009 if an investor makes $100 million dollars from open market sales via a 144 transaction, he will pay $15 million in capital gains taxes at the current 15 percent long-term capital gains rate.

I'm a big believer in keeping these transactions as uncomplicated as possible and making the sales preferably when the company's share price is high, and, if not all at once, then in large blocks. Most of the complicated shelters developed to avoid taxes on executive sales of company stock ultimately turn out to be schemes that either don't work or diminish the precision that is often required by senior executives. For instance, in the late 1990s one of my clients was approached by one of the big accounting firms with an offer to create what is called an *extended settlement contract*, which basically locked the stock sale proceeds into a special tax trust for a period of 10 years. By using complex depreciation and discounting rules, this trust claimed to eliminate a large portion of the capital gains taxes that would need to be paid. My client asked the firm's senior tax advisor how thick the document was that explained this strategy, and the advisor held out his hand like he was holding a Big Mac to indicate a four- to five-inch thick document. My client said no thanks. Four years later we read in the *Wall Street Journal* that the IRS challenged these very shelters, which aimed to avoid capital gains taxes but instead just created legal and accounting headaches (along with hefty IRS penalties) for their investors.

Regarding the after-tax calculator and how it applies to company stock sales, it is important that the owner of the company stock be aware of whether his or her stock is trading at a premium or at a discount valuation to both the broad stock market and the company's particular industry group. This is because if a company is the most expensive in its peer group, it is probably priced above what its privatization yield would be in an acquisition simply because no other company in its industry can buy it without it being a dilutive acquisition. The reason for this is that in a stock-for-stock merger generally the more expensive company acquires the less expensive one by using its shares as currency to finance the deal. But if your company is the most expensive, no other company can really afford to buy your shares. When valuations of your company stock are higher than the market and your peer group and everything seems to be running on all cylinders, this is an ideal time to sell. But the flip side is also true: If your company is cheaper than the market and its peer group, why would you sell it to build a diversified portfolio? In other words, if you have a stock trading at 10 times earnings with a 10 percent earnings yield, why would you sell it to build a portfolio trading at 20 times earnings with a 5 percent yield? Your stock itself will provide a significant equity risk premium over competing asset classes in such a case.

The problem of course with any sale of company stock by the founder of a business is the public's perception of the sale. There is an apparent stigma attached to insider sales, and executives can sometimes be overly sensitive about them. My thoughts on the subject are that if the founder of the company is up front with analysts and the public about the reasons for the sale—that she's selling shares because she's approaching retirement and is of an age where prudent portfolio management requires some level of diversification—then in general the public has been understanding of such sales. By contrast, the consequences of not selling can be drastic if the industry to which your company belongs suddenly enters a major decline. As we shall see in the "train wrecks" chapter (Chapter 15), there are untold numbers of stories of successful businesspeople who flamed out because of an unwillingness to diversify, and there are also stories of CEOs who sold their shares within the right context, and the public barely batted an eye.

FEE OPTIMIZATION

An important part of the optimization process is the fees you pay your advisors. Just a 1 or 2 percent reduction in returns every year because of management fees can have a huge impact on long-term performance. By law, registered investment advisers (RIAs) must disclose their fees in Part II of the Uniform Application for Investment Adviser Registration (Form ADV), which they must file with the Securities and Exchange Commission to become RIAs. Although an RIA designation is not an academic credential indicating any financial training, the ADV at least provides some transparency with regard to fees, and investors should request information about this before hiring an advisor.

Of course, the fee the advisor charges does not necessarily include the fees of the underlying investment products he uses to build clients portfolios. If he is not buying stocks or bonds directly, then there will be additional fees embedded in the mutual funds, hedge funds, or separately managed portfolios. So a 1.00 percent advisor fee can quickly add up to 2.00 or 2.50 percent after including all underlying fees. Some members of the financial planning community attempt to take the high ground by saying that they're "fee-only." Often this means that their fees are a flat rate or percentage and are completely disclosed so they don't have any conflicts of interest or get paid any commissions for distributing products such as mutual funds. As wonderful as that may be, their fee may be equal to or greater than the fees of the fund managers actually investing the money. Thus fee-only is only a good deal if it's a good deal in aggregate. The managed funds in the portfolio may charge only 0.50 percent, but the financial planner may want two times that amount. Such arrangements always make me wonder why the doctor is getting 0.50 percent while the nurse gets 1.0 percent.

There are all sorts of fees, both disclosed and undisclosed. Besides a flat rate or percentage, advisors also get paid by the hour, by commission, or sometimes a fee plus commission leading to the ambiguous term "fee-based advisors" so you don't know if they have any conflicts of interest or not. And these are just fees that are disclosed. What about transaction costs to buy and sell stocks or "soft dollars" paid to brokers that provide research? What about mutual fund trailer or placement fees, or 12b-1 fees as they are sometimes called, that compensate the advisor for selling the investor a fund by giving the advisor a percentage of the assets under management? Some firms are able to disguise fees by disclosing seemingly low asset management or consulting fees while earning higher fees on lending products or money market funds. Often the best way to get rid of these fees is to have as few intermediaries between you and your money as possible. We believe that managing the assets directly for clients for a flat percentage without any underlying funds or additional advisory intermediaries is cost-effective and produces the best long-term results for clients. At the end of the day, many clients simply ask us to invest their money in line with the way we invest our own.

PERFORMANCE REPORTING

Ultimately, we're not really interested in what an advisor's expense ratio is in the abstract. We're not interested in what the gross return is in the abstract. We're interested in what the investor keeps net of all fees and taxes. That is the primary function of the after-tax calculator. And if you get a return from an advisor that is net of fees, you are one step toward understanding whether her fees are reasonable.

In the advisory world I often see two kinds of performance-reporting omissions that lead to a misunderstanding of the fee structure and to overly optimistic projections of returns. Some advisors give clients sales brochures that show only gross returns without the fees taken out, while others don't even provide returns for their firm but for the asset classes the firm invests in. So they show the client a copy of the Ibbotson charts for U.S. stocks since 1926 and basically say that this is what you can expect (pointing to various asset classes on a graph). Both tactics seem blatantly erroneous or naive. A lot of advisors also show Monte Carlo simulations that supposedly give potential best and worst returns but still no actual results net of fees or taxes. Their brochures usually have two or three pages of disclosures in the back, but they are effectively useless because most investors don't read them.

The gold standard for performance disclosure is what is called global investment performance standards or GIPS. The GIPS standard originated at the CFA Institute in the 1990s, and it became the globally accepted performance measurement system. There are strict procedures and actions advisors must follow in order to be GIPS-compliant in addition to disclosing their returns net of fees. For instance, an advisor can't be compliant if she's marketing the performance for an individual account at her firm and that account isn't representative of her firm's overall investment style. GIPS auditors would not allow the advisor to market that account's performance as audited and verified because it is an outlier at the firm.

Generally speaking, GIPS performance numbers are what are known as "composite returns" net of fees for the various styles of asset management offered by the firm. A composite is a group of accounts all managed in the same investment style, be it large-cap growth stocks, small-cap value, domestic or foreign. When GIPS auditors visit the firm, they review the types of securities in the accounts and their performance to come up with a suitable benchmark with which to compare to the composite's performance. So if the advisor buys predominantly blue chip stocks, she may be benchmarked against the S&P 500. The advisor may also have peer-group benchmarks comparing her to other large-cap managers, but regardless of what the benchmark is, any comparison numbers or rankings appearing in a GIPS-compliant report have been audited by an independent third party and the benchmark chosen hasn't been selected simply to make the manager look good.

That an appropriate benchmark is selected can be useful to investors for detecting whether the advisor's fees are too high and thus detrimental to net returns. Because historically one way advisors have been able to juice their performance numbers is by taking on additional risk and buying assets or types of stocks not found in their benchmark. Such practices are commonplace in the advisory world when GIPS standards are not used. I've seen a number of advisors during my career who cherry-pick the index they wish to be compared to so they can show outperformance in their marketing brochures when, in reality, if they chose the appropriate benchmark, it would reveal them to be laggards.

Wealthy investors, of course, don't just need returns net of fees to judge whether an advisor is suitable for them but after-tax numbers as well, calculated at the appropriate income tax rate. Not every advisory firm provides such after-tax returns, but investors should probably steer clear of those that don't. The reason for that is if the S&P 500 has an 8 percent return and the strategy the advisor is recommending produces 10 percent but it has a 200 percent turnover ratio, chances are the S&P wins on an after-tax basis. So failure to report after-tax numbers masks the truth of the performance to the wealthy investor because after taxes, as our calculator so dramatically shows, that high-turnover strategy will probably deliver only 6 percent to someone taxed at nearly 40 percent on short-term capital gains.

Chris Thach, performance analyst for The Gannon Group, developed a system for evaluating after-tax returns for each specific client. The process, called ARAFAT (annualized return after fee after tax), uses input from clients' actual tax returns to extract the net investment return after deductions and actual taxes paid. Another unique performance report was developed by my business partner, Matt Rogers, to report the amount of shareholder earnings produced by the companies in our portfolio for specific holding periods. Since we believe that stockholder returns over time are a function of earnings, this report communicates the level of profitability for their business holdings relative to the amount invested in the company.

PERSONALIZED PERFORMANCE MEASUREMENTS

Although the GIPS and after-tax numbers are useful to evaluate a prospective advisor, ultimately they are not enough once an investor has already hired that advisor. How the firm performs in aggregate net of taxes and fees is different from how an individual client's portfolio performs. This is especially so if the investor has multiple subaccounts invested in different styles with different performance measures from the aggregate of his or her entire portfolio. Also, cash flows into or out of the portfolio from investor contributions or withdrawals will affect its individual performance. So the investor needs a composite performance of her entire portfolio customized and individualized to see if she is meeting her goals.

A composite family performance report will aggregate both the stocks and the bonds and possibly all the family assets, and because the reports are customized, they will require a blended benchmark, a dynamic benchmark that moves with the asset allocation shifts. Such a dynamic benchmark is essential because the investor can see the benefit of the advisor's asset allocation policy. If, for instance, I have a portfolio with $1 million in equities and $1 million in bonds and the equities go down by 50 percent and the bonds stay the same and I as an advisor do nothing, that composite result will be very different from one where I sold half or $500,000 of the equity position before the decline and put it into bonds. And yet if you didn't have a composite report, there would be no way for the investor to see the benefit of that asset allocation shift. Because at the end of the reporting period the remaining $500,000 invested in the stock side of the portfolio would still be down by 50 percent. It is only in the aggregate that you can see the benefit.

Because the cash flow moving into and out of each client's portfolio at a money management firm is so different from one client to the next, it is important not just to have time-weighted returns based on the aggregate firm's performance from one date to the next but a dollar-weighted performance that accounts for all the money coming into and leaving the portfolio to pay for the client's expenses. Such a dollar-weighted performance is essential not for benchmarking the manager against the S&P 500 or some other index, but for benchmarking the client's individual portfolio against his financial goals.

Consider the case of two portfolios each worth $1,000 and invested in exactly the same stocks and bonds at the start of 2010. (See Table 8.3.) On a time-weighted basis the securities selected for each portfolio rise 25 percent in 2010 to $1,250 but fall 20 percent in 2011 to $1,000 so that the net time-weighted return if both investors left the portfolio alone would be 0 percent. In this case the time-weighted return

TABLE   8.3

Time-Weighted versus Dollar-Weighted Returns

	Investor 1	Investor 2
Beginning value 2010	$1,000.00	$1,000.00
Ending value 2010	$1,250.00	$1,250.00
Contribution/withdrawal	–$500.00	$500.00
Beginning value 2011	$750.00	$1,750.00
Ending value 2011	$600.00	$1,400.00
Net gain/loss	$100.00	–$100.00
Dollar-weighted return (annualized)	**6.39%**	**–4.07%**
Time-weighted return (annualized)	**0.00%**	**0.00%**

only takes into consideration the return of the securities in the portfolios and the time the portfolios are invested. It does not take into consideration how much is invested, or whether money is put in or taken out of the portfolios. Put another way, time-weighted returns suggest that if you invest in the market, you're going to get the market's return, no matter how much you invest or if you make contributions or withdrawals to your portfolio.

Now let's look at some hypothetical dollar-weighted returns for these two portfolios. Here, cash flows are important. Let's say that at the end of 2010, Investor 1 who is satisfied with her 25 percent performance and is in need of some cash, removes $500 from her account, leaving her with $750 in her portfolio by the start of 2011. Now let's say that Investor 2 is so excited by the 25 percent gain in 2010 that he decides to add $500 at the end of the year so that his portfolio has $1,750 in it at the start of 2011. As a consequence, during 2011's 20 percent decline Investor 1's portfolio falls from $750 to $600 while Investor 2's portfolio falls from $1,750 to $1,400. Without going into the complexities of applying the specific formula, suffice it to say that it is at this point where the dollar-weighted returns calculation more accurately measures the return on invested capital. In short, the calculation takes note of the fact that even though both portfolios experienced a 20 percent decline, the dollar amount of the decline was more for Investor 2: $350, than for Investor 1: $150. The calculation then adjusts, or weights, the 20 percent decline according to the amount of the dollars lost, hence the name: dollar-weighted returns.

One can already see that by this calculation Investor 2's returns are going to be worse than Investor 1's. Why? Simply because Investor 2 put money in his portfolio before the portfolio declined, while Investor 1 took money out of her portfolio before the market declined and therefore she did not experience the decline on the money she withdrew. By the end of the two-year period, Investor 1 ends up with gaining $100 worth of value in her portfolio, and her dollar-weighted return is 6.39 percent. Meanwhile, Investor 2 actually lost $100 and has a dollar-weighted return of –4.07 percent.

Dollar-weighted returns are important because they make it possible to see if the investors' portfolios are meeting their cash-flow generation goals. If the investor has a standard budget of withdrawing 3 percent of the portfolio's assets each year for expenses and yet his dollar-weighted returns are less than that or even negative, then he may need to adjust his spending habits or accept the fact that his portfolio's value will be depleted sooner than he thought. Dollar-weighted returns are also useful for measuring a client's own investing acumen. In the long history of asset management, most individual investors have a tendency to chase performance, adding money to or investing with money managers at the market's peak and withdrawing assets when the market has bottomed. As a result, their dollar-weighted returns are often less than the money manager's time-weighted ones. If such is the case with clients, advisors may want to instruct them on the perils of performance chasing and the importance of sticking to their investment discipline and stated goals.

CONCLUSIONS

- Building an optimized portfolio is more complex for wealthy, taxable investors than for nontaxable entities.
- Always calculate the expected returns for a potential investment after all taxes and management fees.
- During liquidity events, SEC Rule 144 sales of stock can achieve quick and transparent results compared to more complex strategies.
- Ask that advisors disclose performance net of all taxes and fees.
- The best performance disclosure comes from firms whose composites are audited and verified under GIPS.
- Use dollar-weighted returns to measure your personal performance.

CHAPTER 9

Active versus Passive

How Does an Investor Decide?

The conventional wisdom of passive investing or index funds under the efficient market hypothesis contains more flaws than benefits for the wealthy investor. The proponents of this investment style claim to have superior performance, fees, and tax efficiency than do active managers. Before dissecting the practical application of such claims, we must understand them better. Investors should be very clear on where they stand on the issues of efficient markets and active management. Wealthy families have already proven that they beat the odds since the growth of their wealth was above average, so this group has, by its actions and success, played and won at the active management game. That is, instead of simply taking their seed money and investing it in a market index, they opted to invest it in the family business or businesses, and the end result defied the market averages.

Before falling into the academic chasm of the active versus passive debate, I urge the investor to consider all the available data including the performance history of how the family built its wealth in the first place. If the investor considers this and still concludes that markets are efficient and that active management is a loser's game, then he has effectively declared that his own financial success was either an accident or sheer luck. I'll bet that most hardworking Americans and entrepreneurs would view the active/passive debate differently if they consider their own financial journey.

At the outset of the evaluation of active versus passive management, investors should ask themselves an important question: What is my objective for these investment dollars? Am I interested in making money, or am I interested in tracking the general progress of an economy, sector, or region? Answering this question is key to finding the most appropriate strategy for an individual investor. Jack Bogle, founder of the first index fund in the United States believes that he wants broad exposure to the entire U.S. economy in his equity portfolio. So for him it makes perfect sense to consider a passive investment vehicle to accomplish this objective.

INDEX PERFORMANCE CLAIMS

Many academic studies have concluded that a majority of active money managers fail to outperform their respective benchmark index. This makes complete mathematical sense: In the aggregate all investors make up the market that the index tracks. So after deducting management fees, administrative expenses, and trading costs average managers will lag the benchmark on average. The same even holds true for index funds themselves. A market index cannot be exactly replicated even by an index fund because an index contains no acquisition, turnover, or liquidation fees since the index only exists on paper. An index fund must charge a fee for its maintenance, filing requirements, and transaction costs. Because of this, an index fund will usually underperform its benchmark index by at least the amount of the fees it charges. Or a true index fund would. The fact is there are a lot of index fund managers who tweak the edges of their portfolios, using either derivatives to gain index exposure and bonds to generate extra income and goose returns. You could call such maneuvering a passive-aggressive form of active management.

The likelihood of an index fund imperfectly tracking its benchmark is exacerbated by the fact that its manager must acquire shares of a particular stock on the day it's added to the index. Similarly, the manager must attempt to liquidate shares of a stock the day it is removed from the index.

At certain points in history, index funds have been placed at an unwinnable disadvantage because of the index sponsor's announcements of additions and subtractions to or from the index. In the days before the addition of a stock to the index, some active managers or hedge funds would acquire shares of the target stock in advance of the index funds. The index funds, in order to maintain discipline to their stated objective, must acquire the target stock once it is officially added to the index. When the index funds entered the market with their buy orders, they did not have much control over the price they paid for acquisition so the active managers would enter the market with sell orders to the index funds hoping to trade them at a profit from their entry price in the previous days. This created double jeopardy for the index funds. First, they could refuse to buy the stocks on the first day to avoid being caught by the herd of buy orders. Doing so, however, causes the fund to deviate from its objective of replicating the index or risks the chance of the fund paying an even higher price later. The alternative is to acquire the target stock at any price even if it had risen or sell the removed stock at any price if it had fallen.

According to a 2000 study conducted by Standard & Poor's, on average stocks rise by 8.49 percent from the date of their announced addition to the S&P 500 until the date of addition and then fall by 3.23 percent in the 10 days after the addition. In one extreme example cited by finance professor Jeremy Siegel, dot-com company Yahoo! surged 64 percent in the five days after the announcement in 1999.[1] Managers of index funds had no choice but to buy Yahoo!'s overpriced shares.

INDEX FUND OBJECTIVES VERSUS ACTIVE FUND OBJECTIVES

This may come as a surprise to some readers but index funds do not maintain an objective or a goal of making money for shareholders. From 1966 through 1982 when the Dow and S&P 500 were essentially flat, the index fund performed exactly as it was supposed to by matching that absence of return before dividends. Similarly, from 1998 through 2008, the index fund's objective was fully met by delivering essentially zero performance. In more extreme cases of bear markets, crashes, or corrections, the index fund manager seeks to capture every penny of the market decline. Here we must ask ourselves an obvious question: What or who determines that an index or index fund holds a good portfolio of businesses with the opportunity to deliver shareholder value? Ultimately, the answer is the investor must decide this for himself or herself.

Admittedly, the term "passive index" is a bit of a misnomer. There is a always a human being somewhere designing the benchmark, and that human being is subject to his or her own human biases. So in an abstract sense, there is actually an individual or a group of individuals determining whether an index member is a good or bad business. In the case of the S&P 500, for instance, Standard & Poor's has an S&P Index Committee, a group of economists and equity analysts that meets regularly to determine whether a new member of the index should be added or an old member should be discarded.

Yet the goal of the S&P Index Committee is not to have positive performance but to be a "leading indicator of U.S. equities, reflecting the risk and return characteristics of the broader large cap universe on an ongoing basis," according to an S&P 500 fact sheet.[2] In doing this, the index committee tries to pick viable businesses that are representative of the key industries driving the U.S. economy. But ultimately the committee wants to measure the market, not produce returns. So even if there is a quasi-active selection to the index committee's choices of companies to be added to the benchmark, how effective is that selection for investors seeking to produce cash flow from their portfolios in retirement? And if the primary advantages then of index funds are low costs, low turnover, and a certain level of tax efficiency, why not just seek an active manager who has all those qualities but also seeks to produce positive results?

If the remaining argument for indexing is that markets are efficient and that somehow the market collectively knows better how to value businesses than any individual would, how do the academics explain the existence of bubbles and panics? The idea behind the efficient market is that investors are rational and price businesses appropriately, but every indication throughout history proves that investors are not rational, that in actuality investors are intensely emotional and tend to buy and sell in herds.

So that we do not seem to be overly harsh in our criticism of the indexing crowd, it's worth noting that there is a far more dangerous strategy than index funds: closet indexers. Closet index managers are labeled as actively managed funds (complete with fees and expenses of active management) that essentially replicate or mostly replicate their target benchmark.

FUNDAMENTAL INDEXING

One of the interesting questions about the most popular indexes such as the S&P 500 and the Dow Jones Industrial Average is whether they are truly representative of the U.S. economy. The S&P 500 is a market-cap weighted index, meaning it holds the largest positions in the companies with the greatest total share price value, multiplying each company's current share price by the number of shares outstanding to determine how to weight each stock. But suppose the stock market is in a bubble phase and investors are valuing companies that have minuscule earnings higher than more profitable companies as they did during the dot-com era. As we've seen in previous chapters, tech darlings such as Cisco and EMC commanded share prices and valuations in the 1990s that far exceeded their economic contributions at the time relative to companies such as Gillette, Anheuser-Busch, and Exxon.

Ultimately, what the S&P 500 index represents is not the most economically valuable or representative companies in the country but those companies that are currently the most popular with investors. It is effectively a momentum index, a measure not of fundamental value but of investors' collective emotions about stocks, capturing both their irrational exuberance and their equally irrational panic to the fullest degree.

The Dow Jones Industrial Average, by contrast, is an even more archaic index, which weights its 30 companies by their share prices adjusted for stock splits over time. So a $50 stock will be weighted twice as heavily in the index as a $25 one. This system is a popularity contest also, albeit a more inaccurate one as stock prices are not the same as market capitalization. Why should a company with a $100 stock price and 500 million shares outstanding, and thus having a market cap of $50 billion, be weighed less in the index than a company with a $200 share price but only 100 million shares outstanding, having a lower market cap of $20 billion? That's just the way creator Charles Dow designed it. Do these weightings have any connection to the underlying fundamentals of the companies in the index? None at all. And just as with the S&P 500, the members of the index are selected by committee.

In response to the mismatch between index weightings and economic fundamentals, some money managers have attempted to build a better mousetrap and create fundamental indexes. The most well-known of these are those created by famous quantitative investor Robert D. Arnott, who is chairman of Research Affiliates in Pasadena, California. In

2005, Arnott created what is known as Research Affiliates Fundamental Indexes or RAFI that weight stocks based on their underlying companies' cash flow, sales, book value, total number of employees, and dividends to capture their true economic impact on the economy. Via back-testing, he demonstrated that such a methodology would have beaten the S&P 500 by more than 2 percentage points a year from 1962 through 2004.[3]

While Arnott's research is admirable and a step in the right direction for indexing, his strategy begs the question: How are his decisions in building the index different from those of active management? I have been an admirer of Rob's academic writings over the past decade. If an investor were interested in purchasing an ETF that tracked one of Rob's indexes, I would attribute the success more to the fact that Rob was applying his experience and wisdom than I would to the fact that it was simply labeled an "index fund."

Without the mind of a talented manager such as Arnott, consider the fact that even a fundamentals-based index will generally miss the crucial importance of shifting business dynamics that occur over time, and how once great companies with sizable earnings can suddenly fall by the wayside as smaller more nimble competitors with newer technology or marketing strategies overtake them. So, for instance, even if you had bought such an index of the beer industry in the 1970s, you would gain only a small exposure to newcomer Anheuser-Busch's advance while you would also participate in a more significant way in the decline of then industry leader Schlitz. And if you bought a fundamentally weighted retailer index decades ago, you would have owned Wal-Mart and E.J. Korvette's and Sears, but you would have been exposed disproportionately more to the demise of E.J. Korvette's and Sears than to the advance in Wal-Mart until the index adjusted to the shift in fundamentals.

Ultimately, I think the long-term outperformance of index funds, fundamental or otherwise, is not so much proof of the success of passive investing as the failure of most money managers to create products that treat investors fairly—low-cost, low-turnover products that pay attention to fundamentals, valuation, and taxes. These strategies and managers are available in the marketplace, though they are few in number.

CONCLUSIONS

- Wealthy investors who believe in indexing must accept their own success as luck.
- The indexer's goal is not to produce returns but to match the market's ups or downs.
- The most popular indexes such as the S&P 500 weight companies based on popularity, not business fundamentals.
- There are always human beings behind the index making decisions to add or subtract securities.
- Active managers can have the attractive attributes of index funds—low costs and low turnover.
- The success or failure of an active or passive portfolio will be driven more by stock valuations and earnings growth than the label "active" or "passive."

CHAPTER 10

A New Way to Look at Risk

Since the bear market of 2008 began, many ostensibly conservative investors have been surprised by how much money they've lost. They thought that their portfolios were designed to minimize downside risk. The reason for their surprise is that the financial community—both academic and within the investment advice industry—has been evaluating the wrong statistics to measure portfolio risk in light of the risks investors are most concerned about. As evidence of this fact, one only need go as far as your nearest independent money manager report or mutual fund "honor roll." Under the heading of "risk" or "risk measurement" several statistics dominate the field: beta, standard deviation, peer performance, Sharpe ratio, risk-adjusted peer performance, alpha, information ratio, and Monte Carlo simulation are a few of the most commonly quoted statistics and tools that aim to evaluate the risk or volatility of a portfolio, asset class, individual security, or a particular mutual or hedge fund.

The problem with each of the above statistics is that they do not answer the real question on the mind of the investor: "What is the worst possible loss I could sustain from today's valuation while I own this investment?" When viewing risk in light of this rather simple question, we can observe the main defect in risk measurement in the investment world: Such statistics communicate only observed (past) risk behavior. They do not acknowledge or measure possible (future) risk.

In an eerie reminder of the investment public's inability to effectively measure portfolio risk, a 2007 *Fortune* magazine article highlighted the "conservative and risk averse" portfolio mixes of wealthy investors.[1] One quote from the chief information officer (CIO) of a wealth management firm sums up the confusion: "For the most part, our investors are more concerned with wealth preservation and strategic growth rather than trying to hit a home run." The CIO explained his typical asset allocation for wealthy investors which was surprisingly low in bonds and high in riskier assets. The allocation he recommended was 50 percent U.S. stocks, 15 percent international stocks, 15 percent real estate, 10 percent alternative assets, and 10 percent bonds. The portfolio mix may have displayed an impressive "back-tested" volatility and return characteristics, but it was indeed highly exposed to risk unknown to both the advisor and the investor. The above portfolio mix would have produced a –31.5 percent total return for 2008.[2] This highlights that just because a portfolio mix is labeled as low risk or moderate risk (because of traditional risk measurement techniques) doesn't mean that it will perform as such in the future.

The basis for almost every academically sanctified risk statistic is standard deviation, which measures an investment's historic volatility, generally as a monthly average of the past three years of returns. This backward-looking measure is, unfortunately, used by investors as a gauge for the amount of expected volatility. Stocks considered volatile will have a high standard deviation, while the deviation of a historically stable blue chip will be lower. A large dispersion in monthly returns over the past three years—with very high positive and very sharp negative returns, depending on the month—tells us that in the past an investment has been volatile and reveals how much the return on the fund or stock is deviating from its expected normal returns.

Among the primary challenges of using standard deviation for individual portfolios is the fact that investors are only concerned about how their portfolio will perform in the future. And in this regard using stats such as standard deviation or beta to design their portfolios does them an immense disservice. For instance, a once stable blue-chip stock such as General Motors can suddenly be exposed to enormous risks as it heads into bankruptcy. Admittedly, the study of normalized returns of asset classes can be enlightening in a historical sense, but they offer limited value in predicting the degree of potential volatility an investor faces at a particular point in time.

MISLEADING MUNI FUND STATS

To illustrate how standard deviation can be misleading, let's review the case of the municipal bond arbitrage funds that became popular from 2003 through 2007 before their cataclysmic collapse in 2008. These funds were sold to individual investors as a free lunch of sorts. They invested in long-term municipal bonds and used leverage and short trades of corporate bonds and U.S. Treasury bonds. Historically, municipal bonds have traded at a discounted yield compared to U.S. Treasury bonds and investment grade corporate bonds because of the tax-exempt status of the municipal bonds. The error made by both municipal arbitrage managers and investors is that they assumed that because this relationship in yields had taken place in the past, it would continue to take place in the future.

When the municipal bond curve began to invert in 2007 and traded at a premium to Treasury bonds in 2008, the leveraged position of these funds caused many of them to fail as the value of the margin loans that had been taken out to short Treasuries exceeded the value of their underlying portfolios. The bottom line in this investment postmortem is that the historical volatility statistics were meaningless because they had never included a period of observed premium yields in municipal bonds over Treasuries. This simple fact, along with the speed at which the leverage could destroy the underlying funds, was missed by most investors who claim to have understood the risk of this strategy to be low.

For instance, on March 5, 2007, *BusinessWeek* published an article titled, "Pumping Up the Muni Advantage: Using Financial Engineering, Hedge Funds Can Hike Returns to 8 Percent or 9 Percent." The second paragraph of the article reads as follows:

> Here's a new way, at least for high net worth investors: Give $1 million to a hedge fund. It will pool your money with others to score $100 million of bonds, chop up the interest payments, buy a derivative instrument to protect the investment and *voila*, turn the 4% into 8% or 9%—that's still tax free.[3]

Author's note to reader: If a money manager ever uses the word "voila" in describing his or her investment process, head for the exit. Further into the article a disclaimer was made and then dismissed, "This would be a terrible bet, of course, if the muni-bond yield curve ever inverts . . . . But it never has."

In the case of the municipal bond arbitrage crash, historical volatility was assumed to be future volatility. The underlying credit ratings of the bonds (that carried ratings of AA to AAA) led investors and managers to believe that the strategy also carried a credit rating of AA to AAA. The more appropriate question to be asked by prospective investors in this strategy was: What if the municipal curve inverts or if municipal spreads over treasuries widen? Or equally significant: How does leveraging my bet on municipal bonds versus Treasuries increase my downside risk?

PORTFOLIO STRESS TESTS

In order to gain a more informed view of portfolio risk, it is important to understand that a portfolio is only as strong or weak as the individual securities contained within it. It is useless or incorrect for an investor to say that a portfolio of 10 stocks has a demonstrated a beta of 0.85. The investor should not be concerned about the beta of the portfolio over the past decade, but rather the potential beta in the future. Jeremy Siegel, professor at Wharton, gives the long-term standard deviation of long-term Treasury bonds as 7.4 percent (1871–2006) compared to the long-term standard deviation of U.S. equities (as measured by the S&P 500) as 18.5 percent for the same period.[4] This oft-quoted statistic causes many investors, consultants, advisors, and even money managers to believe that Treasury bonds always bear less risk than stocks. The mistake in this thinking is that the validity of the risk equation can be accurately gauged only by knowing the yield of the bond relative to the price/earnings multiple of stocks.

Let's look at some statistics as of year-end 2008:

- 30-year U.S. Treasury bond yield: 2.6 percent
- P/E of S&P 500: 13.82 times (earnings yield 7.2 percent)

To perform our "what if" risk measurement on these two investments, let's take inventory of a few relevant data points with respect to each of them. In October 1981, the yield on the 30-year Treasury bond was 14.67 percent as the U.S. economy was reeling from high inflation and taxes. The 1981 yield on the 30-year Treasury bond was the highest of the twentieth century. Since the recession of 2008 had been labeled by some in the financial community as the worst economic malaise since the Great Depression, it is reasonable for investors to ponder the implications of high interest rates on the holder of a Treasury bond that now yields only 2.6 percent.

If an investor were to purchase a new Treasury bond on December 31, 2008, she must "stress test" the investment to see how it would perform if high interest rates were to occur. Should the yield on Treasuries rise to the levels seen in 1981 (14.67 percent) the holder of the 2.6 percent coupon Treasury would see her investment valued at 20 cents on the dollar (in response to the repricing of the 2.67 percent coupon bond to the higher interest rate environment). I do not believe that many investors who flocked to Treasuries at the end of 2008 were aware that they could see their investment decline in value by 80 percent.

Rather than look at standard deviation, which you can see is a rather meaningless statistic in this case, it is better to pay attention to current yield and a stat called *duration*, which measures the inverse relationship between bond prices and interest rates. A duration of 15 for instance indicates that bond prices would fall by 15 percent if interest rates were to rise by 1 percentage point. The longer the maturity of the bond, the greater its duration will be because the interest on the bond is locked in for many years, and if interest rates rise during that period, it will be worth less compared to other bonds issued at the new higher interest rate. Needless to say, 30-year Treasury bonds yielding just 2.6 percent will look terrible compared to other bonds if interest rates rise significantly in the next few years. And so prices will fall in that event.

With respect to U.S. equities, it is equally wise for investors to educate themselves as to the depth of potential declines under various possible scenarios. The lowest price/earnings multiples observed in the twentieth century were: 5 in 1921, 5 in 1932, 7 in 1975, and 7 in 1982. (See Figure 10.1.)

FIGURE   10.1

S&P 500 Price/Earnings Ratio versus Interest Rates
(1880–2010)

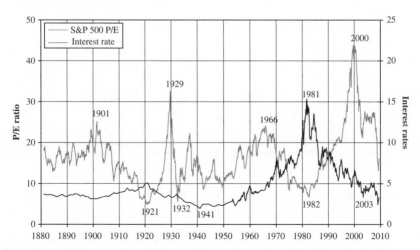

Source: Stock market data used in "Irrational Exuberance" Princeton University Press, 2000, 2005, updated "Irrational Exuberance" Princeton University Press, 2000, 2005, updated, Robert J. Shiller, http://www.econ.yale.edu/~shiller/data.htm.

Therefore, if we were to perform a similar stress test on U.S. equities, we might create a hypothetical model in which the stock market trades at the valuation multiples observed in the worst periods of the last century. In doing so, we would learn that if the market were to trade from a p/e of 13.82 (2008) to a p/e of 5 (as in 1921 and 1932), the equity investor would witness a 64 percent decline in the value of his investment. Similarly, if the market were to trade from a p/e of 13.82 (2008) to a p/e of 7 (as in 1975 and 1982), the equity investor would witness a 49 percent decline in his investment. (*Note*: The above example does not include the possibility of an equivalent p/e multiple on lower earnings.)

What we learn in the above example is that despite the fact that the Treasury bond has demonstrated a lower historical standard deviation than equities, the loss experienced by the bond investor (80 percent loss assuming the highest 100-year U.S. Treasury yield) would be greater than the loss experienced by the equity investor (64 percent loss assuming the 1932 low p/e of 5). Though I do not wish to suggest that either of these outcomes is likely, I believe that the above exercise can and should be performed by investors when they're doing their "what if" due diligence.

BETTER RISK MEASUREMENTS

While such worst-case scenarios as we've illustrated above can prove illuminating for investors who wish to see how they would have fared during historical periods of stress, history unfortunately does not repeat itself. So the question one must immediately ask is whether there are better ways of estimating future portfolio risk and thus minimizing it.

I think, to a limited degree, the answer is yes. Once again, the solution comes down to paying attention to business fundamentals and doing the math.

To me the greatest risk equity investors face over the long term has nothing to do with stock volatility. It is business risk. Ultimately what determines whether you're going to have a positive return from your investment in a company a decade from now is whether or not the company remains in business, whether the number of its customers rises or falls, and whether its profit margins grow or shrink.

Evaluating the sustainability of an individual business takes work and is as much an art as it is a science. Perhaps that is why such analysis is so rarely mentioned in articles and discussions about quantitative risk statistics such as standard deviation, which make measuring risk appear straightforward and scientific. To understand business risk— understand but not calculate—you must analyze an individual company's growth prospects, the health of its balance sheet, and the prospects for its industry. And then you must decide whether the price you're paying for that business is a fair one.

One of the primary reasons clients come to us is that they own a single business and have much of their wealth tied up in it and need to diversify their exposure. We know in such cases that the business risk is high, and it can even be due to the result of factors outside the client's control. So a pharmaceutical executive may be at risk of his company's patents expiring or patients dying from an adverse chemical reaction that was not seen in the early Federal Drug Administration (FDA) studies.

But the question is how diversified must you be in order to protect yourself from individual business risk or industry concentration risk? Is it 5 stocks, is it 50, is it 500, is it 5,000? I've concluded that, at least in the past decade, holding somewhere between 30 and 45 companies allows me to have enough single stock and industry diversification. Beyond that point, I feel that my decisions will have a muted impact on a portfolio's performance. And more to the point, as the number of companies in your portfolio grows, it becomes increasingly hard to measure the individual business risk of each of the stocks in it. The indexer in effect completely ignores business risk. When considering the number of securities necessary to gain true diversification, investors should also recognize that one company may have several divisions, each containing a range of various product offerings.

VALUATION RISK

In many respects, the risk equation is fairly simple for the long-term stock investor. You want to find good businesses, and you want to buy them at the right price. (Of course, executing this strategy is never simple.) Unfortunately, a good business purchased at the wrong price is still a bad high-risk investment. That is the mistake many investors made during the dot-com bubble in 2000. They assumed that, because companies like Cisco and Intel were good businesses, they were good investments at any price. And to this day, those stocks have never returned to their bubble peaks. But at least such investors got half the equation right. Cisco and Intel are still going concerns. Bad businesses that were also overvalued like Enron no longer exist.

But it's important to remember that no investment exists in a vacuum. Investors, as opposed to short-term speculators, are always aware of the risk-reward tradeoff of owning one investment versus another. By making that valuation comparison—of one stock to another or one asset class to another—we can expose the risk if not of loss or business impairment than of opportunity cost, of giving up the risk-free rate of Treasuries or the low-risk rate of high-grade GO municipal bonds to invest in a high-flying tech stock with unsustainable earnings. Volatility measurements such as standard deviation cannot capture either business or valuation risk. All such stats measure is the perceived risk of an investment, not the risk of capital impairment or overvaluation.

Examples of investors just ignoring valuation because a business has a good story are manifold. For instance, Krispy Kreme Doughnuts traded at a p/e ratio of 143 in mid-2001. This meant that it would take 143 years of continuous profitability equal to 2001's nosebleed levels in order for investors to recoup their initial investment. To justify a p/e that high, earnings growth for the next decade would need to be 50 percent every year. If the company was making 2.7 billion doughnuts in 2001 and it grew by 50 percent for the next decade, that would require a consumption level of about 15.5 trillion doughnuts in 2011. This would equal 2,500 donuts per year for each of the world's 6 billion inhabitants. That is a little silly isn't it? Yet investors piled into the stock, and it would subsequently decline from a peak of $46 in 2001 to about $3 in 2009.

Truth be told, a stock with low volatility that trades at an expensive valuation can be far more risky than one with high volatility and a low valuation. A basic concept taught in any class on value investing is Graham and Dodd's notion of the margin of safety from their seminal book *Security Analysis*.[5] And this notion is that a company trading below its book value—or the value of its assets such as plant and equipment if they were sold off—provides a margin of safety to its investors because if that company went bankrupt or was acquired, its assets would be worth more per share when they are liquidated than the company's current share price. So a stock with $10 a share worth of assets in its book value trading for $6 a share would provide a margin of safety or an embedded gain of $4 for shareholders in a sale, assuming its balance sheet is relatively clean. Yet nothing about the stock's volatility would necessarily indicate it's a low-risk investment. To the contrary, for the stock to fall below book value, investors may question whether the book value is appropriately priced. And yet for the long-term investor it represents an opportunity because she knows that even if the worst happens, she should be able to recover close to the book value of her shares.

If anything, assuming you can find good businesses, short-term volatility is actually the long-term investor's friend. Since markets are not efficient, on any given day a company's shares could be trading at a premium to its fair value or at a discount to its fair value. It's the investors' job to assess fair value.

LEVERAGE RISK

Another risk standard deviation and other volatility stats do not measure is leverage or financing risk. It is possible for a company to have a great business and be trading at a cheap price and still implode because it has too much debt or the wrong kind of debt on its books. Certainly some amount of leverage is justified with big, established businesses or even smaller businesses if they can borrow money at a lower rate than they can produce profits by investing the capital internally. There are a lot of companies that have an internal rate of return of 13 or 14 percent on their assets and because they have a highly rated balance sheet, they're able to issue debt at relatively attractive rates.

But it's important to recognize that the amount of leverage truly is an indicator of the risk of a company because sometimes it needs to issue more debt to grow, and there is a limit as to how much debt a balance sheet can take. For instance, in 2009 the United States is experiencing a recession with a slowdown in consumer spending. Drugstore company Rite Aid has a 90 percent debt-to-capital ratio and Walgreens and CVS have much lower numbers. If Rite Aid has a misstep in its product purchasing or if it opens too many stores, it could put itself in a position where it needs to borrow more. And at a 90 percent debt-to-capital ratio, its balance sheet is already reflecting a very high cost to capital for new debt issuance. So it's reasonable to say that a 90 percent debt-to-capital ratio in this kind of economy is a gauge on how long Rite Aid can stay in business on its own without having to rely on the capital markets.

By comparison, Walgreens or CVS might be able to make a misstep in one quarter and still be able to issue debt at a much lower cost than Rite Aid because they are not over-leveraged. And the debt offering will not completely eat into their profits or threaten to kill their business. Bear in mind, these kinds of missteps happen all the time. In 2007, Walgreens suffered in sales because it was a very slow cold-and-flu season, so the traffic in the stores was less than what the company had planned. But because its balance sheet was strong, it survived a tough seasonal sales period. The same would probably not have been true with Rite Aid as the same market pressures would have taken a larger toll on the capital structure of the company.

From a company standpoint leverage is not always so bad because the company has control over the pricing of its products and, if it's healthy, it can often acquire cheap fixed-rate debt. But for investors and money managers, leverage is far more perilous. With margin investing or with leveraged investing of any kind, the debt creates a higher hurdle of return in order for the investor to have a profit. And so, for instance, if margin interest rates are 7 percent and the investor achieves a 7 percent return for the portion of her portfolio she leveraged, her net return after leverage is zero. And if she pulls off a 14 percent gross rate of return in that leveraged portion of her portfolio, this will mean that she netted just 7 percent while possibly having to outperform the market by 100 percent, and that's even before fees are factored in.

With low-cost fixed-rate debt, a company can handle some of the volatility in the economy by raising its prices, building new stores, closing new stores, cutting costs, and so on. By contrast, once an investor puts a trade on the books, we know that over the short term the fundamentals of a company's business can't bail the investor out if the company's stock happens to be volatile. A 50 percent decline in stock prices may not be permanent for Coca-Cola, and it may survive as a business. But if you bought the stock on margin or if you were short the stock in the case of a stock advance, you could be wiped out because business fundamentals do not dictate stock prices over the short run.

From a corporate standpoint a certain amount of leverage can also make sense because sales and profits are, to a limited degree, predictable, depending on the product being sold. But stocks, as we've seen in recent years, can be incredibly volatile. Hedge funds and individuals using margin accounts often borrow at higher rates for shorter periods of time than companies, and the rates on their borrowing are adjustable not fixed, meaning that if interest rates and stock market volatility increases, brokers and banks can raise their cost of leverage at a moment's notice and suddenly the costs increase.

CONCLUSIONS

- Most risk statistics measure only past volatility, not future or possible downside risk.
- Investors should stress-test their portfolios to understand the potential downside.
- Valuations are a better measurement of future risk than past volatility.
- Business risk is hard to measure but is essential to understand.
- Leverage, the amount and the type, is an essential risk component.

CHAPTER 11

The Investing Habits
of Institutions

In this chapter we observe the investing habits and return expectations of two of the largest money management sectors in the United States: defined benefit pension plans and endowments. In addition to understanding the stark differences between these two groups and wealthy families, we will view them on a hypothetical after-tax basis.

PENSIONS

Defined benefit pension funds are investment pools managed by corporations to fund the benefits of current and future retirees. In the defined benefit world the payout to the retiree is guaranteed by the corporation so the risk of investment underperformance does not fall on the shoulders of the individual retirees. In 401(k) plans and other defined contribution retirement plans, the risk of underperformance falls on the shoulders of the individual workers with no specific income or benefit at retirement.

One of the differences between a pension plan and a wealthy family portfolio is that the pension plan knows exactly how many retirees will need to be funded with a somewhat certain date on which the benefits are to commence. The pension plan also has the benefit of operating in a completely tax-free environment. The absence of federal, state, and estate taxes gives the pension plan an insurmountable long-term advantage over the wealthy family portfolio. A few other differences exist with respect to investment performance. A wealthy family investment portfolio, especially if it holds the majority of the family assets, has no "bailout" if the investment plans underperform or fail to materialize relative to expectations. Corporations, on the other hand, can and must fund investment shortfalls out of current income in order to keep the plan in a funded status that is required by law. Should the parent corporation fail completely in the form of bankruptcy, the pension plan assets would usually be assumed by the PBGC (Pension Benefit Guaranty Corporation) of the U.S. government.

The investment habits and return expectations for public corporations are available for review in the annual report or SEC Form 10-K for each individual company. For this discussion we look at 10 of the largest pension funds in the United States. This list, which I call the "Big 10," contains some interesting variances in the approach each corporation has chosen to undertake with respect to its plan. A conservative asset allocation will naturally produce a more conservative expected return on plan assets. Companies that choose low-return expectations for their pension plans do so to reduce the likelihood that they will have to fund investment underperformance out of current earnings. Aggressive asset allocations therefore tend to reflect higher expected returns on plan assets. The higher-return expectations benefit the corporation if its investments perform up to expectations. The greater the return the plan assets achieve, the less likely the plan will result in a charge to earnings.

The Big 10 asset allocations are arguably more traditional in nature in that their reliance on alternative asset classes is generally less than what we see in the endowment world. A few comments with respect to our calculations of expected after-tax returns:

1. Taxation is set at the top tax bracket, effective at year-end 2010 of each classification of return in terms of ordinary income, capital gains, and dividends.
2. A median state income tax rate of 6 percent is included in the calculations.
3. This analysis uses an ongoing taxation modeling (as opposed to full liquidation) in order to account for capital that would be withdrawn from the plan for consumption or investment.
4. Some pension plans choose to disclose asset class expected returns as well as the overall plan expected return. Where specific asset class returns are disclosed, they have been used in the calculation. In the absence of specific asset class return expectations, we have applied the asset class expected returns published by the Yale Endowment. Yale's nominal asset class expected returns are listed as the published real expected return plus an inflation rate of 2 percent.

In observing the average gross and net returns of the Big 10, it is apparent that for the group 30.30 percent of the gross return would have been lost to taxes if identical portfolios were held by high tax bracket investors. In other words, the average after-tax retention rate is 69 percent. The most conservative asset allocation as measured by allocation to fixed income is Procter & Gamble's plan at 50 percent. As one would expect, P&G's expected return on plan assets is also one of the lowest at 7.40 percent (gross). The plan with the lowest allocation to fixed income in the Big 10 is Johnson & Johnson at 21 percent. J&J's expected return on plan assets is also the highest of the group at 9 percent.

The lowest expected return of the group is held by Berkshire Hathaway at 6.90 percent. When reviewing Berkshire's asset allocation, it should be noted that it has chosen conservative returns among each of the asset classes within the plan. Given the public admiration for Warren Buffett's investment expertise, a review of the asset class returns for Berkshire's pension plan might be an interesting case study for conservative investors.

The average gross expected return for the Big 10 is 8.06 percent. The average after-tax return is 5.57 percent. Note that two asset classes in the pension world receive a higher degree of taxation: taxable fixed income (corporate bonds, U.S. Treasury bonds, mortgage-backed securities) and hedge funds. (See Table 11.1.)

PENSION BENEFIT GUARANTY CORPORATION (PBGC)

The PBGC is the safety net above which public pension funds operate. As a federal corporation created by the Employee

Retirement Income Security Act (ERISA) of 1974, the PBGC currently protects the pensions of nearly 44 million American workers and retirees encompassed by over 29,000 defined benefit pension plans. The PBGC receives no funds from general tax revenues. The operations are financed by insurance premiums set by Congress and paid by the sponsors of the defined benefit pension plans, investment income, assets from pension plans trusteed by the PBGC, and recoveries from the companies formerly responsible for the plans. At fiscal year-end 2008, the PBGC's total investments consisted of cash equivalents, investments, and investment income receivables totaling $50.77 billion. The asset allocation of the investment pool at fiscal year-end 2008 were 71 percent fixed income and cash investments, 27 percent equities, and 2 percent alternative investments. The PGBC's allocation is meaningfully more conservative than any of the Big 10 allocations.

Unfortunately for the PBGC, it became yet another victim of investing in "trends" rather than sticking to its knitting. Shortly after the end of the 2008 fiscal year, the PBGC, armed with brand new "Monte Carlo" simulations and hypothetical back-tested studies, implemented what it felt was a new and improved asset mix set to a target of 45 percent equities, 10 percent alternative investments, and 45 percent fixed income. The trustees for the PBGC cited reasons for the changed investment policy as including an observation that they would have had better results with the new allocation and that the increased risk/return profile would increase the probability of closing the PBGC's current funding gap and meeting future obligations. On September 30, 2008, the PBGC held a deficit or underfunded status of $11.15 billion. Only seven months later, PBGC Acting Director Vince Snowbarger reported to the U.S. Senate that the deficit had risen to $33.5 billion by March 31, 2009.

TABLE 11.1

'Big 10' Pension Allocations*

	Asset Class	Weights	Returns	After Tax
Exxon	Equity	75%	8.00%	6.57%
Mobil	Fixed income	25%	4.00%	2.18%
(XOM)	*Total*	*100%*	*9.00%*	*5.47%*
General	Domestic equity	32%	8.00%	6.57%
Electric	International equity	20%	10.00%	5.44%
(GE)	Fixed income	24%	4.00%	2.18%
	Real estate	9%	10.00%	5.44%
	Private equities	9%	13.20%	9.94%
	Other	6%	8.00%	4.35%
	Total	*100%*	*8.50%*	*4.87%*
Procter &	Equity securities	45%	9.18%	7.69%
Gamble	Fixed income	50%	6.00%	3.26%
(PG)	Cash	3%	2.37%	1.29%
	Real estate	2%	10.00%	7.40%
	Total	*100%*	*7.40%*	*5.28%*
JP	Equity	79%	9.80%	8.28%
Morgan	Fixed income	21%	6.00%	3.26%
(JNJ)	*Total*	*100%*	*9.00%*	*7.23%*
Johnson &	Equity	45%	6.95%	5.58%
Johnson	Fixed income	28%	6.00%	3.26%
(JPM)	Real estate	9%	10.00%	7.40%
	Alternatives	18%	10.00%	7.78%
	Total	*100%*	*7.50%*	*5.49%*

Average Pension Returns: 8.06%

* Asset class expected returns are noted where specified in company 10K report, otherwise Yale returns are used.

	Asset Class	Weights	Returns	After Tax
Bank of	Equity	70%	8.50%	7.05%
America	Fixed income	27%	5.75%	3.13%
(BAC)	Real estate	3%	7.00%	5.18%
	Total	*100%*	*8.00%*	*5.93%*
AT&T	Domestic equity	39%	8.00%	6.57%
(T)	International equity	18%	10.00%	5.44%
	Fixed income	27%	4.00%	2.18%
	Real estate	9%	8.00%	5.92%
	Other	7%	8.00%	4.35%
	Total	*100%*	*8.50%*	*4.97%*
Chevron	Equity	64%	8.00%	6.57%
(CVX)	Fixed income	23%	6.00%	3.26%
	Real estate	12%	10.00%	7.40%
	Other	1%	10.00%	5.44%
	Total	*100%*	*7.80%*	*5.90%*
IBM	Equity	47%	9.55%	8.04%
(IBM)	Fixed income	45%	6.00%	3.26%
	Real estate	5%	10.00%	7.40%
	Other	3%	10.00%	5.44%
	Total	*100%*	*8.00%*	*5.80%*
Berkshire	Cash and equivalents	6%	2.37%	1.29%
Hathaway	U.S. government obligations	3%	5.35%	2.91%
(BRK)	Mortgage-backed securities	6%	5.24%	2.85%
	Corporate obligations	14%	7.86%	4.28%
	Equity	59%	6.70%	5.34%
	Other	13%	10.00%	5.44%
	Total	*100%*	*6.90%*	*4.76%*

Average Pension After-Tax Returns: 5.57%

The PBGC's experience with investment policy, asset allocation, and underperformance should be required reading for wealthy families and those who advise them on investing.

It should also serve as a caution to investors and advisors who insist on using Monte Carlo simulations and past performance as a guide for future investment decisions.[1]

ENDOWMENTS

Another practical resource allowing investors to peek inside the investment laboratories of college endowments is found in their annual reports or the NACUBO (North American College and University Business Officer) annual asset allocation report. Since Yale and Harvard were considered by many to be the reigning performance champions through the end of 2007, a review of their annual reports contains many interesting observations on asset allocation, cash flow, and expected returns. Despite the tremendous investment performance accomplished by the investment teams of these two endowments, the reader might be surprised by the absence of lofty expectations for future returns (although the Yale gross expected return is substantially higher than any of the Big 10 pension funds). In the previous section we noted that the pension funds invest with safety nets of their parent corporation or the PBGC. University endowments don't have the benefit of these two sources of assistance, but they have something better: the donations of their alumni and benefactors.

Many in the investment world believe that the Harvard and Yale endowments were able to make such aggressive bets on illiquid alternative assets because the expected cash flow from alumni and benefactors created a steady stream of cash flow with which to make other investments or fund operations. In the following sections we observe the asset allocations and hypothetical after-tax returns of the Yale Endowment, Harvard Endowment, and the NACUBO survey of endowment asset allocation.

Yale Endowment

The 2007 annual report for the Yale endowment contains many helpful notes and references concerning the attitude of David Swensen and his investment team. Mr. Swensen reports expected returns in real terms (net of inflation). The expected real return on the endowment assets is 6 percent. David communicated to me (in early 2008) that his forward inflation assumption was around 4 percent (higher than the Consumer Price Index for the broad economy). It should be noted that to calculate inflation, Yale uses a basket of goods and services specific to higher education. In addition to overall performance, Swensen and his team share their expected return attitudes for each individual asset class. We have added a 2 percent inflation rate to each of the numbers that were reported in real terms. (Yale's 4 percent estimate of inflation is specific to higher education costs rather than the broad economy.)

The expected return of the Yale endowment after taxes is 6.06 percent. The reason for the higher after-tax return of the Yale portfolio versus the Big 10 pension funds can be explained by a lower allocation to fixed income and a higher expected return on each of the asset classes within the portfolio. At first glance, one can understand why so many investors were coaxed into mimicking the Yale asset allocation. Both the pretax and after-tax performance numbers are

TABLE   11.2

Yale Endowment Allocation*

Asset Class	Weights	Returns	After Tax
Domestic equity	11.00%	8.00%	6.57%
International equity	14.10%	9.00%	4.90%
Fixed income	4.00%	4.00%	2.18%
Real assets (private)	27.10%	8.00%	5.92%
Hedge funds	23.30%	8.00%	4.35%
Private equity	18.70%	13.20%	9.94%
Other	1.80%	8.00%	4.35%
Total	*100.00%*	*8.95%*	*6.06%*

* Nominal asset class returns are reflective of real returns plus assumed rate of 2 percent inflation.
Source: Yale University financial report fiscal year 2008.

superior to the allocations of the pension plans. Individual investors should note, however, that it may be unrealistic to believe that one can match the performance of the Yale team. Yale has a size and reputation that allow them to have access to managers who are not available to the investing public. (See Table 11.2.)

Additional insights into Yale's attitudes toward expected returns can be found by reviewing the university's annual report which highlights the financial status of its defined benefit pension plan for faculty and staff. At fiscal year-end 2008, the plan held assets of $845 million. The published expected return on plan assets was listed at 9 percent. (*Note:* This figure is expressed in nominal as opposed to real terms.)

Harvard Endowment

Prior to September 2007, the Harvard endowment was led by Mohamed El-Erian, author of the book, *When Markets Collide*.

The Harvard annual report does not discuss expected returns on the endowment or the specific asset classes within it. However, the report does contain reference to the pension plan for Harvard's faculty and staff. Similar to the defined benefit pension plans, the university endowment is required to select an expected return on plan assets pursuant to ERISA regulations. The Harvard pension is also managed by the same team at the Harvard Management Company. At fiscal year-end 2008, the pension plan held $879 million in assets with an expected return of 7.5 percent. The allocation of the pension plan at Harvard was more conservatively invested compared to the endowment. The pension plan at year-end 2008 held 48.7 percent equities, 19.6 percent fixed income, 6.8 percent real estate, and 24.9 percent marked as "other." We shall assume that the "other" component was a mix of Harvard's absolute return, private equity, and natural resources investments.

For the after-tax analysis of the Harvard endowment, we chose to use the individual asset class expected returns reported by the Yale endowment.

The after-tax expected return of the Harvard endowment is 5.37 percent. (See Table 11.3.)

NACUBO

The North American College and University Business Officer organization is a nonprofit professional organization representing chief administrative and financial officers at more than 2,100 colleges and universities across the country. NACUBO's mission is to promote sound management and financial practices at colleges and universities. The 2007 survey of NACUBO's membership gives a snapshot of the

TABLE 11.3

Harvard Endowment Allocation*

Asset Class	Weights	Returns	After Tax
Domestic equity	11.21%	8.00%	6.57%
International equity	20.83%	9.00%	4.90%
Domestic fixed income	12.67%	4.00%	2.18%
International fixed income	2.94%	4.00%	2.18%
Real estate (public)	0.00%	8.00%	5.92%
Real estate (private)	7.58%	8.00%	5.92%
Hedge funds	18.30%	8.00%	4.35%
Private equity	11.39%	13.20%	9.94%
Natural resources	15.08%	8.00%	5.92%
Total	*100.00%*	*8.18%*	*5.37%*

* Asset class expected returns are from Yale University financial report fiscal year 2008.
Source: Asset class and weights from Harvard endowment annual report 2008.

TABLE 11.4

NACUBO Allocation*

Asset Class	Weights	Returns	After Tax
Domestic Equity	31.68%	8.00%	6.57%
International Equity	25.92%	9.00%	4.90%
Domestic Fixed Income	19.89%	4.00%	2.18%
International Fixed Income	2.21%	4.00%	2.18%
Real Estate (Public)	1.75%	8.00%	5.92%
Real Estate (Private)	1.75%	8.00%	5.92%
Hedge Funds	10.60%	8.00%	4.35%
Private Equity	2.30%	13.20%	9.94%
Venture Capital	0.90%	13.20%	7.18%
Natural Resources	1.60%	8.00%	5.92%
Other	1.40%	8.00%	4.35%
Total	*100.00%*	*7.54%*	*4.95%*

* Asset class expected returns from Yale University financial report fiscal year 2008.
Source: 2007 NACUBO Endowment Study.

allocation habits of a broader slice of the endowment world than viewing solely Harvard and Yale.

The asset allocation shown by the NACUBO report shows a more cautious approach to alternative investments as you can see in the Table 11.4. We did not observe expected returns for endowment assets for the NACUBO study. In order to calculate the after-tax return of this group, we applied the gross asset class returns from the Yale report.

The after-tax return of 4.95 percent can be largely explained by a higher allocation to fixed income (which has a high degree of taxation).

CONCLUSIONS

- Back-tested asset allocations influenced institutional investors to reduce allocations to traditional investments (and increase alternatives) at the wrong time.
- Institutions have different goals and tax status from wealthy investors.
- After taxes most institutional portfolios would exhibit expected returns of 4.95 to 6.06 percent.
- Unlike institutions, wealthy investors cannot be bailed out by the government.
- Illiquid investment portfolios caused endowment managers to reduce spending and cut programs in 2008 and 2009.
- Expected returns by institutions for most asset classes are now in the mid-single digits on an after-tax basis.

CHAPTER 12

The Investment Habits
of Wealthy Families

In Chapter 1, I made mention of the Institute for Private Investors (IPI), founded in 1991 by Charlotte Beyer. The Institute is an educational and networking organization for wealthy families and their advisors. The surveys, research, and insights conducted and communicated by IPI are perhaps the best resource available pertaining to the investing habits (and expectations) of the ultrawealthy. We are grateful to IPI for sharing its wealth of historical observations of this niche of investors. In this chapter, we review the asset allocation mix of this group and provide insight into the returns it might expect to receive net of taxes.

In this chapter I must reiterate that the complexities of an ultrawealthy family are vast. Some families encompass five living generations of members, each of whom may live in different states, with varied individual habits of philanthropy and business-related tax deductions. It is important to remember, also, that some families pass assets to the next generation at the death of the last member of the oldest generation. Others pass wealth to younger generations by utilizing annual gifting or large single gifts (upon which they pay a gift tax of 50 percent). Investment time horizon is, of course, an important variable that helps guide the investment strategy of the various entities within the wealthy family.

Some investment entities may be more sensitive to the character of taxation than others. For example, consider the investment objective of a $5 million trust established for a newborn member of a family. This investment pool may have no requirement to produce any income until adulthood, and principal distributions may not occur until the child reaches his or her thirties or forties. This investment pool, therefore, has an investment horizon of two to three decades and should focus on a tax-efficient long-term strategy rather than attempting to strive for specific investment returns in each given year. In other words, the market value of this investment pool in any given quarter or year (especially the early ones) is immaterial to its long-term success. Only when the need to distribute income or principal is within view (five to seven years) does the value of the investment pool become a material factor in determining the impact it will have on the beneficiary.

In order to gain insight into the asset allocation and investment habits of wealthy families, we will share our observations of the 2008 IPI Family Performance Tracking® survey. Each year the Institute asks family members to submit an anonymous survey of their year-end investment results. Members indicate their asset allocation at year-end, investment returns, annual portfolio spending rate, and other specific data pertaining to the character of their portfolios.

For year-end 2007, the survey respondents indicated remarkably high expected returns of 13 percent. When the investors
were surveyed again in October 2008, the expected returns
for the year dropped to –9.68 percent. By year-end 2008, the
survey results showed a mean return of –18.68 percent (net of
fees). Despite the loss, the IPI group as a whole performed
better than many large institutional investors and college
endowments. The high expected return of 13 percent (at the
beginning of the year) coupled with the reality of a loss of
18.68 percent is not an atypical investor sentiment following
the multiyear gains of 2003 to 2007. As a whole this high
return expectation could have been influenced by the perception of above-average long-only manager selection, a high
allocation to alternative investments, or the effect of the previous year (2006) market return of 15.8 percent. However, any
attempt to encapsulate the attitudes of the group would be
inaccurate because the IPI families represent a diverse group
with varied attitudes toward investment and risk.
Acknowledging this fact, we still felt it would be helpful to
share our observations of the survey results.

The asset allocation for year-end 2008 for the IPI group is
shown in Figure 12.1.

At first glance, the average IPI allocation resembles the
investment allocation in the NACUBO survey of the top 100
college endowments. With respect to alternative investments,
however, the IPI allocation to alternatives (44 percent)[1] more
closely resembles the Yale and Harvard allocations.
Alternative investing has been a hot topic of debate among
wealthy investors over the past decade. Some families are
strong advocates for these assets, while others practice a
"zero tolerance" policy toward alternative investments (15
respondents out of 92 IPI members reported no allocation to

FIGURE 12.1

IPI Member Average Asset Allocation in 2008

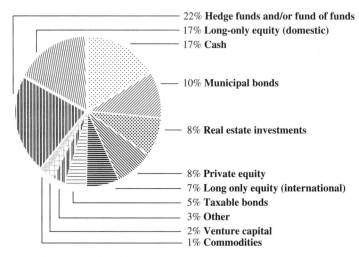

22% **Hedge funds and/or fund of funds**
17% **Long-only equity (domestic)**
17% **Cash**

10% **Municipal bonds**

8% **Real estate investments**

8% **Private equity**
7% **Long only equity (international)**
5% **Taxable bonds**
3% **Other**
2% **Venture capital**
1% **Commodities**

Source: Institute for Private Investors (IPI) Family Performance Tracking® 2008.

the hedge fund category). At year-end 2008 the IPI mix (44 percent allocation to alternatives: 22 percent hedge, 8 percent real estate, 8 percent private equity, 3 percent "other", 2 percent venture capital, 1 percent commodities) was notably higher than the average college endowments (37.8 percent allocation to alternative investments). The IPI alternative allocation also notably dwarfs that of the Big 10 pension funds.

Since 1999, the IPI group has been steadily increasing its allocation to alternative investments and lowering its allocation to long-only equity. This trend mirrors in some ways the trend noted in the 2008 Yale endowment annual report: "In 1988, nearly 75 percent of the endowment was committed to U.S. stocks, bonds, and cash. Today, the [endowment] target allocations call for 14 percent in domestic marketable securities." The changes in allocation from the IPI survey can be seen in Figure 12.2.

FIGURE 12.2

IPI Member Asset Allocation Trends (1997–2008)

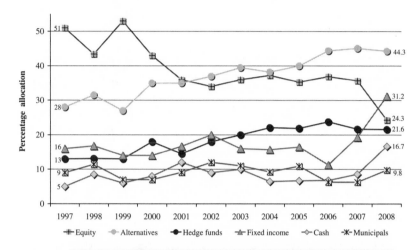

	1997	1998	1999	2000	2001	2002	2003	2004	2005	2006	2007	2008
Long-only Equity	51.0%	43.4%	53.0%	43.0%	36.0%	34.0%	36.0%	37.3%	35.3%	36.9%	35.7%	24.3%
Alternatives*	28.0%	31.5%	27.0%	35.0%	35.0%	37.0%	39.5%	38.2%	40.0%	44.4%	45.1%	44.3%
Hedge funds	13.0%	13.1%	13.0%	18.0%	14.5%	18.0%	20.0%	22.1%	21.9%	23.8%	21.7%	21.6%
Fixed income†	16.0%	16.8%	14.0%	14.0%	16.7%	20.0%	16.0%	15.7%	16.5%	11.3%	19.3%	31.2%
Cash	5.0%	8.5%	6.0%	8.0%	12.0%	9.0%	10.0%	6.5%	6.7%	6.8%	8.6%	16.7%
Municipals	9.0%	11.4%	7.0%	7.0%	9.1%	12.0%	11.0%	9.3%	10.9%	6.3%	6.3%	9.8%

Maximum allocation to asset class over period
Minimum allocation to asset class over period

* Alternatives include hedge funds and/or fund of funds, real estate investments, private equity, venture capital, commodities, and other.
† Fixed income includes municipal bonds, taxable bonds, and cash.

Source: Institute for Private Investors (IPI) Family Performance Tracking® 2008.

Some interesting observations can be made when looking deeper into the 2008 respondent data. The survey included 92 total respondents, 68 of whom reported their portfolio return net of fees. We thought it would be beneficial to study the allocations and portfolio returns of the families with varying allocations to the hedge fund including those who reported no exposure to the hedge fund category. (See Figure 12.3.)

At least in 2008, the heavily hedge-fund allocated portfolios did not outperform those that had no allocation to

FIGURE 12.3

Hedge Funds Did Not Cushion the Downside in 2008

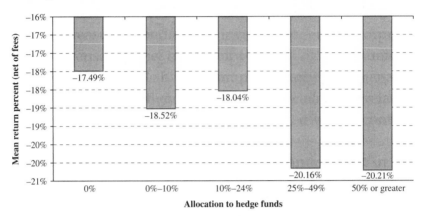

Source: Institute for Private Investors (IPI) Family Performance Tracking® 2008.

hedge. An interesting question was asked in the 2006 and 2007 survey: Do you consider hedge funds to be riskier or risk-reducing investments? In 2006 the respondents voted 75 percent believing hedge funds were risk-reducing to 25 percent believing they were risk-increasing investments. By the 2007 survey, the respondents voted 63 percent risk-reducing and 37 percent risk-increasing. One might assume that after the volatility of 2008 coupled with the accused Ponzi scheme of Bernard Madoff, the respondents might answer this question differently if asked today. Despite the fact that the fees in hedge funds can be tenfold those of traditional investments (when including performance fees) and they employ leverage, this question confirms that the marketing tactics of the hedge fund industry have been remarkably effective. One can also draw the conclusion that the hedge fund industry's historical volatility statistics were misleading to investors in that they disclosed observed as opposed to possible risk. Finally, the tax inefficiency of the hedge fund category has been the primary culprit in the gap separating investor expectations from actual net returns.

EXPECTED AFTER-TAX RETURNS FOR WEALTHY FAMILY TAXABLE PORTFOLIOS

Our work in studying the after-tax equivalent returns of the college endowment and defined benefit pension funds was helpful in determining the expected after-tax returns for the wealthy family portfolios. In the following analysis, we conclude that the expected after-tax return of the year-end 2008 IPI portfolio mix was 4.80 percent.[2] It is important to note that the high allocation to cash at 17 percent of assets can be assumed to earn only nominal rates of return with Treasury bill rates below 1 percent. I would assume that most families do not plan to maintain such a high level of cash as a part of their long-term strategy. In reviewing the allocations excluding cash, the expected after-tax return is somewhat higher at 5.6 percent. This represents approximately a 69 percent after-tax retention rate after taking into account the forward tax rates (effective at year-end 2010) and an implied state tax rate of 6 percent. (*Note*: For this analysis the after-tax return is computed for an ongoing portfolio in which some unrealized portfolio gains remain untaxed.) The postliquidation after-tax return for this portfolio mix is 4.60 percent (including cash). The postliquidation after-tax return on the allocation (excluding cash) is 5.36 percent. The postliquidation rate is useful for families who wish to analyze total portfolio liquidation which may occur in some cases following an estate distribution or in a case in which the family decides to

TABLE 12.1

IPI Family Allocations (Including Cash Allocation)*

Asset Class	Weights	Returns	After Tax Returns
Domestic equity	17.00%	8.00%	6.57%
International equity	7.00%	9.00%	4.90%
Domestic fixed income	5.00%	4.00%	2.18%
Municipal bonds	10.00%	4.75%	4.75%
Real estate (public)	8.00%	8.00%	5.92%
Real estate (private)	0.00%	8.00%	5.92%
Hedge funds	22.00%	8.00%	4.35%
Private equity	8.00%	13.20%	9.94%
Venture capital	2.00%	13.20%	7.18%
Natural resources	1.00%	8.00%	5.92%
Other/cash	20.00%	3.00%	1.63%
Total	*100.00%*	*7.07%*	*4.80%*

* Asset class expected returns are from Yale University financial report fiscal year 2008.
Source: Institute for Private Investors (IPI) Family Performance Tracking® 2008.

deploy portfolio assets toward the purchase of a business. The gross returns for each asset class were extracted from the Yale endowment expected return figures[3] with an implied forward inflation rate of 2 percent. The portfolio mix weightings, expected returns, and after-tax returns are shown in Tables 12.1 and 12.2.

HIGHER RETURNS WITH FEWER MANAGERS

The IPI membership has a wide range of attitudes with respect to the number of money managers they employ in their overall portfolio. At one extreme, one family reported that it employed 83 money managers in 2008. The portfolio

TABLE 12.2

IPI Family Allocations (Excluding Cash Allocation)*

Asset Class	Weights	Returns	After Tax Returns
Domestic equity	21.00%	8.00%	6.57%
International equity	9.00%	9.00%	4.90%
Domestic fixed income	6.00%	4.00%	2.18%
Municipal bonds	13.00%	4.75%	4.75%
Real estate (public)	10.00%	8.00%	5.92%
Real estate (private)	0.00%	8.00%	5.92%
Hedge funds	27.00%	8.00%	4.35%
Private equity	10.00%	13.20%	9.94%
Venture capital	3.00%	13.20%	7.18%
Natural resources	1.00%	8.00%	5.92%
Other/cash	0.00%	3.00%	1.63%
Total	*100.00%*	*8.10%*	*5.60%*

* Asset class expected returns are from Yale University financial report fiscal year 2008.

Source: Institute for Private Investors (IPI) Family Performance Tracking® 2008.

return for this family was –22 percent for 2008. At the opposite extreme, four families reported that they have 100 percent of their money managed by a single manager. The mean return for 2008 for these four families was –17.25, an outperformance of nearly 5 percent compared to the family with the most managers. In general, the survey found a trend of higher returns with fewer managers. (See Figure 12.4.)

TAX STRATEGIES EMPLOYED BY IPI FAMILIES

The various tax minimization strategies used are listed in Table 12.3 by the percentage of respondents who claimed using a particular strategy.

FIGURE 12.4

Higher Returns with Fewer Managers (2008)

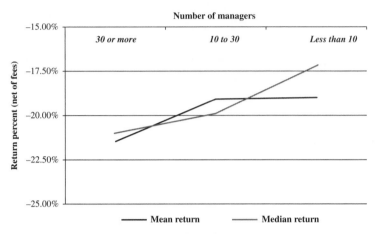

Source: Institute for Private Investors (IPI) Family Performance Tracking® 2008.

TABLE 12.3

Tax Strategies Employed by IPI Families

Respondents	Strategy Employed
61%	Tax loss harvesting
61%	Asset location strategies
57%	Family limited partnership
31%	Life insurance trust
23%	Structures or defective grantor annuity trusts
21%	Customized tax efficient index
8%	Other
2%	Prepaid variable forward contracts

Source: Institute for Private Investors (IPI) Family Performance Tracking® 2008.

WHARTON GLOBAL FAMILY ALLIANCE

In 2008 a group of researchers from the Wharton School of Business at the University of Pennsylvania released a paper with findings of the investment strategies of single family offices. The research presented findings that highlight the nuances of investment management for U.S. and non-U.S. families. Additionally, the research was segregated into subgroups containing those with less than $1 billion in assets and those with above $1 billion in assets. The minimum size of the family portfolios studied by the Wharton Global Family Alliance (WGFA) was $100 million in investable assets.

Notable observations on the role of the family office were presented in the study. We were most interested in the study's results regarding the investment habits of these families. We have made reference at numerous points in this book to the necessity for the investment portfolios to be structured in acknowledgment of the connectivity of the various generations served by a large family investment portfolio. The WGFA study found that in both the United States and in Europe, many family offices cater to up to four generations of members. In its research the WGFA found that the average single family office served 13 households containing 40 family members and 2 to 3 generations.[4]

With respect to investment objectives, the U.S. respondents to the survey reported in the highest numbers that their investment objectives favored a balanced approach. The investment objectives ranked by the highest respondent percentage are presented in Table 12.4.

In general the study found that U.S. families reported a more aggressive attitude toward investment objectives than their European counterparts. (In my opinion, a 20 percent allocation to hedge funds is more aggressive than a 20 percent allocation to the family business.) Wealth management and money-related issues were found to be the most valued aspect of the family office. Additional benefits of the family office were conflict-free advice, confidentiality, sophisticated

TABLE 12.4

Wharton Global Family Alliance (WGFA)
Family Investment Objectives

Respondents	Strategy employed
35%	Balanced approach
34%	Grow
10%	Preserve
14%	Aggressively grow
5%	Preserve very conservatively
2%	Didn't answer

Source: Wharton Global Family Alliance (WGFA).

investment, estate planning, family governance, charitable
and philanthropic issues, and education of family members.

The respondents in the survey reported asset allocation
levels and were grouped by asset size and location. (See
Table 12.5.)

TABLE 12.5

Asset Allocation Levels—United States and European
Investors

Asset Type	U.S. Billionaires	European Billionaires	U.S. Millionaires	European Millionaires
Equities	47%	25%	45%	30%
Fixed income	16%	15%	15%	17%
Hedge funds	20%	12%	12%	13%
Private equity	9%	12%	9%	12%
Real estate	4%	11%	10%	18%
Commodities/timber	3%	4%	4%	3%
Principal investments in companies	0%	20%	5%	6%
Other (wine, art, collectibles, etc.)	1%	2%	1%	2%

Source: Wharton Global Family Alliance (WGFA).

In observing the differences between the U.S. families and their European counterparts, we thought it was notable that European billionaires reported a 20 percent allocation to a principal investment in a company compared to 0 percent for the U.S. billionaires. Another notable difference was observed with respect to investments in real estate. The U.S. millionaire category reported an 10 percent allocation to real estate (highest), while the U.S. billionaire portfolios contained only a 4 percent allocation to real estate (lowest). Exposure to hedge funds was highest among the U.S. billionaires with a 20 percent allocation. The lowest exposure to hedge funds was 12 percent reported by the European billionaires and the U.S. millionaires.

One of the recommendations of the WGFA study was, "Keep it simple," suggesting that the more complex the portfolio and number of holdings, the more difficult the job of performing adequate governance, reporting, and education. The Wharton survey was not the only "think tank" of the wealthy to sound an alarm about investment complexity. The theme of the Institute for Private Investors spring 2008 investor conference was, "The Return to Simplicity." I suspect that private investors and large institutional investors will continue to fiercely debate the merits of complex versus straightforward or traditional investing. My recommendation to wealthy families is to definitively declare their attitude as to the basic drivers of wealth creation and then adopt an investment strategy that captures the essence of their beliefs.

Carefully selecting one or a few managers is often better than having many managers, which cannot be supervised and monitored as effectively.

CONCLUSIONS

- In 2008 the average taxable wealthy investor had a higher allocation (44 percent), to alternative investments than the average nontaxable college endowments, (38 percent) or pension funds (10 percent).
- Carefully selecting one or a few money managers is often better than having many managers, who cannot be supervised and monitored as effectively.
- Keep investment strategies simple, straightforward, and transparent. Complex and opaque asset mixes do not produce superior after-tax returns.

CHAPTER 13

Multigenerational Planning

CAN A PORTFOLIO SUSTAIN A FAMILY'S LIFESTYLE ACROSS MULTIPLE GENERATIONS?

Nearly every culture has some version of the phrase, "Shirtsleeves to shirtsleeves in three generations," which highlights the unpleasant fact that many wealthy families are unsuccessful in preserving the wealth or lifestyle of the founding generation. There are certainly a myriad philosophical and attitudinal factors concerning this statement, which I'll happily avoid in this chapter. What I hope to communicate is the mathematical challenges of wealthy families successfully preserving their lifestyle for future generations. It is important to establish the parameters of the family's definition of "lifestyle" in this exercise. In the strictest interpretation, lifestyle preservation may mean occupying the Biltmore estate as a residence (or a comparable home), a Gulfstream V jet on call at all times, and a 200-foot private yacht with crew.

Before delving into the math, consider how few families have actually been able to preserve and protect both the wealth and the lifestyle of their founding generation. One might consider the British royal family as a good example of maintaining its status. But there are two notable differences between the royals and other wealthy families. First, the royal family was not subjected to the British tax system until 1992, when the queen voluntarily agreed to begin paying taxes. The second notable difference can be best observed by viewing the family tree of Queen Elizabeth II back through history. Only one branch of the tree—the direct heir to the throne—inherited the bulk of the wealth, land, and lifestyle of its predecessor generation. Nonheirs to the throne received a disproportionately smaller inheritance than the future king or queen.

Wealthy families of today experience quite the opposite dynamic to the royal family in that they pay taxes at the highest rates on their income and estates. However, an even greater dilution in wealth occurs with the natural division among siblings in increasing numbers throughout subsequent generations. The founding family, often a husband and wife, enjoys a certain income and lifestyle from their original portfolio. At their death, about half the portfolio is lost to estate taxes with the other half being divided among two, three, or more children. At the death of the second generation, the estate tax is assessed once again, and the division of assets multiplies among an exponentially larger third generation. The process repeats once more as the assets pass to the fourth generation.

The purpose of this chapter is to observe the mathematical effects of portfolio spending rates, income taxes, estate taxes, inflation, and the division of assets among members of subsequent generations. Our research has concluded that preserving the lifestyle of the founding generation (meaning the same inflation-adjusted spending rate is available to each heir) for three generations solely from portfolio income is almost a mathematical impossibility given the current taxation structure of the United States. I make no judgment as to the fairness or unfairness of this fact but feel that this is an extremely important reality which must be dealt with by wealthy families and their advisors. In studying the effects of these variables, families will begin to refine certain aspects of their plan. The most notable (and controllable) is the spending rate they choose to make available to subsequent generations.

In conducting our research on the effects of wealth transfer across multiple generations, we built a model that would allow us to observe varying tax rates, spending rates, inflation, estate taxes, fees, and portfolio returns. Our multigenerational spending matrix (MSM) allows us to plug different assumptions about each of these data points into a spreadsheet that calculates what generation and when the heirs of a founding family will run out of money. In reality, it is unlikely that any of the above variables could remain constant for a period of 84 years as presented in our study. What is important is to formulate reasonable ranges or averages that are helpful in determining the success, failure, or longevity of a particular wealth transfer strategy. This tool has been helpful to me in the advice I deliver to clients in that I believe it has prevented families from engaging in estate planning with overly optimistic assumptions.

The reason this chapter is toward the end of the book is that the study of this material is predicated on a thorough understanding of the material in the previous chapters. Once investors have developed realistic attitudes toward expected return, taxation, fees, and asset allocation, they are ready to ponder the effects of the arithmetic across multiple generations of their family.

THE YALE PORTFOLIO

In considering the portfolio strategies available to clients for multigenerational planning, it is worth examining the Yale portfolio popularized by the university's endowment chief David Swensen as his strategy is remarkably similar to that found to be most common with the Institute for Private Investors. Figure 13.1 (on pages 220-221) is a simulation of this strategy using our multigenerational spending matrix that we ran for a client who was 67 years old.

If you look at the "assumptions" box in the upper left corner, you will see a number of variables that should be explained. The starting age of the client was 67, and it is usually when clients are in their sixties that they begin contemplating retirement and living off their assets as opposed to off the profits from their businesses. If this model were based on a single business with stock and bond assets as a supplement, it would look completely different. Below the starting age variable, life expectancy is 20 years. For someone who is over 65, the average life expectancy is 84 years in the United States, but because an estate plan generally considers both a husband and a wife, there are actually two life expectancies to consider before the second generation receives its inheritance. For that reason and because this client had longevity in his family we kept the estimate at 20 years or an age at death of 87.

The inflation rate variable is essential because it can dramatically affect when heirs will run out of money if they want to maintain the same lifestyle as the founding family. When you calculate what 50 hours on a private jet and a week on a yacht would be for eight great-grandchildren, you begin to understand the mathematical challenges of preserving the wealth not only because you are splitting the money between a greater number of people with each generation, but also because the inflation rate for luxury goods such as private jets, yachts, and beluga caviar tends to be higher than the standard consumer price index. That said, it's not so grim to contemplate if you can preserve some of the portfolio for four generations, maybe the great-grandchildren aren't flying private jets, but perhaps they're flying first class. For the inflation rate I've inputted 3.43 percent, the historical average rate for the past 85 years.

The spending rate variable is of course a key one to discuss with clients. A 3 percent rate on a $100 million portfolio (quite reasonable in my opinion) amounts to $3 million in the first year of retirement for the husband and wife of a founding family. Bear in mind though that to maintain the same lifestyle, the spending increases with inflation, so that $3,000,000 of retirement spending in 2010 is $3,209,329 by year three (2012) with a 3.43 percent inflation rate and $5,889,138 by year 20 (2030). This inflation becomes even more onerous as we move on to the second generation if we assume the second is like the first in that now there are two sets of husbands and wives or four people with the same spending rate, so by 2032 the spending rate of the four heirs in the second generation is $12,600,123.

Just as important is the effective tax rate variable. Although the top income tax rate is currently 35 percent and

FIGURE 13.1

MSM–Yale Endowment Simulation

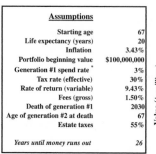

Assumptions	
Starting age	**67**
Life expectancy (years)	**20**
Inflation	**3.43%**
Portfolio beginning value	**$100,000,000**
Generation #1 spend rate *	**3%**
Tax rate (effective)	**30%**
Rate of return (variable)	**9.43%**
Fees (gross)	**1.50%**
Death of generation #1	**2030**
Age of generation #2 at death	**67**
Estate taxes	**55%**
Years until money runs out	**26**

* Generation #1 spend rate is calculated on the initial portfolio value of $100,000,000. The dollar amount is held constant throughout the life of all generations of the family, adjusted for inflation. The assumption is that the lifestyle (i.e., total amount of spending adjusted for inflation) of the first generation is preserved for and maintained by all future generations of the family.

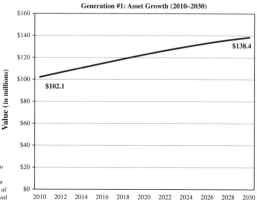

Generation #1: Asset Growth (2010–2030)

$138.4

$102.1

Generation #1: Husband and wife—estate divided by two children

	2010	2012	2014	2016	2018	2020
Age of generation #1	Age 67	Age 69	Age 71	Age 73	Age 75	Age 77
Beginning value	$100,000,000	$104,206,272	$108,416,096	$112,599,385	$116,720,778	$120,738,943
Portfolio returns	9,430,000	9,826,651	10,223,638	10,618,122	11,006,769	11,385,682
Spending *	(3,000,000)	(3,209,329)	(3,433,265)	(3,672,826)	(3,929,103)	(4,203,262)
Fees	(1,500,000)	(1,563,094)	(1,626,241)	(1,688,991)	(1,750,812)	(1,811,084)
Taxes	(2,829,000)	(2,947,995)	(3,067,091)	(3,185,437)	(3,302,031)	(3,415,705)
Ending value	$102,101,000	$106,312,504	$110,513,136	$114,670,253	$118,745,601	$122,694,574

Generation #2: Two children—estate divided by four grandchildren

	2032	2034	2036	2038	2040	2042
Age of generation #2	Age 68	Age 70	Age 72	Age 74	Age 76	Age 78
Beginning value	$53,286,297	$32,586,055	$7,886,722	$0	$0	$0
Portfolio returns	5,024,898	3,072,865	743,718	0	0	0
Spending *	(12,600,123)	(13,479,316)	(8,289,023)	(0)	0	0
Fees	(799,294)	(488,791)	(118,301)	(0)	0	0
Taxes	(1,507,469)	(921,859)	(223,115)	(0)	0	0
Ending value	$43,404,308	$20,768,954	$0	($0)	$0	$0

Generation #3: Four grandchildren—estate divided by eight great grandchildren

	2052	2054	2056	2058	2060	2062
Age of generation #3	Age 67	Age 69	Age 71	Age 73	Age 75	Age 77
Beginning value	$0	$0	$0	$0	$0	$0
Portfolio returns	0	0	0	0	0	0
Spending *	0	0	0	0	0	0
Fees	0	0	0	0	0	0
Taxes	0	0	0	0	0	0
Ending value	$0	$0	$0	$0	$0	$0

Generation #4: Eight great grandchildren—estate divided by sixteen heirs

	2074	2076	2078	2080	2082	2084
Age of generation #4	Age 68	Age 70	Age 72	Age 74	Age 76	Age 78
Beginning value	$0	$0	$0	$0	$0	$0
Portfolio returns	0	0	0	0	0	0
Spending *	0	0	0	0	0	0
Fees	0	0	0	0	0	0
Taxes	0	0	0	0	0	0
Ending value	$0	$0	$0	$0	$0	$0

Source: © 2009 Niall J. Gannon.

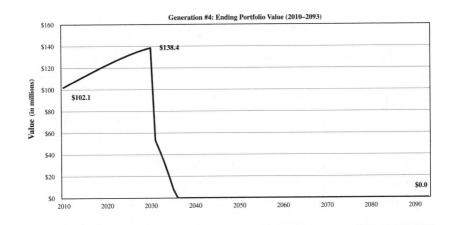

Generation #4: Ending Portfolio Value (2010–2093)

	2022	2024	2026	2028	2030		
	Age 79	Age 81	Age 83	Age 85	Age 87	Generation #1 End Value	$138,424,666
	$124,605,790	$128,265,596	$131,654,025	$134,697,032	$137,309,640	Estate taxes	($76,133,566)
	11,750,326	12,095,446	12,414,975	12,701,930	12,948,299	Amount to heirs	$62,291,100
	(4,496,551)	(4,810,305)	(5,145,951)	(5,505,017)	(5,889,138)	Portfolio per heir (2)	$31,145,550
	(1,869,087)	(1,923,984)	(1,974,810)	(2,020,455)	(2,059,645)	Average annual inflation	
	(3,525,098)	(3,628,634)	(3,724,492)	(3,810,579)	(3,884,490)	adjusted spending per heir	$1,838,117
	$126,465,380	$129,998,119	$133,223,746	$136,062,910	$138,424,666		

	2044	2046	2048	2050	2051		
	Age 80	Age 82	Age 84	Age 86	Age 87	Generation #2 End Value	$0
	$0	$0	$0	$0	$0	Estate taxes	$0
	0	0	0	0	0	Amount to heirs	$0
	0	0	0	0	0	Portfolio per heir (4)	$0
	0	0	0	0	0	Average annual inflation	
	0	0	0	0	0	adjusted spending per heir	$0
	$0	$0	$0	$0	$0		

	2064	2066	2068	2070	2072		
	Age 79	Age 81	Age 83	Age 85	Age 87	Generation #3 End Value	$0
	$0	$0	$0	$0	$0	Estate taxes	$0
	0	0	0	0	0	Amount to heirs	$0
	0	0	0	0	0	Portfolio per heir (8)	$0
	0	0	0	0	0	Average annual inflation	
	0	0	0	0	0	adjusted spending per heir	$0
	$0	$0	$0	$0	$0		

	2086	2088	2090	2092	2093		
	Age 80	Age 82	Age 84	Age 86	Age 87	Generation #4 End Value	$0
	$0	$0	$0	$0	$0	Estate taxes	$0
	0	0	0	0	0	Amount to heirs	$0
	0	0	0	0	0	Portfolio per heir (16)	$0
	0	0	0	0	0	Average annual inflation	
	0	0	0	0	0	adjusted spending per heir	$0
	$0	$0	$0	$0	$0		

will revert to 39.6 percent at the end of 2010, it is important to estimate what the tax rate would likely be for the Yale portfolio. Since Yale runs an endowment that is tax-sheltered, taxes are not a factor in David Swensen's mind, yet they should be for wealthy investors. Our own calculations indicate that the combined asset allocation of Yale's portfolio would be taxed at a 30 percent effective rate, thanks to some holdings that would be taxed at the lower long-term capital gains tax rate. And since his allocations to stocks, bonds, and alternative investments such as hedge funds are similar to the average wealthy investor, it is reasonable to make this comparison. As we shall see in the following example though, by shifting assets to municipal bonds, the gross return declines but the after-tax capture rate increases. So the model facilitates good conversation and suggests thought-provoking changes that could be made because a lower gross pretax return on the portfolio. With lower gross returns, lower fees but a higher after-tax capture rate, these modifications could actually allow the portfolio to last longer.

The portfolio rate of return (ROR) is based on Swensen's own future estimates for the Yale endowment's portfolio—6 percent real returns—which translates into 9.43 percent nominal preinflation returns in this spending matrix. Of course, the Yale endowment has exceeded this return by a significant margin in recent decades, but there's no indication that the endowment's past performance is repeatable, and evidently Swensen doesn't think it is. Moreover, Swensen is acknowledged as one of the world's best investors and has access to some of the best hedge funds and money managers. So assuming a 9.43 percent rate of return for high net worth investors who do not have Swensen's access or acumen is being generous.

Fees are an obvious detriment to portfolio returns, and the lower they are, the better. Expenses, in fact, are one of the few things about performance that are within investors' control. Yet wealthy investors seeking to emulate the Yale portfolio are at a huge fee disadvantage because of the portfolio's investments in high-cost hedge funds. According to the IPI, the average wealthy investor has a 44 percent weighting in alternative investments, close to the Yale model. As a consequence, we've calculated the average gross fee for the entire portfolio to be 1.50 percent (inclusive of consultant fees, custody fees, trading costs, and manager fees).

The death of the founding family couple is anticipated to occur in 2030 in this matrix, 20 years after the 2010 retirement as per the life expectancy column, and we assumed that the second generation heirs would also be receiving the bulk of their wealth at age 67. This of course assumes that no gifting is made to the children during the life of the founders, which, as we shall soon see, is very advantageous taxwise. Finally, for estate taxes we inputted 55 percent. Although in 2009 the top rate is 45 percent and will drop, remarkably, to 0 percent in 2010 because of quirks in the tax code, by 2011 tax rates will revert to their previous 55 percent. All of this reveals how completely unpredictable estate tax rates can be. And yet obviously they can have a huge impact.

As we can see from the results of these inputs for the Yale portfolio, the founding first generation's portfolio has a starting value of $100 million with the couple at age 67 and an ending value of $138,424,666 after all taxes, fees, and inflation when both parents have died by age 87. Unfortunately, the 55 percent estate tax rate consumes $76,133,566 of that, and the two second generation heirs of the founders consequently inherit $62,291,100 when they are age 67. If those two heirs seek to maintain the same lifestyle as their parents, then the portfolio will be quickly depleted thanks to spending, fees, and inflation, so that by age 72 or 2036 the second generation's money will completely have disappeared.

What would it take for this portfolio with current tax rates and fees intact to last through the lifespan of the fourth generation's eight heirs? An annualized return of 18.75 percent, according to the multigenerational tool's calculations, which would produce a $67,111,209 end value to the portfolio in the year 2093. Even Warren Buffett would have trouble earning such a return in the current environment. For high net worth investors, clearly the Yale portfolio may not be enough.

UNCONVENTIONAL CONVENTIONAL THINKING

Since the average wealthy investor has significant exposure to high-cost, high-turnover alternative investments like hedge funds, it's worth considering how a more conventional portfolio of 50 percent stocks and 50 percent high-quality municipal bonds would perform in a similar scenario. Call it an alternative to the alternatives or unconventional conventional thinking, but if we examine Table 13.1, we can see that the results generally improve.

Although for space purposes we have not replicated the entire multigenerational spending matrix, our calculations reveal that the portfolio's ending value for the first generation would be $150,082,948, more than $11 million greater than that of the Yale portfolio. Part of the reason for this is the lower effective portfolio tax rate of 10 percent that a 50 percent

TABLE 13.1

MSM–Core Balanced Simulation

Assumptions	
Starting age	67
Life expectancy (years)	20
Inflation	3.43%
Portfolio beginning value	$100,000,000
Generation #1 spend rate	3%
Tax rate (effective)	10%
Rate of return (variable)	6.50%
Fees (gross)	0.48%
Death of generation #1	2027
Age of generation #2 at death	67
Estate taxes	55%
Years until money runs out	27

weighting in tax-free municipal bonds brings. Another reason is the lower gross fees of 0.48 percent of assets for a core balanced manager.

As a consequence of this shift, though, the pretax return drops to 6.5 percent—a combined return of 4.5 percent for municipal bonds and 8.5 percent for stocks. Unfortunately, the estate tax of 55 percent still consumes a large chunk of portfolio returns, and assets run out in 27 years or by age 73 of the second generation or 2037, one year later than the Yale portfolio. But an additional factor to consider is than this will in all likelihood be a less volatile, lower-risk portfolio than the Yale one as the volatility of the municipal bonds is offset by the stability of principal at maturity. An additional bonus is that a large part of the spending by investors will be covered by a steady stream of guaranteed income paid by the bonds. By contrast, a highly leveraged hedge fund investment's return will be considerably more unpredictable.

What if the client is more frugal and decides to reduce the spending rate to 2 percent? The money runs out by 2043 or age 79 of the second generation—an increase of six years in the portfolio's life. (See Table 13.2.)

If a client were very frugal and kept spending at only 1 percent, then the money wouldn't run out until 2055 and would actually make it to the third generation of the family, but such a spending plan might be too austere for many high net worth investors.

What would it take for the wealth in a 50 percent stock/50 percent muni portfolio to survive four generations with a 3 percent spending rate? A 13.5 percent annualized return with an ending value of approximately $1.5 billion in 2093. With muni yields at a low 4.5 percent currently such a return would be almost as highly improbable as the 18.75

TABLE 13.2

MSM–Core Balance with 2 Percent Spend
Rate Simulation

Assumptions	
Starting age	67
Life expectancy (years)	20
Inflation	3.43%
Portfolio beginning value	$100,000,000
Generation #1 spend rate	2%
Tax rate (effective)	10%
Rate of return (variable)	6.50%
Fees (gross)	0.48%
Death of generation #1	2027
Age of generation #2 at death	67
Estate taxes	55%
Years until money runs out	*33*

percent required return for the Yale portfolio to survive. With a low 1 percent spending rate, the muni/stock portfolio would need a 10.4 percent return to survive, still a tough return to hit in our current environment given the light we have shed on fees and taxes.

Of course portfolio returns depend a lot on the economic and financial conditions at the time when clients start to invest. If bond yields were much higher and price/earnings ratios were much lower than they are today, then sustainable double-digit returns would become possible.

GIFTING STRATEGIES

Of course, the biggest ongoing expense for wealthy families will likely be estate taxes. One key strategy the spending matrix ignores is gifting to heirs during the lifetime of the founding family. Wealthy families have the ability to make annual gifts of $13,000 per heir per donor tax-free, or $26,000 gifted every year from a husband and wife to each of their children. For the family with two children in our example, that amounts to $52,000 a year tax-free and probably a lot more than that as soon as grandchildren arrive. With two children and four grandchildren, that amounts to $156,000 a year tax-free. This gift-tax exclusion should be given if possible using appreciated stock of the founder's business to maximize the appreciation potential outside the donor's estate. In addition to the annual gift exclusion, families also have access to a lifetime exclusion which in 2008 was $1 million. The lifetime exclusion should be considered as an asset to be gifted to younger generations well in advance of a liquidity event.

Paying the gift tax so that heirs can have the money right away makes a lot of sense. In a scenario where the founding family knows their $100 million portfolio may grow much larger than $100 million by the time of their deaths, a couple may figure there is enough money to give a significant portion of their wealth to their children before retirement so that the capital appreciation in the portfolio can occur outside their estate and not be subject to estate taxes.

Often parents in their sixties and seventies want to give their children, in their forties and fifties, the money before they die. Mathematically, it also is advantageous. Gift tax is assessed on what the beneficiaries ultimately receive, but the estate tax is assessed on what the descendent generation inherits on a gross basis. The estate tax effectively taxes both a bequest and the tax on the bequest. Here's a simplified example: If the $100 million of an individual's estate has an estate tax rate of 50 percent, the IRS gets $50 million, and the heirs get $50 million. But note that the IRS has taxed the entire $100 million, not just the $50 million that the heirs receive. But the gift tax is paid by the donor on the net amount the recipients of the gift are to receive. So if the donors planned to give their children $66 million, they would pay the IRS $33 million or 50 percent of the net gift amount before giving it to their children.

Since the founding family generally wouldn't want to gift all of their assets to their children because it would leave them nothing, some sort of balance should be achieved to both minimize taxes and leave the founders enough money to live comfortably. Because such gifting strategies are so individualized, it is hard to model an example in our multigenerational spending matrix. Suffice it to say that gifting to heirs will add a few years onto the matrix so that the portfolio's value will run out later rather than sooner. And advisors should take the time to design a customized gifting strategy for families to stretch the value out as long as possible.

PRIVATE EQUITY

After reading the above, it is clear that if clients truly want to preserve their wealth through several generations, it will take some creative thinking on their parts. Perhaps the best way to sustain the founding family's legacy is to return to the original business-oriented philosophy that created it. Launching or investing in small to mid-sized private businesses may in some cases be the best solution. Although investing in a private equity fund can be expensive, returns are expected to be high going forward—as high as 15 percent according to Yale's Swensen, because prices for private businesses are cheap, and smaller businesses can grow more quickly than larger mature ones. Note that these private equity opportunities are more likely to occur in the early stage businesses rather than in the leveraged buyout sector. Moreover, private equity investing tends to be tax-efficient as turnover is low and gains are generally taxed at the long-term capital gains rate which is currently 15 percent.

But some wealthy families have taken a more hands-on approach to private equity investing. Rather than paying 2 percent of assets plus 20 percent of profits to invest in a private equity fund, successful winemaker Bonny Meyer created Meyer Family Enterprises in Napa Valley, California, with her family office CEO Patrick Gleeson. Gleeson shared with me that the family typically invests in eight private businesses at a time and plans to hold them anywhere from two years to forever depending on how much they like the business. If held forever, returns come from ongoing dividends. The family seeks to generate 10 to 12 percent returns after fees and taxes, enough in their view to sustain the family's wealth through multiple generations.

But the Meyers don't just invest in any private business. They want to be involved in companies for which they have a true passion and that are in fields of industry in which family members possess either some expertise or interest. The goal is not to impose a future career upon the Meyer children but to provide them with the chance to get involved with new businesses they're excited about. "It's not possible to engineer outcomes for the second or third generation but to give them chances," says Gleeson. "If you engineer opportunities, the children are more likely to take a hold of them because it's their idea. Bonny Meyer wants to embrace the entrepreneurial spirit and allow the kids to fail and succeed with their passion and with their areas of interest."

So each family member has his or her favorite private equity investment. One favorite, SureHarvest, taps into Bonny's environmentalist beliefs and her expertise in food and wine while also appealing to her eldest son who is an avowed "techie." A software company, SureHarvest has developed a tracking system and bar codes for food and beverage products that tell suppliers and retailers such as Wal-Mart and Costco what the environmental footprint of a product is all along its supply chain—from the fields where, say, the wine grapes are grown all the way to the shelves in the store. Given the Meyer's expertise in the wine industry, it should come as no surprise that SureHarvest currently serves more than 50 percent of the $20 billion California grape and winery market through a sustainability management information system (MIS). Such an investment perfectly leverages the Meyers' industry expertise.

Of course, there are unique risks to having a portfolio heavily invested in private equity. There is a lack of diversification and the high business risk of investing in smaller companies that may not be firmly established or may be dependent on just a handful of customers to survive. So surely some of the family's wealth should be invested in more conventional stocks and bonds. But building businesses is in all likelihood what made the family wealthy in the first place, and to sustain and reinvigorate that entrepreneurial spirit with fresh blood could be just what the family needs to keep it wealthy through subsequent generations.

CONCLUSIONS

- It is difficult for a wealthy family to maintain the income level of the founding generation for more than three generations because of estate taxes and multiplication of heirs.
- Wealthy families should calculate how many generations their money should last with their current spending habits after deducting fees and taxes, and they should plan accordingly.
- Lowering the family's spending rate or adjusting the portfolio toward more tax-efficient investments can add to the number of years a portfolio will last.
- The gift tax is less onerous than the estate tax because it is assessed on the net amount received by the heirs rather than the gross amount of the estate.
- Direct investments in private companies can help maintain the family's entrepreneurial spirit.

CHAPTER 14

A Case Study to Prove the Correlation between Earnings and Stock Price

Jones Pharma

In this chapter I'll prove once more that there is a strong correlation between long-term stock prices and earnings growth. Jones Pharma or JMED, as I will henceforth call it, was selected for a number of reasons:

1. JMED was named one of the best-performing stocks of the 1990s by the *New York Times.*
2. Dennis Jones, founder of JMED, contributed to this study with his personal experience of launching the company in 1981 and selling it in a merger in 2000.
3. The public record of the initial public offering (IPO) in 1986 along with the sale of the company in 2000 made it an excellent specimen for the study of a successful public company.
4. Dennis Jones hired me as his financial advisor in 1996, so I have an intimate knowledge of the history and workings of his business.

I dedicate this chapter to Dennis and Judy Jones, their family and employees who helped shape this classic tale of free market success. Throughout the chapter I'll make reference to notable events in the history of the company, including the important fundamentals of sales and earnings growth. The study of JMED will hopefully serve as a template for other wealthy families who I urge to chronicle their founding business story if it does not already exist. Most members of a wealthy family are aware of the amount of their wealth. Fewer are truly aware of how they got there in the first place.

Founded in 1981, JMED was a manufacturer of endocrine pharmaceuticals, nutritional supplements, and critical care drugs. The company was named by several analysts in the 1990s as the first of the "emerging specialty pharmaceutical companies" because it carried out virtually no research and development. Instead, Jones focused on acquisitions of products that were deemed to be too small for the major pharmaceutical companies. Dennis Jones once told a group of analysts, "$10 million in annual sales is a rounding error to Eli Lilly." By focusing on these "orphan" drugs, Jones was able to focus on the manufacturing and marketing of products without the costs, delays, and headaches of R&D and drug patents. The story of efficiency and tenacity that ran through every fiber of the company traced its genesis back to the hometown of its founder where he would develop and sharpen his skills for business.

Born to Glenn and Thelma Jones, farmers from Terre Haute, Indiana, who moved to the small town of Marshall, Illinois, Dennis Jones first practiced the art of business while employed by his father's farm equipment business. The lessons he learned would stay with him through his entire business career: Every task, business, or industry has inefficiencies that can be exploited for the mutual benefit of the worker and the customer. After high school and a brief tour in the U.S. Marine Corps, Dennis landed his first sales job with SIG Laboratories, through his mentor, Jim O'Neal. From SIG Labs, Jones and O'Neal would cofound another company, O'Neal, Jones, and Feldman (OJF). The company was subsequently sold in the mid-1970s to Chromalloy American Corporation.

Fresh from this experience, Dennis and his wife, Judy, gathered their entire savings, $100,000, along with an additional $200,000 from friends and founded Jones Medical Industries in 1981. From the beginning, Dennis's goal was to build the company, take it public, and then sell it. The early years would include the acquisition of simple therapeutic compounds and nutritional supplements, repackaging them under their own trademark, and marketing them diligently. Gradually, the company would begin acquiring selected "mature" branded pharmaceutical products that had been on the market for a long time and had since slowed their market growth rates. Jones knew that the major pharmaceutical companies could focus on only a few blockbuster drugs at any given time and that there was always a portion of their drug portfolio that was neglected through poor marketing or stagnant prices. On average, through acquisitions and comarketing agreements, he was able to acquire these "orphaned" drugs for 60 percent of their annual revenues. Because the newly acquired drugs were strategically marketed to physicians and hospitals, the patient and caregiver familiarity increased as did the sales and profits.

By the second quarter of 1986, annual revenues were on pace to hit $6 million. Jones decided it was time to retire some outstanding debt, raise some investment capital, and make an initial public offering at $6 per share on the Nasdaq stock market under the ticker symbol JMED.

Accounting for the six stock splits following the IPO in 1986 until the sale of the company in 2000, the split-adjusted IPO price was $0.54 per share. The closing trade on August 30, 2000, was $35.75. One of the most important points of this chapter is to illustrate the two most important dates relative to an investment: the day it is acquired and the day it is sold. All other days in between are irrelevant in the wealth creation process, except of course for the compounding of dividends. We observe volatility, corrections, and bull phases of JMED stock in this chapter but I continually repeat the point that long-term investing is about getting from point A to point B in the most efficient manner. Because Dennis, the majority of his employees, and certain public investors understood this, they were rewarded with a handsome investment return. Early investors who provided the seed capital at the company's founding in 1981 experienced a greater one. An undisturbed $10,000 investment in founders stock of Jones Pharma saw their investment rise to $45 million by the time the company was sold.

The Jones Pharma example also stresses that over long periods of time the primary driver of equity prices is the earnings growth delivered to shareholders as a function of the price the shareholders paid for those earnings. Unfortunately, chart patterns, index trends, presidential cycles, Super Bowl theories, efficient markets, and bull and bear markets are in most cases distractions to the individual investor, but they tend to receive more attention than earnings. I believe, as do many fundamental analysts and money managers, that stock prices over the short term are essentially arbitrary. The earnings trend is the primary driver of shareholder return

FIGURE   14.1

Jones Pharma Incorporated (JMED) Stock Price
versus Earnings

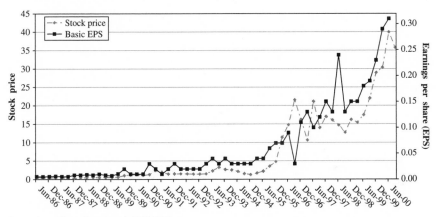

Source: Jones Pharma Incorporated, 1985–2000.

given that the purchase price paid for company stock is reasonable. To illustrate the link between sales and earnings, please review Figure 14.1 and Table 14.1 showing JMED earnings and stock price from IPO to the last day of trading.

From IPO to its last day of trading, JMED demonstrated a compound net income growth rate of 28.90 percent which translated into a compound annual stock price growth rate of 34.45 percent. In order to properly evaluate the factors that contributed to the periods, we'll study them in two phases. First, we'll review the ongoing operations as a stand-alone company until May 2000. In May 2000 discussions commenced between Jones and King Pharmaceuticals which led to King's acquisition of Jones. The "deal premium" that Dennis and his officers received for the company should be studied separately because most companies arguably have two proper valuations at any given time: stand-alone valuation and acquisition or buyout valuation.

TABLE 14.1

Jones Pharma Incorporated (JMED) Annual Sales/Net Income

Yearly	Jun-00	Dec-99	Dec-98	Dec-97	Dec-96	Dec-95	Dec-94	Dec-93	Dec-92	Dec-91	Dec-90	Dec-89	Dec-88	Dec-87	Dec-86	Dec-85
Revenues	97.36	132.54	103.41	88.78	64.18	74.79	47.55	43.22	24.06	20.51	19.65	13.32	10.25	6.79	5.79	4.50
Net income	39.31	48.94	42.34	31.97	18.14	12.39	5.74	6.41	3.73	3.29	2.83	1.59	1.22	0.87	0.70	0.45
Basic earnings per share (EPS)	0.60	0.75	0.65	0.50	0.30	0.22	0.12	0.13	0.08	0.07	0.07	0.05	0.03	0.02	0.02	0.01
Shares outstanding	65.53	65.16	64.80	64.46	63.98	54.51	46.73	45.32	44.64	43.92	43.03	34.98	34.98	34.98	34.98	34.98
Revenue growth (year over year)	28.17%	16.48%	38.33%	−14.19%	57.29%	10.02%	79.63%	17.31%	4.38%	47.52%	29.95%	50.96%	17.27%	28.67%		
Compound growth rate (1986–June 2000)	18.55%															
Net income growth (year over year)	15.59%	32.44%	76.24%	46.41%	115.85%	−10.45%	71.85%	13.37%	16.25%	77.99%	30.33%	40.23%	24.29%	55.56%		
Compound growth rate (1986–June 2000)	28.90%															
Basic EPS growth (year over year)	15.38%	30.00%	66.67%	36.36%	83.33%	−7.69%	62.50%	14.29%	0.00%	40.00%	43.36%	40.23%	24.29%	55.56%		
Compound growth rate (1986–June 2000)	22.21%															

Source: Jones Pharma Incorporated annual reports, 1985–2000.

THE BUILDING BLOCKS OF SUCCESS AFTER THE INITIAL PUBLIC OFFERING

An obvious question one might ask Dennis Jones after knowing the spectacular growth of his initial investment might be, "What do you believe your wealth would be today if you hadn't diluted your ownership to employees and other investors through stock offerings?" I asked this question of Dennis one afternoon, and he replied that the company would never have seen such high growth had it not been for his and Judy's willingness to dilute their ownership. He explained that from the very beginning he wanted his employees to think and act like owners of the business. The most effective way to do this was to make periodic stock option grants to each and every employee right down to the janitor. Dennis gives credit for this idea to the vision of Marion Laboratories founder Ewing Kauffman. The company also made the decision to seed the 401(k) plan with a healthy stake in the company for the benefit of the employees' retirement. Dennis believed that the best way to incentivize the employees to work hard was to let them experience the economic benefits of controlling costs and maximizing profits. It worked.

The year 1998 was a milestone for the company with sales topping the $100 million mark for the first time. The management team, which included Dennis Jones, Judy Jones, Mike Bramblett, G. Andrew Franz, and David A. McLaughlin, was aware of shifting winds in the business which would cause them to focus on the strategic fit of their business mix rather than simply acquire businesses for the sake of growth. The hospital products division, led by sales team Jerry Rose, Tom Boston, Jerry Garner, and Tom Strickler continued to grow market share. The nutritionals business was becoming more competitive and began experiencing margin erosion. Despite the fact that the business was producing over $20 million in annual sales for Jones, the time was right to divest the nutritionals division with a cash sale to Twin Labs for $55 million. Dennis was disappointed to take a step backward in annual sales, but the attractive valuation gave him the mandate to protect shareholder value. In the next 18 months, publicly traded nutritionals companies lost 90 percent of their value on average. Many ceased to exist by the end of the decade. Had Jones chosen to maintain the nutritionals division or sell it to Twin Labs in a stock transaction, the value of the Jones Pharma enterprise would have been severely damaged.

By year-end 1999, annual revenues had topped $132 million with net income of $49 million. One of the flagship products, Thrombin JMI, had gained near exclusivity under the operational direction of Brad Knoll. The management team was keenly aware that another major fork in the road was straight ahead. The following is a summary of the sales and earnings growth of Jones Pharma from IPO to the last year prior to its acquisition by King.

PREPARING FOR THE NEW MILLENNIUM

On December 31, 1999, my wife and I enjoyed a wonderful millennium celebration at Dennis and Judy's home. The *Los Angeles Times* had just named JMED as one of the top 50 stocks for the decade from December 1989 to December 1999 with a cumulative shareholder return of 2,600 percent. The company had just dodged a huge bullet with the divestiture of the nutritionals division. Life couldn't seem to be any better as the stock was trading at an all-time high. At this point, Dennis felt it might be time to hang up the cleats. Not long before, he had confided in me that he had been diagnosed with a heart condition, and he worried that he might not be able to run the company as long as he had originally planned. When reflecting on the reality that he had witnessed such a prodigious rise in both the multiple on his stock and the broad market as a whole, his business and human senses pushed him to explore a sale of the company.

The U.S. stock market had been on a tear in the first quarter of 2000. On February 24, 2000, the *Wall Street Journal* ranked Jones as delivering the largest one-year and ten-year shareholder return in the pharmaceutical industry. Dennis began looking at his company from the perspective of a potential buyer, and it was clear to him that the only company that could afford to acquire Jones with such a rich valuation was a company with an even richer one. King Pharmaceuticals of Bristol, Tennessee, was the only pharma company to fit this mold. So on May 2, 2000, Dennis picked up the phone, called John Gregory, the founder and chairman of King. Dennis said, "John, I have been impressed by how fast your company has grown over the past few years. I am not getting any younger, and I wonder if you would entertain a discussion about King acquiring Jones."

The next 90 days would be harrowing for the Jones management team, but it was able to settle on a stock transaction that gave the Jones shareholders a 38 percent share price premium to the average 30-day trading price. At the announcement of the deal, the shares of both Jones and King would drop precipitously as the Street thought the deal was too expensive and that Jones would slow King's growth rate. By the closing of the transaction, JMED and King would recover a portion of the decline, and both companies would convene their shareholders to approve the deal. G. Andrew Franz was named president and CEO of the Jones division of King Pharmaceuticals. At 4 p.m., on August 30, 2000, Dennis and Judy Jones, along with the officers of King, rang the closing bell on the New York Stock Exchange. Jones Pharma, founded by a couple of high school sweethearts who began their humble lives living in a trailer was sold for $3.6 billion.

TERMS OF THE DEAL

Before Dennis and John Gregory shared the news of their first phone call, they agreed on some basic terms necessary to make the deal work. Dennis recalls giving 10 individual items that were important to him and Jones Pharma's shareholders. Three conditions were nonnegotiable. First, the buyout price had to be a minimum of a 20 percent share price premium for Jones Pharma's shareholders. Second, Dennis and Judy Jones would resign from the company the day the deal was complete. Third, King must take care of Jones Pharma's employees such that a closure of any of the facilities would result in a severance package equal to or greater than the existing policy of Jones Pharma's severance package. Additionally, King would vest 100 percent of employee stock options.

JONES PHARMA: LESSONS FOR INVESTORS

The way for an investor to benefit to the fullest from the Jones Pharma experience was to *own* the stock. There were numerous investment newsletters that recommended buying and selling and even shorting JMED during the 1990s. Writers of these newsletters, I suspect, are still unaware of the fact that a simple long position in the stock was the most profitable investment strategy for this company. It is easy to take a look in the rearview mirror and find successful companies like Jones Pharma. Identifying them and owning them before their growth are of course more difficult tasks. In Jones Pharma's case, there are a few key points that were evident to investors:

- The company had a committed, effective, accessible, and credible management team.
- Annual shareholder meetings included unlimited question-and-answer periods for investors.
- All employees were owners of the company.
- Stock offerings created a currency that provided capital in which to make strategic acquisitions.
- The company had a simple, understandable business plan.
- The stock price reflected net income growth over time.

LESSONS FOR WEALTHY FAMILIES WHO HAVE SOLD THE FAMILY BUSINESS

The most effective way for a family to understand the investment process is to do a postmortem study on how its wealth was created in the first place. The basic ingredients of successful businesses can be easily identified once the emotion of running the business has passed. If the spirit of the entrepreneur and business owner is found to have been vital to the wealth creative process in the first place, does it not make sense to maintain those same ingredients in the diversified portfolio? I strongly believe that it does. Failure to identify how one's wealth was acquired increases the risk of losing it.

LESSONS LEARNED WITH RESPECT TO VOLATILITY OF INVESTMENTS

When reviewing the volatility of the JMED share price, there is a remarkable difference in the visibility of price drops depending on whether annual, quarterly, or daily price plots are used. For example, when reviewing calendar year-end stock prices for JMED, there were two years of negative stock price corrections of 20 percent-plus (1987 and 1994). If you study the quarterly stock prices for JMED for the same period, the volatility is greater, and seven quarterly declines of 20 percent-plus are evident. By viewing daily price plots, the "bear" periods seem to be more frequent and more violent than on either of the other charts. From IPO to the end of 2000 there were six different price corrections of 35 percent or more. Because the corrections were short-lived, they are not evident when you view the charts showing only year-end prices.

If we were to chronicle JMED from 1986 through 2000 with hourly price plots from each trading day, the volatility would be even more amplified. Fortunately for the initial investors in Jones Pharma, the stock price updates were not flashing before their eyes as they sat at their workstations courtesy of an Internet news service as is common today. One of the lessons that we can see when we evaluate how often we "check" on our investments is that the more often we do it, the more the volatility increases. It is a simple mathematical fact. Warren Buffett, who, I'll bet, has a net worth edge greater than most readers of this book, once said this with respect to owning investments: "Only buy something you would be happy to hold if the market shuts down for ten years."

CONCLUSIONS

- Long-term investors should follow a stock's earnings instead of its short-term returns.
- A good business may experience a lot of volatility in its stock price as it grows.
- Motivating employees to feel like owners of the business through their owning shares of stock is beneficial for the business owner, the company, and its employees.
- Half of running a good business is knowing when and how to get out of it.
- Maintaining the spirit of entrepreneurship after the sale of a business is important.
- Wealthy families should chronicle the business decisions which created their wealth.

CHAPTER 15

Train Wrecks

Avoiding the Most Common Mistakes as an Investor

If you have stayed with me for the previous 14 chapters, I owe you a round of drama and excitement. These stories are nothing but drama. They are real stories of real businessmen with whom I was unable to close the deal. Fortunately for me, my name won't appear anywhere on their financial obituary, which reminds me of the phrase, "Some of the best deals I ever did were the deals I never did." I'll apologize in advance that I cannot share their real names or companies with you. I don't have a large enough legal budget to do that. However, you'll see the themes and remember the times in which they occurred, and you'll wonder as I do if things really had to end the way they did. As you read through this section, remember that each of these individuals, like most of us, thought he had a good handle on reality and common sense. There is one common characteristic you should know about each of these gentlemen: their innermost circle of trusted advisors was afraid to tell them when they were wrong. In other words, they surrounded themselves with "yes" men.

MR. TRAIN

Train wreck number one was one of the most spectacular self-destructions I have ever witnessed. I'll call him "Train" as a code name throughout this account. I cold-called Train, founder of a publicly traded financial services company, in 1997. Train possessed a few important characteristics that made him an ideal prospect for me:

- He had hundreds of millions of dollars.
- His net worth was concentrated in one stock.
- His number was listed in the phone book.

Before you read through the story I might as well let you know how it ends. Train never became a client. Train lost everything from his house to his wealth (every penny of it), from his reputation to his company.

Train had all the characteristics of the rock star CEO of the 1990s. He was a self-made risk taker. He attended, but never finished, college. He enlisted in the military right out of high school. By the time I called Train, his company had grown into a multi-billion dollar enterprise listed on the New York Stock Exchange. In those days, CEOs spent a lot of time on the road speaking at analyst meetings to get the word out as to why their stock deserved to trade at a premium multiple compared to the stocks of their peer group. When the analyst road show was not effective at accomplishing a higher multiple, Train began buying his own company stock in the open market, hoping to telegraph his bullish message to the market. The day I called him in the mid-1990s, he had recently completed such a transaction and was particularly happy because he was up a couple of points on the trade. We had a pleasant conversation which he ended by his asking me to stop by to see him if I was ever in his city. Of course, I found myself in his city the next week, and we agreed to meet. The real fun would begin once we met face-to-face.

To say that Train had a nice office would be an understatement. A palace would have impressed me less. In the meeting, Train discussed how the market was finally beginning to understand the real story about his company. His plan was that as the multiple on the stock approached what he felt was an acceptable level, he would begin to diversify significant amounts of capital out of the company. I told him it would be unwise to wait too long to diversify, but he wouldn't listen. As one might guess, the stock never traded at a level acceptable to him.

The next month, Train suffered an ego setback which I believe initiated the chain of events that ultimately bankrupted him. The Forbes 400 list was published, and he was listed on the "near-miss list" because his net worth fell a few million short of the cutoff.

At the same time, a securities analyst who knew the financial services industry well was about to initiate coverage on the company but mentioned very early on that he had concerns about the company's acquisitions and subsequent accounting treatment. By late that year this particular analyst would continue to dig deeper into the company's accounting practices. More analysts initiated coverage on the stock with a "buy" or "accumulate" rating. Train wanted to make the Forbes list with a passion which now consumed him. He had successfully brought most of the analysts in line with bullish ratings, and he was buying his own stock on the open market. The company announced a sizable share repurchase offering which, of course, caused the stock to rally.

By the middle of the following year, I dialed in to the analyst/investor conference call to discuss the recent quarter's earnings. After touching on the earnings report, Train announced that the officers of the company now owned 25 percent of the outstanding shares which they still felt were undervalued. The company had purchased 5 million shares on the open market and would buy more if given the opportunity. In addition to purchasing his own stock and his company purchasing stock, Train struck a deal that would dramatically increase the footprint of his company in a new niche. This acquisition, as it turned out, would eventually bring the company and its officers to their knees.

At my next meeting at his office, Train agreed to "hear me out" on the diversification idea. At the time, his net worth had grown to $600 million. I showed him how even at moderate compounded rates of 6 percent he would have the opportunity to grow his estate to over $1 billion the next one or two decades. At those rates he would be able to live a comfortable lifestyle, make a major philanthropic impact, and sleep at night. He also told me that he had about $100 million worth of Arabian horses and art which were the first assets he purchased as a part of his diversification plan. I did my best to keep a straight face. Keep in mind that those were the alternative investments of the mid-1990s.

By early 1999, Wall Street began to grow uneasy about the accounting methods at Train's company. Train became embroiled with various analysts who published negative reports on the company. One particular analyst, an acquaintance of mine, had been by far the most critical in his skepticism of the stability of the business model at the company. This was to be the first in a series of "wild-west" style shootouts between Train and anyone who dared to question the value of the company. By the mid-part of 1999 the battles with the analysts would reach a crescendo in an elevator at the Waldorf Astoria in New York.

The event was a financial conference where CEOs and their senior management would make presentations to Wall Street analysts and buy-side money managers. Train's presentation lasted one hour, and the answer to every possible question had been carefully rehearsed. Hundreds of portfolio managers and analysts were in attendance that day. At the break I had the misfortune of riding the elevator with him to the banquet room where lunch would be served. Train made an announcement to the nine or ten people crammed into the elevator: "Do any of you guys know Niall Gannon? He manages money for high net worth individuals, and he has been trying to get my account. I told him that things might get better if certain analysts would *stop kicking my ass!*" Train chuckled. Nobody else on the elevator, including me, thought that was funny at all. I'll never know who the other gentlemen were who took that elevator ride that day, but I have to assume that any ounce of bullishness they may have maintained for Train's company had immediately dissipated.

Train began buying his own stock, on margin, as the share price began to fall. He had negotiated a line of credit for several hundred million dollars which would finance his purchases. I would have only one more conversation with him that year. He continued to rant that Wall Street didn't understand his company and its true value. He also used the mother of all swear words in describing the analysts who had sell ratings on the stock. A few months later, with the stock in the single digits, Train resigned from the company with a negative net worth. The amount he owed the bank was multiples greater than the value of his stock, his home, all his jewelry, wine, sports cars, and Arabian horses. Train was wrecked.

TRAIN WRECK 2

I'll refer to train wreck 2 as Casey Jones since he was an engineer on a train to the poor house. Coincidentally, I met Casey only a few months after witnessing the demise of our friend Train. Casey was the founder and CEO of a Southern health-care products manufacturing company. He would also make a series of bad judgment calls which would strip him and his family of the bulk of their wealth. Obviously, my view of the necessity of diversification and the dangers of leverage had been strengthened.

Near the end of the 2000 the concept of fundamental analysis to which I have made reference throughout this book had nearly breathed its last on Wall Street. Nobody really cared about high multiples, earnings purity, or accounting gimmicks, and Casey knew it. Acquisitions those days were often financed in "pooling of interests" stock transactions meaning the higher multiple at which a company traded, the easier it was to make accretive trans-actions by buying lower multiple companies. Like most com-panies still managed by their founders, Casey spoke to analysts and investors with authority. He issued financial reports delivering exactly what the Street wanted, and everybody was happy—for a time.

In my first conversation with Casey, I inquired about his personal level of liquidity and whether he had plans to diversify out of a portion of his concentrated holdings in the company. He indicated that the SEC-approved window allowing him as a senior executive to sell shares of his company was currently closed for him as earnings for that quarter had not yet been released but that he was considering the implementation of a diversification plan in the near future. He also indicated that he would not hesitate to sell the entire company at the right multiple.

Each conversation I would have with Casey over the next year seemed to make progress in terms of his willingness to sell stock. Casey was fearful, however, that large-scale sales in the open market under SEC Rule 144 could send a negative signal to the market, depress the stock price, and make him vulnerable to lawsuits. To settle this concern, he felt that a 10b5-1 plan would be more appropriate for him. A 10b5-1 plan would allow company insiders to place large amounts of stock into a "blind trust" administered by a third-party custodian who could make open market sales in certain proportions during the year without input or direction from the individual shareholder. My concern for Casey was that this process could take years to accomplish a significant amount of liquidity and that the current multiple on the stock made it a good time to sell immediately. The other reason I favored open market sales under Rule 144 was that we had witnessed an increase in large-scale institutional block trades which he could access as a seller. The best approach might be to simply have Casey announce to the Street that over the next year he would be making some open market sales in order to gain some liquidity and for estate planning purposes. His stock was trading at an earnings multiple of nearly 70.

Casey didn't like my idea, and the next month he and other officers of the company placed several million shares into blind trust 10b5-1 plans in order to begin their diversification. He concurrently placed $40 million worth of stock into an exchange fund. His comment was, "If this whole thing tumbles, at least I should have something."

Over the following months, Casey began to receive relatively nominal amounts of proceeds from the blind trusts which prompted him to open an account with me. At this point in our relationship, I felt confident that I would be effective in strengthening the financial position of this family. Despite its wealth, family members still held their stock in joint name rather than in trust. Their estate plan was little more than a simple will with some unfunded trust plans. Casey thanked me for making suggestions on the title of the stock and for pushing him to complete and fund his estate plan. He asked me to write a letter to his attorney outlining all of my concerns with respect to liquidity and estate planning. What I didn't know then was that as he was giving me this directive, he was on a private jet on his way to the Masters golf tournament in Augusta, Georgia, as a guest of one of my competitors.

Over the next few months, our conversations became less productive. Casey would ask me, "What stocks are you buying?" and I would ask Casey if he had moved any closer to protecting his capital and his estate. As one would expect, I wasn't interested in having a conversation with him about stock tips, and he wasn't interested in talking about the big picture. A few weeks later I would receive a call from Casey's attorney thanking me for bringing the estate planning issues to his attention. He indicated that he agreed that Casey should hold his assets in a revocable trust in order to keep these assets out of probate at his death but that Casey had replied, "I'm not too worried about all of that" The attorney recommended that we convene on a conference call the next month.

Over the next month Casey's stock rallied by 25 percent, and it was time for me to use stronger language in our communications. I called his office and said, "Casey, you need to do a 4 million share block trade when your SEC Rule 144-stock sale window opens next week following the earnings announcement." "That's what you think I should do, huh?" he replied. At the time I was aware of at least three firms that would be willing to compete for the highest bid on the block. The volume on the stock had swelled to a point where he could sell 4 million shares while not violating the Rule 144 volume limitations. Casey stated to me, "A 4 million share block trade? But what if I find an acquisition I was to buy between now and then? If we acquire someone, the stock will trade higher, and I can always sell some stock then." Despite Casey's hesitation, I felt that the 4 million share block trade seemed to be in the best interest of all parties because he could take down close to $200 million in one transaction, and it might take his mind off his binge for making acquisitions. Several conversations ensued during the next week, but Casey decided against the block trade because he still felt that the stock was undervalued. As it turns out, Casey's stock rallied another 12 percent in the next few months, and he agreed to another meeting.

"Niall, I have decided against your idea to sell a large amount of stock at these prices. I think it would send the wrong message to the shareholders, and I still think it will rise more," he said. My reply to him stressed that even in light of the 12 percent rally, I recommended that he diversify and increase the amount sold to $300 million. My thinking was that he could take the first $150 million to build a high-quality municipal bond portfolio and use the remainder to buy a diversified portfolio of high-quality multinational businesses. Casey said, "Niall, you are too conservative. If I were to do that, I would buy $220 million in stock and $80 million in municipal bonds." He added that they were looking at several large acquisitions and that in order to fund them, he would need to do a secondary offering on the stock. He agreed that when that time came, he would sell 3 million shares as a part of the stock offering.

On the plane home that afternoon, I remembered that train wreck 1 had been waiting his whole life to make the Forbes 400 list. It was possible, I thought, that if Casey made the Forbes list that year, he would have reached a personal "summit" and would be more realistic about his wealth and the work that remained to be done to plan for his family. After the recent rally in the stock price, I was sure that Casey would make the list, and when I checked with *Forbes* editor Peter Newcomb, it turned out that he did.

When I called Casey to tell him the news, he said, "Wow. Thank you!" I thought about saying, "Now will you consider a block trade?" but I didn't want to spoil his moment. It wasn't important at that point, however, because he would file for the secondary offering the next month including a block of his "founder's stock" within the prospectus. The offering was to be priced on Halloween night, October 31. Casey called me at 4:30 in the afternoon to tell me that they were considering increasing the offering by another 5 million shares and if I would render an opinion as to whether that was a wise move. What I would learn is that the sellers of the company he was trying to acquire were demanding a higher price despite the fact that Casey's stock had fallen in the previous weeks. Increasing the size of the offering was the only way to finance the purchase of this company. After negotiating with the sellers until nine that evening, Casey walked away and pulled the offering. He was sure that his investment bankers had "ganged up" on him to try to force the price of his stock lower. The stock fell over the next couple of days, and Casey relented and agreed to lower the price of the offering. He retained some cash for the payment of capital gains taxes and agreed to start our relationship with $30 million.

The $30 million was indeed a good start for his portfolio, but it was still only a fraction of his net worth and therefore could really not make a significant impact on the family. Unfortunately, Casey's stock dropped 30 percent over the next six months. I recommended that he terminate the blind trusts and simply make open market sales under Rule 144 since the stock was still richly valued compared to his peer group and the rest of the market. He refused, stating that the current litigious environment made him uncomfortable. I reminded him that if he were to sell stock under Rule 144, he would not be breaking the law, but he was still fixated on the possibility of a lawsuit. In the next few months Casey would retire from the company. He had been correct to fear a lawsuit, however. In the months following his retirement, the SEC launched an investigation into the company's accounting practices which unleashed at least a dozen shareholder lawsuits.

Casey's stock eventually lost 85 percent of its value from its peak. Of the $30 million he had placed under my management, he continued to liquidate the municipal bonds and core equity positions for "personal reasons" and asked us to wire the cash to his bank account. Casey had taken approximately $100 million of the funds he had accumulated from his diversification strategy and through his private investment fund he purchased four $25 million positions in "pink sheets" and Nasdaq-listed small capitalization stocks, each of which also lost 85 to 100 percent of their value.

LESSONS LEARNED

As painful as the above stories may seem, there were hundreds of stories just like them in the late 1990s and early 2000s. The bull market from 2003 to 2007 yielded a bumper crop of new ultramillionaires who would repeat the same mistakes in their own way by taking their once-in-a-lifetime fortune and gambling it away in overconcentrated positions, margin, commodities, trading schemes, and alternative investments. My only hope in telling these stories is that perhaps one day a successful entrepreneur will read this book and decide to try to make a "safe landing" with his or her fortune.

That said, there are also plenty of happy stories of successful business people who divested themselves of enough shares of their businesses to live comfortably without damaging their companies' images. Their stories may be just as instructive to wealthy investors, albeit not as much fun to read. Consider the case of Craig Sullivan. On July 12, 2002, the then 62-year-old CEO of household cleaning products and food company Clorox issued a press release that was titled "Clorox CEO to Diversify Holdings." The press release stated that he had filed a notice with the SEC that he intended to sell up to 857,728 Clorox shares between July 1 and December 31 of 2002, and it also stated that he had further plans to exercise and sell other tranches of stock options. A quote by Sullivan stated, "I remain fully dedicated to delivering solid results and building the value of the company for all Clorox shareholders. This is about planning for my future and diversification is an important aspect of a sound financial strategy particularly at one's later years. At the age of 62 it simply makes sense to diversify a portion of my holdings."[1]

Clorox stock did not take a beating in the market the day of that news release. It was hardly a concern, and I believe that's because the company and the CEO were so clear and so forthright with the press release stating that he didn't have anything up his sleeve and that he simply wanted to diversify his holdings because he was getting up in years. Sullivan could have even added to that and said that selling now was actually a benefit to shareholders because if he were to die with most of his estate in Clorox shares, the family would be forced to liquidate a huge amount of the stock in an uncontrolled fashion in order to pay the estate taxes. Regardless of that omission, the release was so straightforward that I believe the market did not fear that Sullivan was bearish on the stock or that there would be a enormous amount of liquidity overhanging the market because the sale program was to take place over several months. Thus, it is an excellent example of a well-executed liquidity strategy on the part of a public company CEO.

So why don't more wealthy investors follow such a strategy? There's no surprise in the fact that hubris is one of the greatest enemies of successful businesspeople and that part of that hubris is businesspeople often think that investors care immensely about what they say or do as opposed to the fundamental strengths and weaknesses of their businesses. CEOs often falsely believe that buying their own stock is going to send a major bullish signal to the market and that selling their stock is going to send a major bearish one. For this reason they often try to hide their selling and tend to favor prearranged trading programs and 10b5-1 programs where the stock is sold slowly over months if not years.

The reason I believe the Clorox example is also worth noting is that Sullivan was the right age and in the right environment to sell because the company was performing well and he was approaching retirement. It made complete sense for him to diversify at the age of 62. His stock was trading, in my opinion, at a fair valuation and the SEC Rule 144 volume limitations on sales actually allowed him to sell stock in the open market fairly easily. And it makes sense for anyone of his age in similar circumstances to do the same thing because who knows what might happen? Two years from now you could have cancer or the stock price could be half of what it is today.

By contrast, with a slower 10b5-1 trading program, it can take two or three years to execute the sale plan. As a result, an investor might not be able to purchase that portfolio of municipal bonds with yields at 4.75 percent as they are today because rates could be 3 percent by the time she's done with her sale program. And she might not have the downside protection bonds provide in a bear market. So while public company executives should make sure that they're running their businesses and making their SEC filings with the clearest disclosure possible, they shouldn't be afraid to do what Sullivan did and diversify when it makes sense for their families.

That said, such aggressive sales aren't appropriate for everyone. A 35-year-old founder of a new or young company ought to have a lot of skin in the game, and I think it would be more alarming to shareholders for him to sell a significant portion of his holdings without an explanation. But an executive who is approaching retirement age and is truly acting with prudent goals of diversification in accordance with all securities laws should have nothing to fear.

CONCLUSIONS

- Hubris (on the part of investors and advisors) is the greatest enemy of successful wealth management.
- A carefully executed liquidation strategy by a business owner can be acceptable to shareholders if communicated properly.
- Waiting for the "perfect" moment to sell your shares in your business can lead to significant losses.
- Don't let tax worries determine the timing of your stock sales.

CHAPTER 16

Wealth Management Strategies and a Comparison of Various Models

Family Office, Full-Service, and Direct Wealth Management Firms

Given that the entire focus of my book has been on maximizing after-tax returns for wealthy investors, I would be remiss if I didn't address the benefits and drawbacks of different types of wealth management firms and how they can affect performance. Traditionally, high net worth investors have employed one of two types—a family office or a full-service wealth management firm. Somewhere in between these two models lies the Gannon Group or what I like to call direct wealth management. Direct wealth management differs from the most common wealth management models in that the family maintains a direct relationship with the principals of the money management organization. I don't claim that it offers the best of both worlds, but for the right kind of wealthy family it does address some of the shortcomings of both models. But first, let's review what those two models are and then we can examine how the Gannon Group operates in practice.

FAMILY OFFICE

For the top tier of wealthy investors, a family office makes a lot of sense. The most popular family office model is one in which families who have in excess of $500 million establish a separate operating entity, which is charged with the task of overseeing the investments, taxes, legal strategies, cash flow issues, household staff, insurance, and even some concierge-level services for the family members. The traditional family office structure is expensive, but at a certain dollar level—and a lot have agreed that $500 million is a good starting point—the family would be able to hire a highly qualified family office executive, and this would usually be someone who has a background in accounting or law, or possibly investment management. This executive would be in charge of hiring all the other people in the office and making sure that everything runs smoothly. Typical costs for operating a family office can be upwards of $1 million a year.[1]

Ideally, such an office would operate for the entire family as a cohesive unit, so that certain cost-saving synergies would result. In other words, fees charged would be for the family's assets as a whole rather than the assets of each of the family members individually. Collectively then, the family should achieve certain economies of scale and thus increase its total after-tax return net of fees.

One of the great benefits available to the family office is what I like to call in-sourcing. Most institutions and even wealthy families currently follow an investment approach in which a consultant, advisor, or other intermediary brings money managers and clients together under the framework of a diversified portfolio. The purpose of in-sourcing is to seek to eliminate intermediaries so that the investor is dealing directly with those who make investment decisions on behalf of the family. This can be accomplished by hiring a portfolio management staff to work within the family office or by employing a boutique firm that may be willing to provide truly customized portfolio management. We've observed that one-third of the members of the Institute for Private Investors currently employ this model and deal directly with investment managers without the use of a consultant. The remaining two-thirds of the membership employ a consultant in order to aggregate and coordinate the investment managers. The consultant-driven model dominates the market.

Certainly hiring their own full-time portfolio management team may make economic sense to families with portfolios in excess of $500 million. When a family that outsources its investment management reviews the expenses it currently pays to consultants and money managers, the results may be comparable to the salaries of professionals who could work for the family exclusively.

But the benefits of in-sourcing go beyond lower management fees. A portfolio management team that works exclusively on behalf of one family can bring significant customization and cost savings. Consider for a moment that most families possess a number of different portfolios with different investment objectives, tax exposure, and time horizons. Consider the fact that over time, some securities are sold at a taxable gain for the family, while others may be sold for capital losses.

The family foundation, for instance, may be the recipient of annual gifts from family members including initial seed money from the year of a liquidity event such as the sale of a business or of public stock. If a family holds a position with a large embedded capital gain which is a candidate for sale (as the position may be overvalued), the portfolio manager may "gift" the appreciated shares into the family foundation which establishes the value of the donation. The appreciated shares may then be liquidated by the foundation in order to be reinvested into the overall investment allocation. Because the foundation pays only a minimal excise tax of 2 percent,[2] the postliquidation value of the shares is higher for the foundation than it would be for the family portfolio which would have otherwise been responsible for the payment of long-term capital gains taxes. We work with families that regularly gift appreciated portfolio shares into their family foundation rather than use cash.

For obvious reasons, the benefits of the in-sourced portfolio management could be negated if the family is unable or unwilling to hire a capable and adaptable portfolio management team. Certainly, a disadvantage of the in-sourced portfolio management concept would be evident for those families that typically practice a high turnover of investment managers in an attempt to maintain top quintile, "best in class" managers. All money managers exhibit cycles of outperformance and underperformance. Failure to understand this dynamic could lead to unrealistic expectations by the family. For the family that is willing to engage in an intensive search to find a portfolio management team that has demonstrated quality investment management experience, adaptability to the family's investment mores, and a commitment to work for an extended period, the in-sourced concept is a sound and viable option. I suspect that as more of the college and endowment market hire in-house portfolio management teams, the wealthy family market will follow.

Families looking to hire wealth managers may want to consider joining the Institute for Private Investors (at www.memberlink.net), which maintains an advisor data bank and gives members the ability to screen for managers and advisors. For example, a family that wishes to interview firms that serve exclusively taxable investors with returns certified according to official global investment performance standards (GIPS) could easily screen for them with this resource. If the investor wishes to screen for managers who report performance after-tax, this option is available. The IPI advisor data bank also enables private investors to submit blind requests for proposals (RFPs). Using this system, the investors maintain their anonymity and receive responses and proposals through the Advisor DataBank® system.[3]

In addition, the Chartered Financial Analyst Institute (CFAI) maintains a job posting site at www.cfainstitute.org connecting its membership with those interested in interviewing or hiring investment professionals. A family seeking to interview portfolio managers would do well to begin its search process here as the CFAI is one of the largest and most respected organizations in the world for investment professionals.

FULL-SERVICE WEALTH MANAGEMENT

Full-service private wealth management firms are generally the big names in financial services you've probably heard of—Merrill Lynch, Citigroup, UBS, Morgan Stanley, Northern

Trust, Bessemer Trust, U.S. Trust, and so on. These firms have wealth management units that pretty much maintain a soup-to-nuts product offering. Most of them have a consultant-based model in which the family is dealing with a consultant/relationship manager and that person is designed to be the quarterback, to interface with money managers, attorneys, accountants, art advisory teams, insurance agents, and the like. Such a turnkey operation is attractive to some clients, and they may be willing to pay significant fees for these services. The full-service option can be expensive when you view the fees of all vendors in aggregate. Some advisors who have abandoned full service firms and trust companies to join smaller boutique operations have done so because they felt their clients were simply paying too much for over-head and infrastructure which was not adding value.

Here for instance is a list of services provided at one full-service firm:

- Investment monitoring and pooling
- Financial and estate planning
- Personal, partnership, and trust accounting
- Tax planning and preparation
- Banking and credit management
- Bill payment
- Trust administration
- Insurance coordination
- Family communication and meeting planning
- Manager selection and oversight
- Asset allocation
- Performance measurement
- Philanthropy/foundation support
- Operating business consulting

- Real estate management
- Aircraft/yacht management
- Travel coordination
- Educational programs for younger generations
- Nuptial planning

One of the downsides of this model is that families that don't require all those services may wind up paying for them anyway. For those in the upper echelons of wealth, consulting fees can range from between 0.40 percent and 1.0 percent of assets plus another 0.40 percent to 0.90 percent to hire the money managers. Then when you consider that on average 44 percent of wealthy investor assets are invested in "alternatives" such as hedge funds, which charge 2 percent of assets plus 20 percent of profits, the fees really start to add up. Aggregating all these fees, I have estimated the total costs to be between 1.8 percent to 2.0 percent of assets per year at full-service firms (if alternative investment fees are included), which can consume as much as a third of an investor's after-tax return.

The full-service model can also have its drawbacks from a tax perspective if the consultant is outsourcing the money management through funds or exchange-traded funds (ETFs). A portfolio manager who is investing, say, $50 million of a private account for one family, but who has $12 billion in assets under management for hundreds of institutions in a mutual fund, cannot possibly be mindful of the unique traits of that one family. She just doesn't have the time. So what usually happens with regard to the portfolio's tax management is that the money manager waits for a phone call somewhere between October and December asking her to generate some tax losses. The portfolio management team then sells everything in the portfolio that is trading with a capital loss and then hopes they can buy it all back in 31 days to avoid the wash-sale rule. That winds up being a poor tax strategy because the clients are not benefiting from the portfolio manager's due diligence and tax loss harvesting opportunities throughout the year.

Another drawback to outsourcing the money management is that management fees are often not tax deductible (for funds, ETFs, and alternative investments). If you're dealing with one private manager who charges his fees directly to your account as opposed to a pooled investment vehicle like a fund, many families may choose to take those investment advisory fees as a deductible item on Schedule A of their tax forms. In such a situation, the reason they are able to do this is that the fees are deductible to the client, not to the firm that charges them. But with a mutual fund or hedge fund, though you might be paying the same fee or even a higher fee, you're paying it to the company, so the client is not able to take it as a tax deduction. If a manager charges 0.50 percent of assets to invest a portfolio for a high net worth client directly, not only can that portfolio be customized specifically to that client, but because the manager's fees may be deductible, after taxes the client in the highest tax bracket pays an effective rate of only 0.30 percent.

"Open architecture" has become a catchphrase in the wealth management industry often used to describe financial supermarkets. It is meant to convey that a firm maintains a completely unbiased advisory model with no in-house product offerings or "pay to play" arrangements with outside vendors. Open architecture firms promote the practice of finding "best in class" managers, products, and services. Unfortunately, the term has become overused and has been adopted by both fee-only financial planning firms and full-service wealth management firms. Clients who have abandoned open architecture firms complain that the business model lacks substance. They don't want to be advised that they can buy anything, from anyone, at any firm, at any price. Such firms often recommend money managers who are "best in class" based upon their performance record only to recommend firing the manager when they determine that the manager is "worst in class." The net result of this practice is that the managers are usually fired and replaced after the damage to the portfolio has been done.

It is important to discuss whether full-service firms are acceptable to clients who are less fee-sensitive. We own shares (in our equity portfolios) of two public wealth management companies because we believe them to be highly profitable businesses. Members of one family told me in an initial interview that they were so happy with the relationship they had with their current financial advisor that even if my fee was 1 percent less and my performance was 1 percent better, it wouldn't change their mind about working with him. Despite the fact that this could be an additional $20 million on a $100 million portfolio over 20 years, performance and fees simply didn't matter. This example does point to the fact that there is no magic formula for serving the wealthy family market, and firms that try to be all things to all people will ultimately deliver mediocrity at best.

DIRECT WEALTH MANAGEMENT

Of course, the problem with in-sourcing and managing money for clients directly is figuring out how to do it in a cost-effective way for families with less than $500 million in assets. One solution growing in popularity of late is the multifamily office. The classic example of this is the Rockefeller & Co. family office, which was founded by the Rockefellers in 1880 to manage the family fortune. It became a registered investment advisor in 1980 and started taking on new clients with a minimum net worth of $50 million.[4] Today the firm has $6 billion in assets under management[5] with about 180 families.

The problem with such a model is that the founding family—in this case the Rockefellers—has the final say on the firm's investment policies, offerings, and structure. Because of this there is the potential for bias and conflicts of interest at the firm, which may serve the founding family first and other clients second. Ultimately, the purpose of the founding family's office shifts from managing the money of that family effectively and exclusively to being a profit-making stand-alone enterprise. The ultimate goal (in the beginning at least) is to generate additional revenue or cost sharing by pooling the assets of multiple families. So the interests of the managers of such offices and their clients are not perfectly aligned.

Clearly, one of the positives of the multifamily office concept is that many families would prefer to join forces with other families that have successfully developed a framework for managing the complexities of wealth rather that set out to build such a structure from the ground up.

By contrast, the model I've developed is called direct wealth management (DWM). The Gannon Group exists as an independent entity utilizing the structure and benefits of a large investment bank. However, we are not wealth management consultants, and we do not outsource our money management services to external funds or vendors for the core components of our portfolios. Our goal is to eliminate intermediaries and have as direct a relationship with our clients and their assets as possible and, by doing so, keep a lid on costs and portfolio risk. And we've succeeded in doing this while still being able to provide a lot of individual attention for our clients. We currently manage assets for just 14 families. Our fees are inclusive of trading commissions which means that the client does not bear additional costs for trading or tax-driven portfolio turnover. We earn the same fee, regardless of the asset class, which eliminates another potential conflict of varying margins on different asset classes.

The reason it is so important that the firm be limited in the number of families it serves is that above a small number of families (20 to 25) truly customized portfolio management solutions become difficult if not impossible to execute. A typical wealthy family may encompass as many as four or five living generations, each with its own philanthropies, wealth transfer entities, and qualified retirement accounts. Because of the number of members and financial entities contained within a single family, a boutique firm serving 25 families could ultimately oversee 500 individual entities. Beyond 25 families it would seem a difficult task for the principals and portfolio management staff to have enough familiarity with the entities in order to render truly customized portfolio management service.

At The Gannon Group, 50 percent of our time is spent on managing money. The other 50 percent is spent on the clients themselves—getting a better understanding of their estate planning strategies, their investment objectives and risk tolerance, their charitable intent, their wishes with respect to cash flow, and all of the facets that stem from or relate to these issues. We provide what we believe to be the highest value-added services of a full-service firm. Most of these services revolve around the coordination of the direction of cash flows for the family, the interconnections of family trusts and trustee relationships, tax planning and coordination, and legacy planning. We coordinate their documents and maintain a secure family office archive, with all copies of trusts, because a lot of clients wind up being successor trustees for other members of their family. And, we also maintain copies of tax returns, so that on a portfolio management basis, we are able to know what entities of the family are connected to one another and where tax efficiencies can be utilized.

In our group, Cindy Feaster performs the role of family office manager, and she does it with great skill and diligence. The cash flows for a wealthy family can be as complex as those of a business. Charitable gifts of securities must be disbursed, documented, and archived. Gifts of cash or stock to family members must be verified as to the correct cost basis to the recipient. Gift tax returns may need to be filed and coordinated. Gift tax liabilities must be accounted for and segregated for payment at the proper time. A family's pilot, yacht crew, or household staff must receive their wages. Large purchases of art may be transacted in euros or rubles, while the delivery of such items may be handled by vendors who speak a foreign language. On several occasions, we identified transferable state tax credits which were available for purchase toward the payment of state taxes in the year of a large liquidity event for a family. Cindy's coordination of these purchases, along with the coordination of tax filings with the client's CPA saved thousands of dollars in taxes. On one occasion, a tax credit acquisition saved more in taxes than the entire amount of our fees for the previous year. The fact that the family office manager is integrally woven into the wealth management team also means that there is a limited likelihood that assets would ever have to be sold in adverse market conditions to cover an expense.

But we don't offer every service. Concierge services can be cost effectively obtained by a specialist vendor or exclusive credit card such as the American Express black card or the Citigroup Chairman Card. Bill payments can also be easily coordinated, reviewed, and controlled through a service like Quicken. Of the 14 families we serve, 13 like to pay their own bills because they believe it is the best way to keep themselves abreast of their spending. Two of our clients had actually hand-signed the payroll checks when they had an operating business as a way of introducing systematic accountability and oversight to their companies. We wholeheartedly agree with this decision because spending has the biggest impact on the long-term values of portfolios, followed by taxes, inflation, and fees.

One decision I had to make as I was building our group was how to deploy capital and how much I was willing to spend on staff and technology, realizing that the more employees and services I added, the more we would have to charge the client. And since fees reduce the client's available return for either spending or growth in the portfolio, we wanted to make sure that we struck the right balance. When I considered building a turnkey solution and reviewed the costs, I realized how difficult it is to hire a great attorney or a great accountant at salaried wage levels. The $100,000 or $150,000 it costs to hire a very junior-level attorney, with salary and benefits, wasn't going to capture the legal mind and experience that would be commensurate with the complexities and demands of our clients. So it was a very conscious decision then that we would rather build a model that would fully interface with the client's attorney or accountant. We didn't want to replace that person, because in a lot of cases, the attorney has been named as a successor trustee of the family. He or she may have personal knowledge as to why certain legal or financial entities in the family were established and even why certain entities were reviewed and subsequently rejected. When a client or advisor is able to develop a long-term relationship with a professional, the result is a higher-quality plan with the depth and scope that would be expected of the chief legal counsel of a large corporation. I feel equally as strong that if the client maintains a high level of trust and history with a CPA or tax attorney, everyone benefits if this relationship can be maintained and sewn into the fabric of the master plan for the family.

Our business is structured to maintain independence, even to the point where we contractually mandate that our trading occurs on an agency basis (away from Smith Barney's or Citigroup's principal trading desks). If the client requests it, we are able to manage the assets even if they are held by another custodian such as a bank or trust company. Though we lose certain efficiencies in this arrangement, it communicates that our role is to deliver for the clients in the most effective manner possible. In this way, we are able to offer the best possible execution and have access to the entire Street's research and bond offerings. In other words, we are able to compete as a truly independent buy-side asset manager. We avoid proprietary products, and this independence is appreciated by clients and prospective clients alike.

FINDING THE RIGHT ADVISOR

In many ways an advisor's relationship with the family is so personal that it's a lot like a marriage. In assessing the right fit, personality and common philosophy usually dominate the factors influencing the decision to hire or not hire an advisor. I recommend that this process be taken seriously and that the costs be completely disclosed up front, including the economic effect the costs will have on the net returns after taxes, spending, and inflation. I also caution investors from hiring multiple advisors in order to see who does the best job at the end of three or four years. The math is simple: If a portfolio is split among four different advisors in order for the client to select the best one, the end result will be that 75 percent of the money was in the hands of the wrong advisors. Take your time and get it right the first time. To summarize, I've compiled a list of questions to ask before hiring an advisor with occasional notes to explain what isn't self-evident:

1. Why did you decide to become a financial advisor?
   Note: Although it's unlikely that advisors will admit they became advisors simply for the money, it is still important to ask this question just to gauge their reaction. If the advisor has a true passion for the job, that passion and devotion will shine through in the answer.
2. What is your personal asset allocation?
   Note: Advisors should "eat their own cooking." If they want to put you in a portfolio of stocks and bonds and yet won't invest in the same portfolio of stocks and bonds with you, why should you trust that the investments they're putting you in are really their best ideas?

3. What percentage of your personal net worth is invested alongside your clients?
   Note: If an advisor has 90 to 100 percent of his liquid assets invested alongside his clients, this is different from a smaller allocation of 15 to 25 percent.

4. What is the biggest mistake you have made in your career and what did you learn from it?
   Note: If a prospective advisor says she has never made a mistake, move on to the next candidate. Mistakes and willingness to disclose the lessons learned from them are very revealing of an advisor's character, her investment style, and her willingness to admit when she's wrong.

5. What will be the annual amount of all fees received by you or your firm from my assets, including expense ratios, commissions, 12b-1 fees, and consultant fees? What outside fees to other firms, vendors, brokers, or funds will I pay?

6. Are the total amount of fees subtracted from the expected-return modeling you do for clients?
   Note: Although past performance is essential for evaluating advisors, so is an analysis of their return projections and how those returns match your investment goals. If they are not adding fees into their expected returns calculations, the numbers will be inaccurate.

7. How often are performance reports prepared and presented to clients?

8. Are your performance numbers GIPS compliant and certified by an independent auditing firm? Do you produce dollar-weighted after-fee, after-tax

performance specific to my family? May I see a copy
of the audit?

9. Will you prepare, discuss, and adopt a written
statement of investment policy specific to my
family's expectations, and attitude toward risk?

10. How many families do you work with?

11. On average how many total entities do you serve
within each family—foundations, charitable trusts,
family limited partnerships, Uniform Gifts to Minors
Act (UGMA) accounts, cash flow accounts?

HOLISTIC FINANCIAL PLANNING

Although we don't offer as many services as the big private
wealth management firms (such as insurance, tax preparation, legal documents, concierge services), we believe in inte-
grating our services into a holistic financial plan for each of
our clients. So, in building our wealth management office
architecture and our record-keeping system, and in handling
the cash flow side of clients' accounts, we do not encroach on
their attorneys' or accountants' turf, but we have found ways
to work with them. We know, for instance, how to anticipate
the data that clients' CPAs need. When they are preparing gift
tax returns, it's important for them to be able to get detailed
information about the timing of the gift and whether the
taxes owed were already set aside for the payment of gift tax.
We are happy with this integrated system because we have
not had to charge clients anything more for this, and they are
able to maintain their relationships with other trusted
advisors. And, though we are very knowledgeable about the
tax and legal issues, we feel it's important not to step across

that line and present ourselves as tax or legal experts. We believe that we are money managers first and that we want to interface with the clients' very best people on the legal and accounting side of the relationship.

To ensure that our services are integrated into the whole of a client's financial life, we have developed a Venn diagram planning model called the Gannon Group wealth management process. (See Figure 16.1.)

The reason we employ this holistic model with clients is that it is critically important to us that the money management side of things not be viewed as a commoditized, separate entity that is simply a tool in a bag of financial services offered to clients. The money a client invests with us is the financial result of the success of his or her family in building a business and then moving it into a diversified portfolio. As you can tell from the diagram, we want to see the relationship between the family and the money invested with us as part of one holistic entity in which there is a cycle of cash flow

FIGURE   16.1

The Gannon Group Wealth Management Process

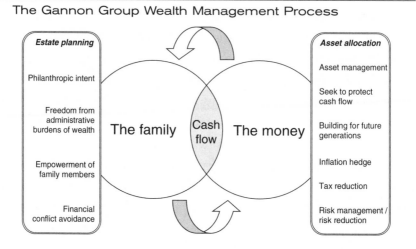

coming into the portfolio from the family's investing with us and coming out of the portfolio to the family to pay for expenses. It is extremely important as an advisor to remember that the primary reason investors hire an advisor is so that they can either maximize the return on their capital or to maximize the protection of capital.

Although the money side of the diagram should be fairly familiar to readers by this point, it is of equal importance to review the family side too. The first step in our wealth management process is to discuss estate planning with our clients. It is essential, for instance, that they understand the risks of dying intestate—that something could happen to them today after they leave my office, or when the whole family is on the private jet together.

It's shocking how many people with incredibly successful businesses neglect their personal affairs. There are individuals with hundreds of millions of dollars who don't have a will or a trust for their estate. I was introduced to one executive who was a member of the Forbes 400 yet held all his shares of his company's stock in joint name with his wife without an estate plan. This meant if he and his wife were to die suddenly, that $750 million worth of assets would have been publicly adjudicated and then distributed through the probate process in the state court system—a nightmarish prospect for that kind of sum.

That's why it's important to ensure that clients have an estate plan first before we design their asset allocation strategy. To facilitate that, we arrange a meeting with the client's trusts attorney or help find the client a trusts attorney (often clients don't have an estate plan because they don't have an attorney), and we work with that attorney to develop a plan for the client. Trusts can be complicated because of the size of some wealthy families. Every family member is different and has different financial needs.

As part of a wealthy investor's overall financial plan, we discuss his or her philanthropic intent—the next step in the Venn diagram of our wealth management process. We want to do this early in our relationship with a client because, generally speaking, there is a certain amount of philanthropy that every wealthy family is going to perform over their lifetimes and it is always wise to plan for this before a liquidity event occurs. If members of a family are considering selling the family business and if, for example, they wanted to tithe 10 percent of the gross proceeds to a foundation, they would also want the gain on those assets to occur in the foundation, so they would limit the taxes on the gain. And the sooner this is done, the better from a tax perspective.

When families don't want to start a foundation but are still interested in philanthropy, I ask them to think ahead to the next decade or two and try to determine how much they'd like to give away in that period and to prefund the donations of those assets today in a donor-advised fund that will safeguard the money even though they have not yet identified the recipients for those gifts. This way if they are about to sell their business, which will create the greatest tax liability they will ever pay in their life, their charities can avoid some of the taxes on those appreciated assets.

In the diagram, "freedom from wealth"[6] is simply getting the family to acknowledge that money isn't everything and that the most important thing about this financial planning process is enabling them to live their lives without having to worry about money. One client declared at the end of a three-year process of restructuring the affairs of his family, "Now I can sleep at night knowing that my tombstone won't read,

'Here lies the dumbest guy who ever lived.'" A harsh statement, perhaps, but it was important that this individual free himself from those things that were keeping him awake at night. Freedom from wealth often feeds into the next step of the process—empowerment of family members. There are people who really don't own the wealth but they are beneficiaries of the wealth. The stereotypical albeit sometimes true example of "trust fund kids" often do not have the ability to manage their financial affairs properly because they've never been given the chance. They are simply income beneficiaries of entities that exist and are managed by attorneys or trust companies. A good example of the sterile relationship between these parties is best illustrated by recalling Mr. Drysdale, banker to the TV family, the Clampetts on *The Beverly Hillbillies.*

I completely understand the motivation of some families that feel that their heirs are best served by limiting access to the funds through complex trust structures. I feel strongly, however, that the best way to empower members of the next generation is to allow them to own a certain amount of the wealth at an appropriate time, even if that means their making some mistakes. Each of the families I advise has a different story with different circumstances. One thing I try to do is to remind individual clients that they should view themselves as the first generation even if the bulk of their wealth came from a parent or grandparent. In this way, the members of the family begin to think about their decisions based upon future generations and on society instead of viewing their grandparents' decisions as affecting them. Perhaps the best example of this was a family whose daughter and son-in-law decided to establish and fund their own family foundation in concert with the sale of a family business. This action certainly provided the daughter with a great deal of satisfaction, set a great example for her own children, and made her parents beam with pride. From a purely mathematical standpoint, the daughter should have kept every nickel and funded all of her philanthropic commitments from her parents' charitable foundation. But she would have none of that; she wanted to give from her own storehouse rather than from someone else's. The spirit of the entrepreneur and the philanthropist did not die in the case of this family. It multiplied.

To help my clients achieve freedom from wealth, I try to educate them about the financial planning process so that they can learn how to manage their own affairs (or effectively supervise those who do). This can be a complex learning experience depending on how many generations of the family are involved. Once I've done this, I try to get inside my clients' heads with respect to gifting, or passing the money down the generations. It is important to remember that if a husband and wife live to their actuarial expectancy of their mid-eighties or even nineties, the children may not inherit the money until they are sixty-five or seventy. That creates a picture that is often unappealing to the members of the first generation because they want their children to enjoy their money before their golden years. So if parents want to give their children some of the money earlier, we explain the economics—that it is cheaper to gift assets even if they have already used up all their $1 million lifetime gift tax exclusion, because the growth on those assets occurs outside their estate, and then the gift tax is assessed on what the beneficiaries ultimately receive as opposed to the estate tax, which is taxed at a gross amount of the founding family's total estate.

All of this planning and education is to satisfy the last stage of the family side of the diagram—financial conflict avoidance. If an adequate estate plan is in place and all the children of the family are adequately taken care of in advance, then conflicts should be avoided when the parents die. Experience has also taught me that there should be as few "secrets" in the will as possible.

Once these issues with the family are resolved, we are then ready to move on to the asset allocation side of the diagram. And if that's done correctly, then the central part of the diagram, cash flow, is something the family doesn't and shouldn't have to worry about. Our approach to cash flow generation is counter to the conventional wisdom of spending total return as opposed to portfolio income. If the family's cash flow needs can be funded from visible sources of interest and dividends, this prevents the family from having to liquidate assets in down markets. Clients in a bear market worry just like everybody else about account values, but what they do not want to worry about is that their monthly income is going to stop, and so that goes back to doing a great job with the portfolio management. If we understand the family's needs on the left side of the diagram correctly, then the asset allocation on the right side will provide the necessary cash flow to fully fund the vacations, the educational goals, the philanthropic intent, and all the things that family members want to do so that they can rest easily at night.

Ultimately the goal of financial advice should be to help clients move beyond their financial situation. Although everyone likes to get paid, for the best advisors money is only part of the equation. I will never forget Dorothy Garrison, my very first client, who died in January 2006. She was in a hospice for the last nine weeks of her life, and I'm grateful that I was able to say good-bye and thank her for the impact she had on my life. At that point, risk premiums, asset allocation, and sector weightings didn't seem to matter as much as they did before. What mattered to her was that her affairs were in order and that the money she had so diligently saved and invested for her family would be managed by someone she trusted after she was gone. As her advisor I knew that proving I was worthy of that trust was my primary job. And knowing that it comforted her just a little bit in her final days meant a great deal to me.

When I called Dorothy on Christmas morning, a few days before she died, she was in good spirits and bid me farewell as I was leaving the next day for Cancun. Her parting words: "Make sure you don't drown and stay away from the sharks."

ENDNOTES

CHAPTER 1

1. Brett Nelson, "Secrets of the Self-Made 2008," *Forbes*, September 17, 2008, http://www.forbes.com/2008/09/16/self-made-secrets-ent-manage-selfmadesecrets08-cx_0917 secretsgreatest08.html.
2. Statistics and representative yields obtained from *The Bond Buyer*, New York.
3. http://www2.standardandpoors.com/portal/site/sp/en/us/page.topic/indices_500/2,3,2,2,0,0,0,0,0,0,5,0,0,0,0,0.html.
4. Brett Nelson, "Secrets of the Self-Made 2008," *Forbes*, September 17, 2008, http://www.forbes.com/2008/09/16/self-made-secrets-ent-manage-cx_bn_selfmadesecrets08_0916secrets2008_land.html.
5. Institute for Private Investors, "Family Performance Tracking® Survey 2008, 92 Private Investor Respondents" (Survey conducted February 2009).

6. Ibbotson Associates, *Stocks, Bonds, and Bills after Taxes 1925–2005* (Chicago: Ibbotson Associates, 2006).

7. Niall J. Gannon and Michael J. Blum, "After-Tax Returns on Stocks versus Bonds for the High Tax Bracket Investor," *The Journal of Wealth Management*, Summer 2006, 1–11.

8. Duncan Greenberg and Matthew Miller, "The Forbes 400," *Forbes*, September 2008, http://www.forbes.com/2008/09/16/richest-american-billionaires-lists-400list08-cx_mm_dg_0917richintro.html.

9. Dan Popkey, "What's Next for Simplot Estate?" *Idaho Statesman*, June 2008, http://www.idahostatesman.com/simplot/story/397147.html.

CHAPTER 2

1. Benjamin Graham and David L. Dodd, *Security Analysis*, 6th ed. (New York: McGraw Hill, 2009), 26.

2. Adam Shell, "Tech Teetotalers Have the Last Laugh," *USA Today*, January 10, 2001, http://www.usatoday.com/money/perfi/funds/2001-01-10-value-funds.htm.

3. John Kenneth Galbraith, *A Short History of Financial Euphoria* (New York: Penguin Books, 1994), 28.

4. *Ibid.*, 49.

5. *Ibid.*, 7.

6. Harry S. Dent, *The Roaring 2000s: Building the Wealth and Lifestyle You Desire in the Greatest Boom in History* (New York: Touchstone, 1999), 29.

7. John Maynard Keynes, *The General Theory of Employment, Interest, and Money* (New York: Houghton Mifflin Harcourt, 1964), 159.

8. Galbraith, *A Short History of Financial Euphoria*, 19–20.

9. Katrina Nicholas and Abigail Moses, "Credit Swaps Market Cut to $38 Trillion, ISDA Says," Bloomberg.com, April 22,

2009, http://www.bloomberg.com/apps/news?pid= 20601087&sid=a4AtVMqwawtc&refer=home.

10. Alan Greenspan, "Risk Transfer and Financial Stability," remarks by Chairman Alan Greenspan to the Federal Reserve Bank of Chicago's Forty-first Annual Conference on Bank Structure, Chicago, Illinois, May 5, 2005, http://www.federalreserve.gov/Boarddocs/Speeches/2005/20050505/default.htm.

11. Peter Lynch, *One Up On Wall Street* (New York: Penguin Books, 1989), 11.

CHAPTER 3

1. Standard & Poor's Web site: www.standardandpoors.com contains the history of the index dates to 1923, with an expansion to include 500 companies in 1957.

2. Ten-year rolling returns studied 1957–1967, 1958–1968, and so on. Twenty-year rolling returns studied 1957–1977, 1958–1978, and so on.

3. For rolling 10- and 20-year periods the lower of "annual return" or "postliquidation" was used.

CHAPTER 4

1. Gary P. Brinson, L. Randolph Hood, and Gilbert L. Beebower, "Determinants of Portfolio Performance," *Financial Analysts Journal,* January/February 1995, Vol. 51, No. 1, 133–138.

2. Thomas Friedman, *The World is Flat* (Farrar, Straus and Giroux: 1st ed., 2005).

3. U.S. Bureau of Labor Statistics, http://www.bls.gov/cpi/#tables.

4. The Bond Buyer, statistics obtained by request.

CHAPTER 5

1. Institute for Private Investors, *Advisor Databank*® (New York: Institute for Private Investors, 2007).

2. Wharton Global Family Alliance, *Single Family Offices: Private Wealth Management in the Family Context* (Philadelphia: Wharton School, University of Pennsylvania, 2008).

3. Northern Trust, "Wealth in America," executive summary findings, 2008.

4. http://www.investinginbonds.com/learnmore.asp?catid=5&subcatid=24.

5. www.bondbuyer.com.

6. U.S. House of Representatives, HR6308, September 9, 2008, as reported with an amendment, committed to the Committee of the Whole House on the State of the Union.

7. George H. Hempel, Washington University in St. Louis, "The Postwar Quality of State and Local Debt," National Bureau of Economic Research, 1971, 9–32.

8. http://www.publicbonds.org/public_fin/default.htm.

9. Andrew Ward, "State Bankruptcy Fears May Be Overstated," *The Bond Buyer*, January 12, 2009, http://www.thebondbuyer.com.

10. U.S. House of Representatives, HR6308, September 9, 2008, as reported with an amendment, committed to the Committee of the Whole House on the State of the Union.

11. Standard & Poor's, "A Complete Look at Monetary Defaults during the 1990's," June 2000.

12. http://www.hawaii.gov/tax/pubs/08outline.pdf.

13. This calculation includes the effect of the federal deduction of state income taxes.

14. The black swan theory (in Nassim Nicholas Taleb's version) refers to a large-impact, hard-to-predict, and rare event beyond the realm of normal expectations.

CHAPTER 6

1. David Swensen, *Unconventional Success: A Fundamental Approach to Personal Investment* (New York: Free Press, 2005), 126, 133.
2. Robert Huebscher, "David Swensen Speaks Out: Are Hedge Funds of Funds a Cancer?" *Advisor Perspectives*, 2009, http://www.advisorperspectives.com/newletter09/pdfs/David_Swensen_Speaks_Out.pdf.
3. Mohamed El-Erian, *When Markets Collide* (New York: McGraw-Hill, 2008), 216.

CHAPTER 7

1. David Silverman, "Taxes in Ancient Egypt," *University of Pennsylvania Almanac*, Vol. 48, No. 28, April 2, 2002, http://www.upenn.edu/almanac/v48/n28/AncientTaxes.html.
2. Charles O. Hucker, *China's Imperial Past* (Palo Alto: Stanford University Press, 1995), 190.
3. Edwin R. A. Seligman, *The Income Tax: A Study of the History, Theory and Practice of Income Taxation at Home and Abroad* (New York: The Macmillan Company, 1911), 62.
4. *Ibid.*, 106.
5. Gary Giroux and Sharon Johns, "Financing the Civil War: the Office of Internal Revenue and the Use of Revenue Stamps," paper presented at the Academy of Accounting Historians International Accounting History Colloquium, 2000, http://acct.tamu.edu/giroux/financingcivil.htm.
6. Seligman, *The Income Tax*, 444.
7. Sheldon David Pollack, *The Failure of U.S. Tax Policy: Revenue and Politics* (University Park, PA: Penn State Press, 1999), 55.
8. The Tax Foundation, "Federal Individual Income Tax: Exemptions and Treatment of Dividends, 1913–2006," http://www.taxfoundation.org/taxdata/show/2090.html.

9.   Mark T. Green and Fred Thompson, *Handbook of Public Finance* (Boca Raton: CRC Press, 1998), 487.

10.   Jeremy Siegel, *Stocks for the Long Run: The Definitive Guide to Financial Market Returns and Long-Term Investment Strategies*, 4th ed. (New York: McGraw-Hill, 2007), 74.

11.   Leonard E. Burman and Deborah Kobes, "Preferential Capital Gains Tax Rates," *Tax Notes*, January 19, 2004, 411, http://www.taxpolicycenter.org/publications/url.cfm?ID= 1000588.

12.   John R. Luckey, "A History of Federal Estate, Gift, and Generation-Skipping Taxes," Congressional Research Service, April 9, 2003, CRS-7.

13.   *Ibid.*, CRS-9.

14.   Fein, Such, Kahn, and Shepard, "New Tax Laws: Separate New Jersey Estate Tax," 2002.

15.   Baseline (Thomson Financial) value of S&P 500 index on March 31, 2008:1322.7, value on March 9, 2009: 676.53.

16.   Luckey, "A History of Federal Estate, Gift, and Generation-Skipping Taxes," CRS-1.

17.   Darien B. Jacobson, Brian G. Raub, and Barry W. Johnson, "The Estate Tax: Ninety Years and Counting," *SOI Bulletin*, Summer 2007, 122, http://www.irs.gov/pub/irs-soi/ ninetyestate.pdf.

CHAPTER 9

1.   Jeremy Siegel, *Stocks for the Long Run: The Definitive Guide to Financial Market Returns and Long-Term Investment Strategies*, 4th ed. (New York: McGraw-Hill, 2007), 352–353.

2.   Standard & Poor's, "S&P 500 Fact Sheet," The McGraw-Hill Companies, http://www2.standardandpoors.com/spf/pdf/ index/500factsheet.pdf.

3.   Robert D. Arnott, Jason Hsu, and Philip Moore, "Fundamental Indexing," *Financial Analysts Journal*,

March/April 2005, 83–99, http://www.researchaffiliates.
com/ideas/pdf/fundamentalIndexation.pdf.

CHAPTER 10

1. Katie Benner, "Why the Wealthy Avoid High Risk," *Fortune*,
    February 26, 2007, http://money.cnn.com/2007/02/20/
    magazines/fortune/benner_wealthy_invest.fortune/
    index.htm.
2. 5 percent allocation Barclays Capital U.S. Aggregate Bond
    index, 5 percent Barclays Capital Municipal Bond Index, 65
    percent S&P 500 index, 10 percent CS/Tremont HF index, 15
    percent NAREIT (all real estate investment trust) Index.
3. Nanette Byrnes, "Pumping Up the Muni Advantage,"
    BusinessWeek, March 5, 2007, http://www.businessweek.
    com/magazine/content/07_10/b4024098.htm.
4. Jeremy Siegel, *Stocks for the Long Run: The Definitive Guide to
    Financial Returns and Long-Term Investment Strategies*, 4th ed.
    (New York: McGraw-Hill, 2007), 13, 15.
5. Benjamin Graham and David Dodd, *Security Analysis: Classic
    1934 Edition* (New York: McGraw-Hill, 1934), 108.

CHAPTER 11

1. Source: www.pbgc.gov, 2008 PBGC annual management
    report.

CHAPTER 12

1. Includes investment categories of hedge funds, private
    equity, venture capital, commodities, real estate, and assets
    marked "other."

2. Assumptions of tax rates effective at year-end 2010: ordinary income, 39.6 percent; dividends, 39.6 percent; long-term capital gains, 20 percent.
3. 2008 Yale endowment annual report, Yale University, New Haven, CT, 2009, 5–14.
4. Raphael Amit, Heinrich Liechtenstein, M. Julia Prats, Todd Millay & Laird P. Pendleton, Single Family Offices, "Private Wealth Management in the Family Context," survey conducted by the Wharton Global Family Alliance, University of Pennsylvania, 2008, 10.

CHAPTER 15

1. Business Wire, "Clorox CEO to Diversify Holdings," July 12, 2002, http://findarticles.com/p/articles/mi_m0EIN/is_2002_July_12/ai_88829662/.

CHAPTER 16

1. Robert Frank, "How to Bank Like a Billionaire," *Wall Street Journal*, June 10, 2004.
2. Council on Foundations, www.cof.org/files/documents/government/06_excise_tax.pdf.
3. Institute for Private Investors, *Advisor Databank®* (New York: Institute for Private Investors, 2007).
4. Robert Frank, "How to Bank Like a Billionaire," *Wall Street Journal*, June 10, 2004.
5. Rockefeller & Co., "At a Glance" PDF fact page, http://www.rockco.com/files/factsheet_lr.pdf.
6. Charles Lowenhaupt, "Freedom from Wealth," *Journal of Wealth Management*, Spring 2008, http://www.iijournals.com/doi/abs/10..3905/jwm.2008.701847.

INDEX

Accountants, 275–276, 279
Acquisition (buyout) valuation, 237
Acquisitions, 240–242
Active investing, 161–162, 164–166, 168
Advisors:
  fees of, 151–152
  herd mentality of, 20–22
  performance of, 152–159
  selecting, 277–279
After-tax calculator, 60–62, 105, 140–146
After-tax returns, xiv, 35–52
  of bonds vs. equities, 49–52
  on equity investments, 10
  of Harvard endowment, 198
  of IPI members' investments, 207–208
  and liquidation rates, 48–49
  of NABUCO allocation, 198, 199
  in performance reporting, 154–155
  and portfolio turnover rates, 44–48
  and state of residence, 43–44
  on stocks, 19, 39–43
  for wealthy investors, 35–39
  of Yale endowment, 195, 196
"After-Tax Returns on Stocks versus Bonds
    for the High Tax Bracket Investor"
    (Michael Blum and Niall Gannon),
    11, 35
AIG (American International Group), 30
Alternative investments, 103–116
  commodities, 105–108
  currencies, 108–109
  hedge funds, 109–112
  for IPI families, 203–205
  private equity funds, 112–115
  for wealthy investors, 38, 250
American Express black card, 275
American Recovery and Reinvestment
    Act, 80
Amsterdam Stock Exchange, 23
Anheuser-Busch, Inc., 70–72,
    167, 168
Annual gift tax exclusion, 136–137, 227
Annualized return after fee after tax
    (ARAFAT), 155
Arnott, Robert, 167, 168
Asset allocation, 53–78

after-tax calculator for, 60–62, 140–141
and cash flow, 62–65
in Gannon Group wealth management
    process, 285
and index funds, 36
by IPI families, 203–207
market and stock valuations in, 70–72
municipal bonds in, 74–78
in pension plans, 188–189
and picking stocks, 67–70
and portfolio management,
    65–67, 72–74
and portfolio performance, 53–54
and taxation, 9–10
and valuations of market, 55–60
in Wharton Global Family Alliance,
    212–213
of Yale endowment, 195
Assets, 10, 27–31, 66, 133
Assumed returns, in after-tax calculator,
    142, 144
AT&T, 57, 193
Attorneys, 275–276, 279

Bank of America, 57, 193
Barbell portfolio strategy, 94–95
Baruch, Bernard, 20
Bear market of 2008, 27
Bear Stearns, failure of, 67
Beebower, Gilbert L., 53
Benchmarks, 154, 156–157, 162–163
Berkshire Hathaway, 57, 190, 193
Best Buy, 31–32
Betas, of portfolios, 175
Beyer, Charlotte, 201
"Big 10" companies, 56–57,
    188–190, 192
Black swans, 99–100
Blind trusts, 253, 256
Block sales, of stock, 253, 255–256
Blum, Michael, 11
Bogle, John C., 36–38, 162
The Bond Buyer (newspaper), 81
Bond Buyer Index, 49–52,
    77, 81, 82
Bond ratings, 87, 89, 91–92, 175

295

ABOUT THE AUTHOR

Niall J. Gannon is the lead member of the Gannon Group at Morgan Stanley Smith Barney. Niall's role is advisor to ultra-high-net-worth investors. At Morgan Stanley Smith Barney, Niall manages a group of four professionals that has over 35 years combined experience assisting Forbes 400 families, CEOs and other investors of substantial means. Niall has been recognized as one of the nation's top 100 financial advisors by three leading industry journals and investor publications.[1]

Niall is an active member within the Institute for Private Investors and has made enduring commitments to professional and civic associations in the St. Louis region and the State of Missouri. Niall is on the board of directors of the

---

[1] Barron's "America's Top 100 Brokers," September, 2004, as identified by Barron's Magazine, Registered Rep. Magazine, 2003 and "The Winner's Circle," 2005 using quantitative and qualitative criteria and selected from a total annual pool of over 3,000 nominations. Advisors who are selected have a minimum of seven years of financial services experience. Quantitative factors include, but are not limited to, the amount of assets under management. Qualitative factors include, but are not limited to, compliance record, interviews with senior management, and philanthropic work. Investment performance is not a criterion. The rating may not be representative of any one client's experience and is not indicative of the advisor's future performance. Neither Morgan Stanley Smith Barney nor its financial advisors pay a fee to Barron's in exchange for the rating. Barron's is a registered trademark of Dow Jones & Company, L.P. All rights reserved.

Junior Achievement of Mississippi Valley, Connections to Success and St. Louis Variety. He is also musical director of the St. Louis Irish Arts Youth Instrumental Group; honorary chairman of the Niall J. Gannon Scholarship at The Citadel Military College of South Carolina; former president of the St. Louis Irish Arts; and former chairman of the 2006 Annual Catholic Appeal.

For his outstanding work in these and other areas, Niall is a four-time recipient of the President's Volunteer Service Award in 2004, 2005, 2006 and 2007. In 2008, he received the Bill Eager Portfolio Manager of the Year Award.[2]

Niall completed The Wharton School, University of Pennsylvania's "Institute for Private Investors: Private Wealth Management Professional Track Program" in 2005. He received his undergraduate degree from The Citadel Military College of South Carolina and subsequently held the rank of lieutenant in the U.S. Army Reserve as an M1 Abram's tank platoon commander.

---

[2] The Bill Eager award, as selected by the Board of Directors of the Portfolio Management Institute (PMI), is PMI's highest honor. To receive the reward, the recipient must be a person who is dedicated and committed to the client, always striving to improve their knowledge and skill set, with a passion for the markets, willing to share their knowledge and expertise, committed to hard work and persistence, dedicated to helping partners and employees achieve full potential, who enjoys determined and competitive people, who is dedicated to their community through volunteerism, who is considered good natured, benevolent and committed to family, with unwavering commitment to their faith. The Bill Eager award is bestowed annually to only one member of the Portfolio Management Institute among all its members. Currently there are 300 members of the PMI.